✦ FOR GRADES 1-6 ✦

TRUTHQUEST HISTORY

AMERICAN HISTORY FOR YOUNG STUDENTS III
✦ 1865-2000 ✦

IN A CHRONOLOGICAL INVESTIGATION ENLIVENING THE TRUTHS OF HISTORY

BY MICHELLE MILLER

In honor of my beloved grandfather, Harold McVean Gingell,
for whom the years covered in this guide
were not history, but real life.
His life embodied the American spirit...
for this Michigan farm boy and his brother
raised and then peddled their potatoes door-to-door
to make their way and improve their lot
which resulted in them building a town
as well as its church, school, firehouse, store, hardware, and service station.
Oh, the changes he saw in his lifetime!
It's an honor to be his granddaughter.

Thank you, Scott Cottrill, for the proofreading!

TruthQuest History guides are not affiliated with the TruthQuest Inductive Study Bible.

ISBN 0-9752908-9-4
Printed in the United States of America

TruthQuest History
PO Box 2128
Traverse City, MI USA 49685-2128
info@TruthQuestHistory.com
www.TruthQuestHistory.com

We'd love to have you join our online discussion group. Simply send an email to:
HIStoryQuesters-subscribe@YahooGroups.com

Notes for Mom:

"How does one 'do' TruthQuest History?
Isn't it just a lot of words and booklists?
It looks too easy.
Are my kids just supposed to read?
Aren't they going to 'do' something?
Where are the activities and the daily lesson plans?
How will I know if they're learning anything?"

Good questions! They show your spirit of excellence. But you're about to leave *regular history* behind.

" Regular history. What do you mean by that?
History is history! It's the people and events of the past.
It's the story of mankind! "

Is it? Where did you get that definition?

" Are you crazy?! I went to school. I sat through many a history class.
That's what we studied!"

Ah, but this is where I must challenge you, as I've been challenged. We only *think* that's what history is, because that's what was in our history books. So, we were learning not only the history they taught us, but also the *definition of history* they taught us. As Christian adults, though, we must hold every definition up to His blazing light. Is history indeed the story of mankind? Could the secular minds that birthed our history textbooks also have had a secular definition of history itself? Is it possible?

" Okay, okay! You yak a lot. Just let me think. "

Gladly. That's just what I hope you'll do. I hope you think about history in a brand new way, for it is *not* first the story of mankind, but of the One who *made* mankind! Yes, the Lord God Creator initiated all life and, of course, the laws that govern life. He towers over all human existence. Thankfully, He chose to make us in His image; He chose to make our humanness special by giving us free choice. In other words, we have the privilege of deciding how we will *respond* to His preeminence!

God's initiation and *our response*...that's history. To the degree that we choose to believe and obey truth, to that degree our lives are blessed, our nations free and healthy, our science beneficial, our laws wise, our businesses prospering, and our art glorious. Each of these spheres of life cannot be understood without grasping the spiritual issues at their base. Again I say, *now that's history!*

" Then that means...er, that means the opposite is true!"

You hit the nail on the head! For a couple hundred years now, western civilization has put God on the sidelines of life, so that most history is taught as the story of mankind, as if people were the 'prime force' of the universe, as if they were the makers of themselves and of truth. How presumptuous! But there's more! After Darwin, little reason was seen to learn about the past; folks believed they were moving–on their own power–toward a perfect future. Since then, history has become a dull, meaningless 'obligation.' (No wonder it was so boring!) It should be a *personal* encounter with the King of the Universe, the Maker of our souls! It should be one of the most inspiring, personal, real, and intimate topics because it hooks us up with the truths that make life work! And our practical-minded boys *especially* need to know that history is about *right now*...about truth and power and law and right and good government...and all the other things for which this world is secretly hungering. Now *that's* something into which kids can pour their energies and ambitions!

" *I admit that my history classes were dull and meaningless, but I never wanted to admit that to my kids.* "

Well, isn't it good to know all that's behind you?! Because history *is different* than what you were taught, you can teach history in a *different way* than you were taught. You won't need the artificial motivations of 'questions at the end of the chapter' and 'multiple-choice tests.' Why? Because you're not giving your kids dead material! Their eyes won't glaze over! Real truth is a spark that lights its own fire! All you have to do is convey truth to your kids in the way the Bible often does: through story. Hence, the copious booklists in this guide, and the happy fact that your children's 'history time' will be spent basking in great reading. Since all your children can learn together, they will play it, eat it, dream it, and talk it. Besides, as Jeremy Jackson put it: *history is philosophy* [beliefs] *teaching by example.* All these great books give lots of great examples. But...

" *What do you mean 'but?' That was sounding good!* "

All that good reading will still be mere humanistic fluff unless your kids have first been 'primed' to look for the deep spiritual issues at work in the lives of all those people and events they're reading about. Otherwise, your child will just be impressed by the human heroics. Ooh, more humanism, even though well-meant! That's where this guide's commentary comes in (the emboldened text). You'll see that a paragraph or two introduces each new topic. It does that 'priming' for you, and incrementally and subtly weaves together the deepest issues of this era of history. By the end of the guide, the veil will lift. History will be truly connected. The key importance of God and of beliefs will be seen, and the consequences of truth and untruth will be personally grasped by your children. If you, Mama, can just read the emboldened text too, you'll find yourself much better able to lead–and enjoy–vivid and profound conversations with your kids on some of the most important topics in life...and isn't that why we're homeschooling?! (It isn't absolutely necessary, but it's great if you can!) To help your kids think deeply, *ThinkWrite* exercises focus their seeking and synthesizing. (Sample answers are provided for you in Appendix 1.)

" *OK. So what about Day One. Tell me how I should plan each week.* "

Well, that's up to you. But you mustn't panic! Remember, this history is a new kind of history. You'll see that it takes on a life of it's own. You'll gather the little kids on the couch to read aloud to them, or you'll have kids sprawled around (or sitting in an orderly row) as each is absorbed in their books. At dinner time or while driving to piano lessons you'll have the most fascinating conversations, guaranteed! Older students can more deeply research special topics. Yes, this can be enough. It's that simple.

But you may want more, as befits your style. You can arrange special bi-weekly or monthly evenings where you gather as a family, or with other families, to give oral reports, put on skits, show off projects, and eat 'historical' food. You can all talk about what you've learned. Believe me! Your mother-in-law will be thunderstruck by the good, deep stuff flowing out of your child's heart! You can make notebooks, do narrations, or create timelines. You can draw, paint, sculpt, or build Lego towers. You can 'publish' a newspaper reporting on 'breaking news' and mail it to friends and family. (Many ideas are shared on our online discussion loop.) Or, you can do none of the above. You can simply immerse in and discuss great living books (as listed in this guide).

You'll be spending a great deal of time in this era, and the learning (both factual and ideological) will be quite impressive. You won't need any tests to show that your kids are learning; they'll be living what they learn, playing what they learn, talking what they learn, and praying what they learn!

As for overall planning, it's good to jot down a general plan. How many years do you have left with your students? How many historical eras do you need to cover? (There is a *TruthQuest History* guide for each era, after the Old Testament epoch.) If you have plenty of time, you can 'play' this guide by ear (knowing that the content of this guide has been carefully planned) and go at the rate of interest in your students, allowing time for greater or lesser depth as you feel led...*or* you can divide the number of units in this guide by the number of months you have available, and then see to it that you get through them in a timely fashion. Either way is fine.

You know what's best because you're the one who is seeking God for His plan for your family! He certainly doesn't have a one-size-fits-all-plan for His children. He has made each one uniquely, and has a unique plan for their lives; how and what they learn is part of that plan! Assuredly, I don't know what that plan is, so what right do I have to schedule your day?! Heaven forbid! (Literally!)

Enough said.

Let me just close, then, with a few 'housekeeping' details:

1.) This era we're studying includes many 'touchy' topics. If you question your children, you may be surprised to find they have already been exposed to the common worldly thinking on these topics, despite your best efforts. You see, the secular worldview is everywhere! I've heard it coming from video tapes playing in children's clothing stores, for example. That's why, in this guide, we try to *lightly* introduce the biblical worldview on these 'touchy' topics. So please don't assume, when reading the Table of Contents, that we are trying to make your children 'politically correct.' On the contrary! We're trying to gently alert them to truth where falseness is widespread.

This era also includes many horrific events, such as the world wars, sinking of the Titanic, etc. I've included these topics for those who are able to study them, but, parents, you alone can decide that. Be assertive! You know what needs to be learned by your child, which ideas you'd like to defer until your child is older, and you know Whom to seek for wisdom and direction!

2.) All worrying about acquiring listed books is hereby outlawed! You can see that I've listed oodles of books so you have as many choices as possible! Certainly, you're *not* supposed to read each book on each topic. It's a smorgasbord; enjoy the delicious options! Don't try to be such a 'good mother' that you bore your kids to tears by reading a million books on the each topic! Wondering which books to select? Probably, the newer the book, the more *post*-Christian is its outlook, but there *are* new books which are very good, especially in the picture book section.

3.) Books which were known or deemed to be *in-print* at the time of this writing are marked with an asterisk. (*) The asterisk does *not* mean it is a 'preferred' book, as is often assumed.

4.) The following books provide a narrative 'spine,' *if* you like to use spine books. They are not at all required. Be completely assured that you can use this *TruthQuest History* guide *without* using any of them, as we also cite oodles of topic-specific books:

Story of the Great Republic, by H.A. Guerber	Gr. 3-7
This Country of Ours, by H.E. Marshall	Gr. 3-8

5.) Be aware that, at the request of parents, I've included more of the current books you're likely to see on your library shelves. I have not personally reviewed each of these books. Parents, you'll have to determine what is actually read by your children!

6.) Remember, the grade levels marked on the booklists denote estimated independent reading, *not recommended* reading level. I would have to live for a thousand years to evaluate all the books in this guide! Besides, only *you* know what is best for your children!

7.) Some kids have favorite book series, so the series names are in parentheses in the listings.

8.) Searches through your library's database will be more effective if you do *not* use a book's subtitle. So why did I include them in the booklists? They give a glimpse of the book's content. But few library databases include subtitles, so don't nullify your searches by including them.

9.) What happens if you can't find a book on a topic? Be creative. Use an encyclopedia or some other general resource. Hey, when you decide to use 'living books' and to learn through real literature, you're automatically committed to using whatever you can find. That's true no matter which curriculum guide you choose. See why I list so many books here? I'm trying to increase your chances of finding gems. A *copyrighted* list of books cited in this guide is also included in Appendix 2. It may *not* be copied for others, but you may make a copy to keep in your purse during book hunts!

10.) I have not listed each American president in this guide, only those who were most influential. If you'd like your children to follow each presidency, simply add that information from a resource of your own.

11.) You would do well to highlight your own state's history when we're covering your region.

12.) This is a large guide! Feel free to move through it more quickly by skipping topics you feel are unnecessary. You're the executive! This guide is only a tool!

13.) One last thing...enjoy!

Table of Contents

Notes for Mom

TruthQuest History

American History for Young Students III
✦ 1865-2000 ✦

TruthQuest History
❂
American History for Young Students III (1865-2000)

Okay, I'll admit it. When I was a girl, about your age, I once ran away from home. I packed an outfit and stomped out the front door. I was *so* mad!

I'd had enough of my mother telling me what to do and how to do it! Couldn't she tell that I could run my own life? I wasn't a baby anymore! Didn't she see how good my ideas were? Why couldn't she understand that I already had life figured out and didn't need her interference?! After all, I was eight years old!

My life was filled with *important* things— kickball games, tree forts, football fests, doll houses, bike trails, tadpoles, and great books! But my mom was gettin' in the way! She made unreasonable demands! She insisted I clean my room, help around the house, and do nice things for my little sister. How on earth was I going to do everything I wanted to do if I had to mess around with all that nonsense?!

"So, who needs her?!" I thought. "I'm outta here! She'll be sorry once I'm gone." She'd realize what a mistake she had made telling me what to do and acting like I couldn't make it on my own just fine. But by then I'd be gone. Ha! How sweet it was to think of the regret she'd feel!

You might have felt this same feistiness once or twice. I think it's probably the best way of describing the 'sin nature' that's in us all. We all want to run our own show. Funny thing is, the reason we think we can make it on our own is because the big

people in our lives have done so much to take care of us and teach us!

Well, guess what. Since America is filled with people, and people all have this same desire to be their own boss, what do you think happened to this country when things were going pretty well–after the hard times were mostly past, when the Revolutionary War was over, when the Civil War was behind us, cities were growing, and pioneer farms were prospering?!

You can guess, right?! Many Americans started thinking like I was thinking. They figured they had 'proven' they could take care of themselves. Maybe they admitted they had needed God at the beginning when they were a baby country; they needed His truth to get the government and the laws and their businesses on the right track. But they thought they were too grown up to need God *now*. They thought they'd figured out life all by themselves! They started thinking *they* were the ones who had made their own success! So they didn't think they needed any Boss-God telling them what to do!

Truth be told, I can see how the Americans of the 1800s fell into this trap so easily. There *had* been a lot of progress. Trains crossed mountain ranges. Pioneers tamed the wilderness. Factories were whirring away. Telegraphs flung messages clear across the nation, while farm reapers, sewing machines, cotton gins, and steam engines churned away, making hard labor so much easier.

But here's the thing: people started thinking progress had come *only* because they were so super-de-dooper. And that brings us to the 'hot potato' of history: what do we *choose* to believe is the truth about God and about people? I call those the *Big 2 Beliefs*. They are the absolute heartbeat of history. Why? Because what folks believe to be true shapes everything they think and everything they do.

Now, God has made it absolutely clear in the Bible, in the very laws of nature, and even in the starry sky that He is the Creator.[1] He is the boss. (That's the true answer to the first big question in life: *Who is God?* It's the right *Big Belief #1*.) What He says goes. He made up the game, so He gets to make up the rules. And whatever He says is true is *absolutely* true for everyone and everybody because God doesn't just tell us truth, He IS truth,[2] and He is the same yesterday, today, and forever.[3] Since He doesn't change, truth doesn't change. It's that simple. The happy thing is that He's such a loving God that all His plans happen to be best for us! They bring us health, safety, peace, creativity, prosperity, good family life, and all those other fantastic things that make families and nations solid and free! Neato!

Actually, the truth about *Big Belief #2* (which answers the question–*Who is mankind?*) is hidden inside that last paragraph. Did you catch it? It's pretty simple. If God created us, then we didn't make ourselves. We do not have the power to create people, but God does. That means God is more powerful than us. If someone more powerful than us made us, then we are *not* the boss of ourselves. On the other hand, the fact that God *wanted* to make us because He wanted to know us, talk with us, and love us...well, that shows how precious we are! He even made us in His own image, so that we have powerful choices about what we want to believe and do. Double neato!

Ah, but hidden in *that* last paragraph was the 'hot potato' of history. We get to choose what we believe. Phew-ee! That's a whopper choice! Bigger than you probably know right now! We can believe what's true...or what's not true.

Why are we talking about all this right now? Because that 'whopper choice' is the real story of this last chapter of America's history. It's so easy for us to get carried away, thinking that history is all about people and the things they do. But it's not, because we're not the boss of the universe! History is *really* about what God has said and done... *then* what we believe and do about it.

Yes, we will meet many people in this guide, and we will see the things they did. But I want you to look deeper, like when you try to glimpse the bottom of a lake or a river. See what's deep down in history too!

'Whopper choices' are always at hand, but it seems that the folks who lived during the last century-plus we're exploring (1865-2000), had ultra-whoppers because so many hoity-toity ideas were swirling around. And, ooh, were they tempting! They all boiled down to one thing. All these new ideas said that people were just fine on their own. They could use their own brains or their own feelings to figure out the truth about life...and run the

---

[1] *...that which is known about God is evident within them; for God made it evident to them. For since the creation of the world His invisible attributes, His eternal power and divine nature, have been clearly seen, being understood through what has been made, so that they are without excuse. (Rom. 1:19-20)*

[2] John 14:6.

[3] Hebrews 13:8.

whole world perfectly! Anything God might say would just get in their way. Yep! Those are the same goofy thoughts I had when I ran away from home!

I'll tell you a little secret. None of these smarty-pants ideas were possible if people admitted that God had created all people and the entire universe, because that would automatically make Him boss, as we just said a couple minutes ago. *So folks decided to believe that God did not create us.* Then, they used science to look for 'proof.' Of course, that makes for bad science, when you aren't just observing what really exists, but are instead trying to find something you want to find. But, that's what folks did anyway (during this time we're studying, and just before it).

Let me say it another way: many people wanted to believe the world could *run* without God (and could instead be run by people), so they tried to 'prove' the world was *made* without God. The first person to 'prove' this in a way that seemed convincing enough was a man named Charles Darwin. He said the world was getting a little better all the time; it was *evolving*. But, it was evolving without God, Darwin said; it was evolving with its own earthly power! Ah, that was even better, folks thought! Not only could they ignore God, but they could also believe they were getting smarter and better and that they'd soon be *so* evolved they could make a perfect world!

Yes, it was with human power that people now intended to rule the world. Since the power of one person is small, they decided to link the power of many people through governments. Then, they could make what they believed to be perfect schools, perfect laws, perfect towns, perfect businesses, and even perfect people! They had only to get

rid of the old ways of thinking–the Christian ways–and they could then remake the world with their new beliefs! They had only to convince people that human progress would rule the universe!

And that's just what they set out to do... through schools, books, speeches, political campaigns, science, and more! Surely it was a slow process, but as you watch this part of history you'll see that even many Christians fell for all this silliness because many of the leaders of the church had flocked to these flattering ideas. How terribly, terribly sad. They forgot, or ignored, the right *Big 2 Beliefs!*

Well, when I ran away from home, I made it just half a block before I realized how silly it was to think that I could take care of myself. I got scared, and rightfully so! I *couldn't* make it on my own. I *didn't* have life all in hand. I admitted that the good things in my life came from my parents! I whirled around and ran into my mother's arms as fast as my eight-year-old legs would carry me. I had to humble myself and admit that I needed Mom and Dad, and that I needed to learn the good things they had to teach me.

So, here's the question of this history exploration: what did people believe, how did their beliefs affect history, and if they got too big for their britches, did they hurry back to God?

Well, let's find out! Let's dig in! And don't forget! We're discovering the most recent years of American history–the world of your grandparents, parents, and *you!* So, you're not just watching history this time, you're living it!

1 ♣ Picking Up the Pieces (Reconstruction)

When we left off in the last guide, America's tragic Civil War between the northern states and the southern states had just ended, and Abraham Lincoln had just been assassinated. That was a pretty sad place to stop our story, but we can now look ahead. Trouble is, what happened right after the war isn't very nice either, especially in the South. War is a serious thing, and picking up the pieces is tough, but it's part of our history so we had better tackle it. We'll be able to move on to happier topics later. As always, though, you'll see there were people who did the right thing and were kind to others! Of course, those who were selfish and bossy hurt those around them.

This time after the Civil War is called *Reconstruction*. That's a big word, but it simply means "building again." You see, the South had been hit hardest by the war since almost every battle was fought there and they had lost so many of their men in the fighting.[4]

After the South surrendered, the northerners got to decide if the southerners should be allowed back into the American government. *What a sticky situation!* You can imagine that it was hard for many northerners to give southerners power because they were afraid the government would be ripped up by the same arguments all over again. So for a while, the southerners didn't have any real voice in the American government, and that was a terrible feeling for them, especially since many of them had fought the Civil War (or the *War Between the States*) because they were worried about the government in Washington getting too bossy and overpowering. It seemed like their worst nightmares had come true! In fact, the government was trying to decide if the southern leaders should be punished for treason—for turning against the United States—and that is a very serious crime with a very serious punishment. Both sides hardly trusted each other! Besides, they were mad at the other side for killing their soldiers—their sons and husbands and fathers and brothers!

Too, the South had always had, by and large, just one kind of business: farming, especially growing cotton. It was the slaves that did most of the work on the big farms (plantations) and the southern slaves had been freed. So now the postwar, burned-out plantations went to weeds. There was no money to buy seed, no money to pay workers, and few trains to take the crops to market if there had been crops. You see, before the war, the southerners had put almost all their money and effort into building bigger farms and buying more slaves. They hadn't built many factories or bridges or canals or railroads or any of the other things that make good businesses possible, and without good businesses there isn't any way for people to work to buy food for their families. This made the mess after the war even worse!

It seems that President Lincoln had intended a gentle plan for Reconstruction, but he had been killed. Tricky fellows started taking advantage of all the troubles; they were called carpet-baggers and scalawags. Because most Americans, I'm ashamed to admit, weren't very excited about living next to or hiring ex-slaves (because they were black and because they were

---

[4] Clarence Carson, *A Basic History of the United States—Volume 3* (Wadley, AL: American Textbook Committee, 1985) 178. The North lost more men, but the South lost a higher percentage. Carson's ideas are throughout this section.

4

uneducated), there really wasn't anywhere the former slaves could go. Isn't that sad?! Many of them ended up working on the same plantations they'd been on before the war, but they still weren't getting paychecks. They had to give part (a "share") of their crops to the plantation owner in return for the use of his land, so they were called sharecroppers. Most lived in the same slave quarters (which were often dreadful) and remained uneducated. It was hard for them to get ahead, too, because they weren't used to taking care of money. It was going to be a long road back for the former slaves. (They are now called African-Americans too.)

One man who wrote about this time, Clarence Carson, didn't pull any punches in describing it: "Reconstruction was a sorry episode in American history...."[5] But as sad as this topic is, we can always look for the folks who did the right thing, even in hard times, and that's inspiring!

❧ Reconstruction:

Story of the Great Republic, by H.A. Guerber, Ch. LVIII, LXb	Gr. 3-7
This Country of Ours, by H.E. Marshall, Ch. 92-93	Gr. 3-8

Reconstruction, by Brendan January (Cornerstones) This provides a very succinct overview.	Gr. 3-7
Reconstruction, by Judith Peacock (Let Freedom Ring)	Unknown

Fiction/Historical Fiction:

Be Ever Hopeful, Hannalee, **and**, *Turn Homeward, Hannalee*, by Patricia Beatty Story of Southern girl who tries to survive during difficulties of Reconstruction	Gr. 3-10
Little Colonel, by Annie Fellows Johnston Dear Kentucky girl helps reunite a family torn by the Civil War; 1st in a series.	Gr. 4-10
Forty Acres and Maybe a Mule, by Harriette Robinet Ex-slaves try face great difficulty in the first year of Reconstruction.	Gr. 5-10
Sounder, by William Armstrong This is the story of a (later) sharecropping family and their beloved dog. Very poignant.	Gr. 5-12
The Wound of Peter Wayne, by Leonard Wibberley	Gr. 5-12

---

[5] Carson 3:174 (for this quote, and for other ideas in this section).

2🌿 Westward Ho!

For many Americans, the best hope for a fresh start lay in the 'new' lands out west, especially after Abraham Lincoln's *Homestead Act* gave federal land to settlers who would improve their lot. The railroads were a-growin'! They soon connected east and west in an engineering marvel, and travel was now much easier. Cowboys and farmers, merchants and traders, all were pouring into the west. In fact, the Great Plains area–first seen merely as a huge obstacle on the way west, and thus dubbed the 'Great American Desert'–was now viewed as good settling land too, especially when a tough kind of wheat was found that could thrive there, but that's a story in itself!

But these lands weren't empty! Not only were the western Indian tribes living there, but many of the eastern tribes had been sent out west to live on reservations–land that was just for them. Now white settlers were moving even onto their reservations! They were breaking their promises and treaties!

Do you remember in the last *TruthQuest History* guide we talked about this thorny issue? We won't talk much about it again here, but do know that Native Americans (Indians) are still affected by the wrongs of the past. God alone fully understands all that happened and all that He wanted to happen, and if we want to understand too, we need to ask Him for His truth and wisdom. All lands and people are actually His. He lifts people up in blessing and puts them down in judgment. But His purposes and judgments are surely beyond me! All I know is that they are always for the best...in the long run. I don't know *what* the Lord wanted to have happen on this land between the white man and the Indians, and I don't know that God was judging anybody, but I do know that both sides needed the Lord and His good ways. Any time you see people rejecting God–whether it be a greedy white settler or a pagan Indian who ignores all that the heavens reveal about the Lord God (before hearing about Jesus Christ), let's be willing to admit where people were wrong. And then we can try to make things better as God would lead us! Yeah!

(And parents, you should know that much of the current treatment of these issues is rather 'politically correct.' Please be careful about the worldview of the books you select on this topic, even being careful about the books listed below. They represent what you're likely to find at your library; you must filter!)

Well, we've been talking about the Indians, but so much of their story involves their fight with the white newcomers, that it may be best to first learn about the big wave of settlers. Then you'll better understand what the Indians were facing. If you'd like to alter this order, of course you may! Either way, make sure to include the history of your own state if we're discussing your home area. Hang on to your hat, pardner! We're off!

2a🐾 Prairie pioneers, many of them immigrants

Note: In books containing info on many phases of pioneering, please read only the info on *prairie pioneers* since we studied other pioneer phases in earlier *TruthQuest History* units.

Wagon Wheels (I Can Read)   Gr. K-2
       by Barbara Brenner
       Based on a real story, an African-American family heads west.

> Here are some amazingly poignant books about the prairie. Don't miss 'em!
>
> *What You Know First*   All ages!
> *All the Places to Love*   All ages!
> *Three Names*   Gr. 1-5
>   all by Patricia MacLachlan
> *If You're Not from the Prairie* All ages!
>   by Dave Bouchard
> *Heartland*, by Diane Siebert All ages!

Clara and the Bookwagon, by Nancy Levinson (I Can Read)   Gr. K-2
       Prairie pioneer girl is thrilled when first traveling library arrives.

Prairie Primer A to Z, by Caroline Stutsman   Gr. K-3
       Beautifully illustrated book provides A to Z snippets of warm pioneer life.

True Book of Pioneers, by Mabel Harmer (True Books)   Gr. K-3

Sod Houses on the Great Plains, by Glen Rounds   Gr. 1-6
       What a fun style Rounds has! Boys especially love it!

The Story of the Homestead Act, by R. Conrad Stein (Cornerstones)   Gr. 2-7

The Story of the Conestoga Wagon, by Kenneth Richards (Cornerstones)   Gr. 2-7

The Seasons Sewn, by Ann Paul   Gr. 2-8
       This precious book uses quilt patterns to reveal the yearly flow of pioneer life.

Pioneering on the Plains, by Edith McCall (Frontiers of America)   Gr. 3-7
Pioneer Traders, by Edith McCall (Frontiers of America)   Gr. 3-7
Pioneer Show Folk, by Edith McCall (Frontiers of America)   Gr. 3-7

Pioneer Stories for Boys, by C. Richard Schaare   Gr. 3-7
       This book is unusually designed and illustrated, so is good for reluctant readers, but its rarity makes finding a copy very unlikely.

First Book of Pioneers, by Walter Havighurst (First Books)   Gr. 3-8

To Be a Pioneer, by Paul Burns   Gr. 3-8

The Winning of the West, by Harold McCracken   Gr. 3-8

The Treeless Plains — Gr. 3-10
    by Glen Rounds
    What a fun style Rounds has!
    Boys especially love it!

Frontier Home, by R. Bial — Gr. 3-10
    Photographs show reality.

Frontier Leaders and Pioneers — Gr. 3-10
    by Dorothy Heiderstadt

19th Century Frontier Fort — Gr. 4-8
    by Scott Steedman (Inside Story)

Heroines of the Early West — Gr. 4-12
    by Nancy Ross (Landmark)

You'll want to learn about the **Orphan Trains** which stopped at various stations where families could see if there were any orphans they wanted to keep. Can you imagine?!

Orphan Train Rider: One Boy's True... — Gr. 5-12
    by Andrea Warren
Fiction/Historical Fiction:
Train to Somewhere, by Eve Bunting — Gr. 1-5
*The *Orphans' Journey* series — Gr. 3-9
    by Arleta Richardson
*The *Orphan Train* series — Gr. 3-9
    by Joan Lowery Nixon
Film:
*Orphan Train — Parental decision
    I've NOT seen this! Content unknown!

Famous Pioneers, by F. Folsom — Gr. 4-12
Chapter biographies on many pioneer leaders.

Sketches of America Past, by Eric Sloane — Various
    Three books in one, about pioneer tools, woodworking, etc., with meticulous drawings which can be enjoyed by all ages.

☞ Just for fun: *History Alive Through Music: Westward Ho!* by Diana Waring — Various
    This audio features real songs sung by the pioneers!

Fiction/Historical Fiction:

The *Little House* series, by Laura Ingalls Wilder — Various
    The original nine books in the series can be read by students in Gr. 2-8, but even younger children enjoy them as read-alouds. Also, a lovely new series (*My First Little House*) of picture-books relate to even younger children many of the precious scenes from the main series. Sample titles are: *Sugar Snow, *Prairie Day, *A Deer in the Wood, *Going to Town, *Farmer Boy Birthday, *Winter on the Farm*, etc. As if that weren't enough, there is a lovely *Little House Cookbook*, by Barbara Walker, the *Laura Ingalls Wilder Songbook*, by Eugenia Garson, lovely paper dolls, and even many books about Laura Ingalls Wilder herself, such as: the tenderly illustrated *Pioneer Girl*, by William Anderson (Gr. 1-5), *Laura Ingalls Wilder*, by Gwenda Blair (Gr. 1-4), *The World of Little House*, by Carolyn Collins (stories, activities, and foods for Gr. 3-10), and both *Laura Ingalls Wilder Country* and *Laura Ingalls Wilder Country Cookbook*, by William Anderson (Gr. 4-12). Roger MacBride carried on the tradition by relating the life of Rose Wilder Lane, daughter of Laura Ingalls Wilder, in the *Rocky Ridge* stories (Gr. 3-8).

Long Way to a New Land, **and,** *Long Way Westward*, by J. Sandin (I Can Read) Gr. K-2

Pioneer Bear, by Joan Sandin (Step Into Reading 2)   Gr. K-2
    Based on a true story!

Dakota Dugout, by Ann Turner   Gr. K-3
    Another don't-miss book!

Going West, by Jean Van Leeuwen   Gr. 1-3
    A very lovely, evocative book.

New Hope, by Henri Sorensen   Gr. 1-4
    Gorgeous illustrations tell of Danish founder of Minnesota town.

High Wind for Kansas, by Mary Calhoun   Gr. 1-4
    This story is actually based on fact. Someone *did* attach a sail to their Conestoga wagon
    so it would travel faster!

McBroom and the Big Wind, by Sid Fleischman   Gr. 1-5
    Hilarity ensues when a zany prairie family faces a storm! Just for fun.

Sarah, Plain and Tall, by Patricia MacLachlan   Gr. 1-6
    Beloved story of mail-order bride from Maine. You might also enjoy the sequels:
    Skylark, and *Caleb's Story*.

Pioneer Sodbuster, by Irene Estep   Gr. 1-6

Dandelions, by Eve Bunting   Gr. 1-7
    The tremendously poignant writing in this book capture the loneliness of prairie life.
    Though sad, this book is quite special.

Dear Levi: Letters from the Overland Trail, by Elvira Woodruff   Gr. 1-7
    Boy's letters show life on the way west.

Little Obie and the Flood, by Martin Waddell   Gr. 2-6

Willow Whistle, by Cornelia Meigs   Gr. 2-6

Klara's New World, by Jeanette Winter   Gr. 2-6
    Swedish pioneer girl settles in Minnesota.

Addie Across the Prairie, by Laurie Lawlor   Gr. 3-8
    Girl adjusts to difficulties of pioneer life in the Dakota Territory.

Caddie Woodlawn, **and**, *Magical Melons*, by Carol Ryrie Brink   Gr. 3-9
    Wonderful, funny escapades of Wisconsin pioneer girl. Don't miss these!

Trouble River, by Betsy Byars   Gr. 3-9
    Boy's raft is only hope of escape from Indians.

The Children Who Stayed Alone, by Bonnie Worline   Gr. 3-10
    Highly esteemed story, originally titled: *Sod House Adventure*.

Old Yeller, **and**, *Savage Sam*, by Fred Gipson   Gr. 4-12
    Powerful, beloved stories of Texas settlers' brave dog, Old Yeller, and his son, Sam.

Hannah's Brave Year, by Rhoda Wooldridge   Gr. 3-12
    Pioneer children are orphaned in Texas. There are at least three sequels.

Sod-House Winter: They Came from Sweden, by Clara Ingram Judson   Gr. 4-10

The following books are in the esteemed *American Heritage* series from Aladdin, not the more well-known series by that same title:
    Homestead of the Free: The Kansas Story, by Aileen Fisher   Gr. 4-10
    Back of Beyond, by George Cory Franklin (set in Colorado)   Gr. 4-10
    Green Grows the Prairie: Arkansas in the 1890s, by Charlie May Simon   Gr. 4-10
    Sons of the Big Muddy: The Dakota Territory in the 1880s, by W. Granberg   Gr. 4-10

Song of the Pines, by Walter & Marion Havighurst (Land of the Free)   Gr. 4-12
    Award-winning story of Norwegian settlers lumbering in Wisconsin.

A Lantern in Her Hand, by Bess Streeter Aldrich   Gr. 5-12
    Beloved tale of a pioneer woman's hard, but rich, life in Nebraska. *Very good!*

Young Pioneers, by Rose Wilder Lane (formerly titled, *Let the Hurricane Roar*)   Gr. 5-12
    Laura Ingalls Wilder's daughter tells an *excellent* story of a newlywed pioneer couple.

☞ If you enjoy the *American Girl* books, the series about Kirsten tells of an immigrant pioneer girl into Minnesota. There are two Christian series about pioneer girls, though each family must determine their literary worth: the *Sadie Rose* series by Hilda Stahl, and the *Suzannah* series by Elaine Schulte.

2b❧ Prairie wheat

I hope you have time to read at least the first book listed below because it tells the amazing, providential story (or so it would seem) of how better wheat was brought by the Mennonites to the American prairie–wheat that made the farmers prosperous and made the Great Plains a source of food for the entire world!

The King of Prussia and a Peanut Butter Sandwich, by Alice Fleming   Gr. 2-8
    I love this book!

Turkey Red, by Esther Vogt   Gr. 4-9

> This book may be as good as the one above, but I've not read it. Being from a Christian publisher, it focuses on the Mennonites who brought this great wheat to America.

2c❧ Locust/grasshopper plagues

Fiction/Historical Fiction:

Clouds of Terror, by Catherine Welch (On My Own)   Gr. 1-4

The Middle Sister, by Miriam Mason   Gr. 1-6
> Girl tenderly cares for her apple tree during a grasshopper plague.

Grasshopper Summer, by Ann Turner   Gr. 2-8
> Reluctant pioneer boy faces grasshopper plague!

2d❧ Mayo Brothers, frontier doctors

Want to meet two frontier doctors? The famous Mayo Clinic still bears their name.

Value of Sharing: Mayo Brothers, by Spencer Johnson (ValueTales)   Gr. 1-4

The Mayo Brothers, by Jane Goodsell (Crowell Biography)   Gr. 1-4

Frontier Surgeons, by Emily Crofford (Carolrhoda's Creative Minds)   Gr. 1-6

Will and Charlie: Boy Doctors, by Marie Hammontree (Childhood)   Gr. 1-6

3❧ The Wild West!

But it wasn't just the homesteading farmers headin' for the hills. No, sirree! The West was becoming the *Wild West!* Everywhere there were cowboys and cattle drives (as up the Chisholm Trail); there were even a few camels! Add to that, miners and ghost towns, marshals and outlaws, dusty heat and blizzards, as well as the terrible slaughter of the buffalo and its effect on the Indians, and you're starting to get the picture! But remember, these people were starting a new life. They faced a 'fork in the road.' They had to choose whether to build on themselves or build up God's way in their lives and in their towns. Sadly, more than a few people went west because they thought they could 'run their own show.' And that's why there was some ruthlessness and lawlessness out west. It wasn't all glamour and adventure as you might think from watching movies. Remember, good laws are a great gift. They protect us from harm. Don't ever let yourself be made to apologize for law. It's a big part of God's good plan for us.

3a✦ Cowboys and other western goodies!

My Cowboy Book, by B. Grant   Gr. K-2

*Where the Buffalo Roam   Gr. K-5
     by Jacqueline Geis (I love this!)

*Cowboys, by Glen Rounds   Gr. 1-3

*Cowboy ABC, by C. Demarest   Gr. 1-3

*Cowboys, by D. & M. Gorsline   Gr. 1-3

Big Book of the Wild West, **and,**   Gr. 1-4
Big Book of Cowboys, by Sydney Fletcher

*Old Chisholm Trail   Gr. 1-4
     by Rosalyn Schanzer

No wonder you Texans are so high and mighty! ☺ Look at some of the books written especially about your exciting history!

Real Book about the Texas Rangers   Gr. 3-8
     by Allyn Allen (Real Books)
Indians Who Lived in Texas   Gr. 3-8
     by Betty Warren
Lost Lakes (Winston Adventure)   Gr. 3-9
     by Catherine Peare
Ten Tall Texans, by Lee McGiffin   Gr. 3-12
Texas Rangers (Landmark)   Gr. 4-12
     by Will Henry
Ten Texas Tales, by R. Gilstrap   Gr. 4-12

Fiction/Historical Fiction:
Texas Star, by Enid Meadowcroft   Gr. 1-6
Johnny Texas, **and** *Johnny Texas on the*   Gr. 2-9
     San Antonio Road, by Carol Hoff

*Yippe-Yay! A Book about Cowboys and Cowgirls, by Gail Gibbons   Gr. 1-4

Indians and Cowboys, by Sanford Tousey   Gr. 2-6
     Very rare, but very precious. Also printed as separate volumes.

Camels are Meaner than Mules, by Mary Calhoun   Gr. 2-6
     US Army tried to use camels in Texas!

The Story of the Chisholm Trail, by R. Conrad Stein (Cornerstones)   Gr. 2-7

Cowboys and Cattle Drives, by Edith McCall (Frontiers of America)   Gr. 2-8

Cowboys and Cattle Trails, by Shannon Garst (American Adventure, older ser.)   Gr. 3-7
     Orphan cowboy becomes governor!

First Book of Cowboys, by Benjamin Brewster (First Bks)   Gr. 3-7

Silver and Lead, by Ralph Moody   Gr. 3-8
     This wonderful author tells of a western ghost town.

When Cowboys Rode the Chisholm Trail, by James McCague (How They Lived)   Gr. 3-8

Real Book about Cowboys, by Michael Gorham (Real Books)   Gr. 3-8

Real Book about the Wild West, by Adolph Regli (Real Books)   Gr. 3-8

The Book of Cowboys, by Holling Clancy Holling   Gr. 3-9
    This book is really a favorite; I hope you can locate a copy.

Up the Trail from Texas, by J. Frank Dobie (Landmark)   Gr. 3-9

Camel Express, by Olive Burt (Winston Adventure)   Gr. 3-9
    Army uses camels in Texas!

Lawless Land, by Mark Boesch (Winston Adventure)   Gr. 3-9
    Boy helps Montana vigilantes.

Texans Ride North: Story of the Cattle Trails,
    by John Jakes (Winston) Gr. 3-9

Bandannas, Chaps, and Ten-Gallon Hats
    by Bobbie Kalman   Gr. 3-9
    One of several in a series.

Cowboy Trade, by Glen Rounds Gr. 3-12
    Rounds's books are exceptional!

Trail Boss in Pigtails   Gr. 3-12
    by Marjorie Stover
    Gal drove herd from Texas to
    Chicago!

Book of the West, by C. Chilton Gr. 4-10

Copper Kings of Montana   Gr. 4-10
    by Marian Place (Landmark)

Cowboy (Eyewitness)   Gr. 4-12
    by David Murdoch
    Photos seem like museum visit;
    no narrative text.

Cowboy's Handbook, by T. Cody Gr. 4-12
    Factual overview.

Cowboys of the Wild West   Gr. 5-12
    by Russell Freedman
    Authentic photos and account.

Take a gander at great western art. It will really give you a feeling for the life of the Indians, pioneers, cowboys, animals, etc.

Art of the Old West, by Shirley Glubok Gr. 5-12

Frederic Remington:

Frederic Remington (Childhood)   Gr. 1-5
    by Clyde Moore
Child's History of Art, by Hillyer & Huey, (*Painting* sect., Ch. 31a) OR, *Young People's Story of Fine Art: Last Two Hundred Years*, pp. 96-99   Gr. 2-8
Frederic Remington (Art for Children)   Gr. 3-9
    by Ernest Raboff
Frederic Remington: Artist on Horseback   Gr. 4-12
    by LaVere Anderson
Painter of the Wild West (Messner)   Gr. 5-12
    by Robin McKown

Charles Russell:

Cowboy Artist, by S. Garst (Messner)   Gr. 5-12

George Catlin:

Man Who Painted Indians, by N. Plain Gr. 3-7

☞ Hopefully, you'll also view Karl Bodmer's & Albert Bierstadt's paintings.

Wild, Wild West, by James Daugherty   Gr. 5-12

☞ **Kickin' Up Some Cowboy Fun*, by Monica Hay Cook   Various
    Fun activities, games, and recipes!

☞ Want to learn some cowboy songs? *Cowboy Jamboree*, by Harold Felton   Various

☞ For activities, recipes, games, projects: **Wild West Days*, by David King   Various

Fiction/Historical Fiction:

☞ **The *Cowboy Sam* and the *Tom Logan* series are both super!** (by Edna Walker Chandler) These old 'graduated readers' have drawn many reluctant boys into the joy of reading! Each series gradually becomes more challenging to read, as the student's ability grows. Sadly, these are rather rare. (Gr. 1-5)

☞ **Another fantastic series begins with *Whitey Ropes and Rides!*** (by Glen Rounds) You're much more likely to find these warm, funny books in your library. (Gr. 1-5)

Thunderhoof, by Syd Hoff (I Can Read)   Gr. K-1

The Strawberry Roan, by Glen Rounds   Gr. K-2
    Another funny western story from Rounds! You'll love it!

**The Brave Cowboy*, by Joan Walsh Anglund   Gr. K-2
    Every child who has ever imagined himself as a cowboy will *love* this little book!

**Cowboy Country*, by Ann Scott   Gr. K-3
    An older cowboy tells of his hard, yet rewarding, life's work.

The Contests at Cowlick, by Richard Kennedy   Gr. 1-4
    Soooo funny! A clever boy takes on a whole gang of outlaws!

Cowboy Tommy's Roundup, by Sanford Tousey   Gr. 1-5
    A rare antique, but delightful!

Why Cowboys Sing, In Texas, by LeGrand   Gr. 1-5
    Always funny, LeGrand tells the story of a funny, singing cowboy.

Did you know there were cowboys and pioneers moving into new areas back East, such as Florida?! Here are some good stories:

**Brave the Wild Trail*, by M. Howard Gr. 3-8
**Strawberry Girl*, by Lois Lenski   Gr. 3-12

Mr. Yowder... (several in series) Gr. 1-6
    by Glen Rounds
    Do not miss these hilarious stories!

**Texas Roundup* (Adv. in Fr. Am) Gr. 2-4
    by Catherine Chambers

Me and the Man on the Moon-eyed Horse, by Sid Fleischman	Gr. 2-6
Young Sand Hills Cowboy, by Frances Kroll (Young Heroes Library)	Gr. 2-8
Pioneer Buckaroo, **and**, *Pioneer Tenderfoot*, by Irene Estep	Gr. 2-8
We Were There on the Chisholm Trail, by Ross Taylor (We Were There)	Gr. 3-8
We Were There with the California Rancheros, by Stephen Holt (We Were...)	Gr. 3-8
*Renegade in the Hills, **and**, **Sheriff at Waterstop*, by Andy Thomson Two Christian tales of the West.	Gr. 3-9
Ride a Northbound Horse, by Richard Wormser	Gr. 3-9
*Journal of Josh Loper, a Black Cowboy, by W. Myers (My Names is America)	Gr. 3-9
Cowboys, Cowboys, Cowboys, edited by Phyllis Fenner A collection of short stories by various authors.	Gr. 3-12
Cowman's Kingdom, by Edmund Collier (Aladdin's American Heritage) This story is set in Montana and Wyoming.	Gr. 4-9
*Brighty of the Grand Canyon, by Marguerite Henry Exciting story of western prospector and his burro.	Gr. 4-10
*Mustang: Wild Spirit of the West, by Marguerite Henry Now might be a great time to enjoy a classic Western horse story.	Gr. 4-12

☞ There are several Christian series about the West, such as those written by Janette Oke, the Thoenes, Michael Phillips & Judith Pella, Stephen Bly, etc. There isn't space here to list them all, but they're readily available from your homeschool supplier or local Christian bookstore.

☞ Of course, there are oodles of films you could watch! I won't even try to mention them all.

3b☙ Famous westerners–cowboys, cowgirls, marshals, explorers, and more!

*Buffalo Bill and the Pony Express, by Eleanor Coerr (History I Can Read)
     'Buffalo' Bill Cody was just 15-years-old when he rode for the Pony Express (which we
     covered in the last unit).
	Gr. K-2

John Muir, by Glen Dines (See & Read)   Gr. 1-3
     Life of early Western explorer, naturalist, and author (of famed dog story, *Stickeen*).

**Little Sure Shot: The Story of Annie Oakley*, by S. Spinner (Step Into Reading 3) Gr. 1-3

**Bill Pickett: Rodeoridin' Cowboy*, by Andrea Pinkney   Gr. 1-4
     True story of gutsy, black rodeo star, the son of former slaves.

*Buffalo Bill, by Ingri & Edgar Parin d'Aulaire   Gr. 1-4
     Don't ever miss a d'Aulaire picture-biography!

John Muir, by Charles Graves (Crowell Biography)   Gr. 1-4

Adam Bradford, Cowboy, by Don Russell (Garrard Americans All)   Gr. 1-4

The Value of Humor: Will Rogers, by Spencer Johnson (ValueTales)   Gr. 1-4

John Muir: Friend of Nature, by Margaret Goff Clark (Garrard Discovery)   Gr. 1-4

Annie Oakley: The Shooting Star, by Charles Graves (Garrard Discovery)   Gr. 1-4

**Shooting for the Moon: Amazing Life and Times of Annie Oakley*, by S. Krensky   Gr. 1-4

You'll enjoy these tall tales about a legendary cowpoke–Pecos Bill!

Pecos Bill Finds a Horse, by K. Darling   Gr. 1-4
*Pecos Bill, by Steven Kellogg   Gr. 1-4
*Pecos Bill, by Brain Gleeson   Gr. 1-4
Pecos Bill and Lightning, by Leigh Peck   Gr. 3-8
Pecos Bill, by Harold Felton   Gr. 4-12

Buffalo Bill (Garrard Discovery) Gr. 1-4
     by Mary Davidson

*Buffalo Bill (Childhood)   Gr. 1-5
     by August Stevenson

*John Muir (Childhood)   Gr. 1-5
     by Montrew Dunham

Will Rogers (Childhood)   Gr. 1-5
     by Guernsey Van Riper, Jr.

*Annie Oakley, by Ellen Wilson (Childhood)   Gr. 1-5

**Black Cowboy, Wild Horses: A True Story*, by Julius Lester   Gr. 1-5
     The true story of Bob Lemmons, a great cowboy and former slave.

Who's That Girl with a Gun? A Story of Annie Oakley, by Robert Quackenbush   Gr. 1-5

Buffalo Bill, by Frank Beals (American Adventure, older series)   Gr. 2-7

Wild Bill Hickok, by Sanford Tousey   Gr. 2-7
    Too rare to seek, but if you have it, enjoy!

Will Rogers: Cowboy Philosopher, by Eliz. Montgomery (Americans All)   Gr. 2-7

Nat Love, Negro Cowboy, by Harold Felton   Gr. 3-7
    The adventures of the former slave nicknamed "Deadwood Dick."

Wild Bill Hickok, by A.M. Anderson (American Adventure, older series)   Gr. 3-8

*Bull's-Eye: A Photobiography of Annie Oakley, by Sue Macy   Gr. 3-8

The Story of Buffalo Bill, by Edmund Collier (Signature)   Gr. 3-8

The Story of Annie Oakley, by Edmund Collier (Signature)   Gr. 3-8

John Wesley Powell: Canyon's Conqueror, by Marian Place (Piper)   Gr. 3-8

Wyatt Earp: U.S. Marshal, by Stewart Holbrook (Landmark)   Gr. 3-9

Wild Bill Hickok Tames the West, by Stewart Holbrook (Landmark)   Gr. 3-9

Buffalo Bill's Great Wild West Show, by Walter Havighurst (Landmark)   Gr. 3-9

*Hats Off to John Stetson, by Mary Christian   Gr. 3-10
    Story of famous cowboy hat maker.

Down the Colorado with Major Powell, by James Ullman (North Star)   Gr. 4-10

Buffalo Bill, by Shannon Garst (Messner)   Gr. 4-12

Wes Powell: Conqueror of the Grand Canyon, by Leonard Wibberley   Gr. 4-12

Muir of the Mountains, by William Douglas (North Star)   Gr. 4-12

Buckey O'Neill of Arizona, by Jeanette Eaton   Gr. 4-12

Calamity Jane, by Doris Faber   Gr. 4-12

Butch Cassidy; Judge Roy Bean; Wyatt Earp; Buffalo Bill; Wild Bill Hickok   Gr. 4-12
    all by Carl Green

Will Rogers: Immortal Cowboy, by Shannon Garst (Messner)   Gr. 4-12

Gene Rhodes, Cowboy, by B. F. Day (Messner)   Gr. 4-12

Black Robe Peacemaker: Pierre de Smet, by J.G.E. Hopkins (Am. Background)   Gr. 4-12
    Story of frontier Catholic priest.

In Search of the Grand Canyon, by Mary Ann Fraser   Gr. 5-8

Bat Masterson, by Dale White   Gr. 5-12

Young Bat Masterson, by Richard O'Connor   Gr. 5-12

Films:

Richard "Little Bear" Wheeler has done a video presentation/re-enactment about the life of Wyatt Earp, titled: *Showdown at O.K. Corral*.

Gunfight at OK Corral, starring Gary Cooper

3c☙ Stagecoaches, such a part of Western travel

William Fargo (Childhood), by K. Wilkie   Gr. 1-5

Stagecoach Days and Stagecoach Kings   Gr. 3-8
    by Virginia Voight (How They Lived)

Wells Fargo, by Ralph Moody (North Star)   Gr. 5-12

> Want to read about an incredible western blizzard?
>
> *The Blizzard of 1896*   Gr. 1-6
>   by E.J. Bird

Fiction/Historical Fiction:

Stagecoach Sam, by Sanford Tousey   Gr. 1-5
    A rare antique, but delightful!

Charlie Drives the Stage, by Eric Kimmel   Gr. 1-6
    Hysterical!

Danger at Dry Creek, by Irving Werstein   Gr. 4-10

☞ You can make a paper stagecoach! *Built Your Own Wells Fargo Stagecoach*, by Richard Mansir.

4⚜ Choo-Choo! (Trains across America)

What really opened and changed the West was the railroads! After years of *very* hard work (much of it done by Chinese immigrants called *coolies*), the eastern and western rails met at a spot in Utah. The last spike they hammered in was golden! It could now be called the Transcontinental Railroad (*trans-* means across). America's two coasts—and the continent between—were finally connected. People and news could travel much faster and easier. Farmers, ranchers, and miners could get their goods back to eastern markets, and that is so important to building businesses. Pioneer homesteaders no longer had to raise everything they needed to live (*subsistence farming*); instead, they could raise crops to sell in far-away cities thanks to the railroads. These farmers then earned real cash and could *buy* things they needed. But the railroads made life much harder for the Indians: their lands were crisscrossed with snorting trains and these trains were bringing even more settlers!

Story of the Great Republic, by H.A. Guerber, Ch. LXa   Gr. 3-7

We can't talk about railroads without meeting legendary John Henry!

John Henry: An American Hero Gr. 1-5
  by Ezra Jack Keats
John Henry: Steel-Drivin' Man   Gr. 2-6
  by Adele deLeeuw
John Henry and His Hammer   Gr. 3-10
  by Harold Felton

Iron Horses, by Verla Kay   Gr. 1-4
  Don't miss this strong, energetic book!

George Pullman: Young Sleeping Car Builder   Gr. 1-6
  by Elisabeth Myers (Childhood)

James J. Hill: Young Empire Builder   Gr. 1-6
  by Mildred Comfort (Childhood)
  Story of founder of Great Northern Railroad.

Coolies, by Yin   Gr. 2-6

Men on Iron Horses, by Edith McCall (Frontiers of America)   Gr. 2-7

The Story of the Golden Spike, by R. Conrad Stein (Cornerstone)   Gr. 2-7

Ten Mile Day, by Mary Ann Fraser   Gr. 3-8

When the Rails Ran West, by James McCague (How They Lived)   Gr. 3-8

Building of the First Transcontinental Railroad, by Adele Nathan (Landmark)   Gr. 3-8

Golden Age of Railroads   Gr. 3-12
  by Stewart Holbrook (Landmark)

End O' Steel: Men and Railroads Gr. 4-9
  by Glenn Dines

Railroads Yesterday and Today   Gr. 4-9
  by Walter Buehr

Don't miss the exciting, true, story of Kate Shelley, who tried to...well, I better not tell!

Kate Shelley and the Midnight Express   Gr. 1-5
  by Margaret Wetterer (Carolrhoda)
Kate Shelley: Bound for Glory, by SanSouci Gr. 1-6

19th Century Railway Station, by Fiona Macdonald (Inside Story)   Gr. 4-12
        Cutaway views.

Across America on an Emigrant Train, by Jim Murphy   Gr. 4-12
        This book is based heavily on notes made by the famous English author, Robert Louis
        Stevenson, as he traveled on the Transcontinental Railroad with many emigrants (to
        Stevenson they were 'emigrants') searching for new lives out west.

Full Steam Ahead, by Rhoda Blumberg   Gr. 5-12

Fiction/Historical Fiction:

Train Song, by Diane Siebert   Gr. K-4
        This evocative poem gives a great sense of railroads. Nice illustrations.

Pioneer Engineer, by Irene Estep   Gr. 1-6

The Journal of Sean Sullivan, by William Durbin (My America)   Gr. 3-9

We Were There at the Driving of the Golden Spike, by David Shepherd   Gr. 3-9

The Railroad Book, by E. Boyd Smith   Gr. 3-12
        This lovely book, originally published in 1913, gives a nostalgic look at old trains.

Footprints of the Dragon, by Vanya Oakes (Land of the Free)   Gr. 4-12
        Story based on life of Chinese coolies working on the railroads.

5♣ *More* Gold!

Remember?! You learned about the California Gold Rush in the last guide, but that wasn't the only gold rush! No, indeed! Soon, gold was found in Alaska and in the Klondike part of Canada near Alaska. Seattle (in what is now Washington State) became a booming city because it was the jumping-off-point for miners headed to the gold fields!

When a Ton of Gold Reached Seattle, by E. Montgomery (How They Lived)   Gr. 3-8

When Men Panned Gold in the Klondike, by Edward Janes (How They Lived)   Gr. 3-8

Alaska Gold Rush, by May McNeer (Landmark)   Gr. 3-10

If You Lived in the Alaska Territory, by Nancy Levinson   Gr. 4-8

Yukon Gold, by Charlotte Jones   Unknown

Fiction/Historical Fiction:

The Klondike Cat, by Julie Lawson   Gr. 2-5

We Were There in the Klondike Gold Rush, by Benjamin Appel (We Were There) Gr. 3-8

Gold Miners' Rescue, by Dave & Neta Jackson (Trailblazer)   Gr. 3-9
     Fictional kids meet real Christian hero (Sheldon Jackson) of the Gold Rush.

☞ I should mention a poignant book which takes place in the Northwest around this same time: *Only Opal*, by Opal Whiteley (Gr. 1-3). It is the heartrending story of an orphaned Oregon girl who tries to have a positive attitude during a very hard life.

6☙ Native American Indians

Phew! Now you can see what the Indians were facing, right?! Well, let's now learn more about the Indians themselves! First, I'll list some general books, and then we'll get to specific tribes, Indian leaders, and special topics! Don't forget to focus on the Indians of your home area, if we're covering that area now. And don't forget what we said about this issue earlier; you need to be careful about the viewpoint in the books you read. Now, let's dig in!

6a☙ General resources

North American Indians, by Marie Gorsline   Gr. K-2

True Book of Indians, by Teri Martini (True Books)   Gr. K-3

Plains Indians, by Henry Pluckrose (Small World)   Gr. K-3

Meet the North American Indians, by Elizabeth Payne (Step-Up)   Gr. 1-5

Indians: The First Americans, by Patricia Miles Martin   Gr. 1-5

Famous Indian Tribes, by William Moyers   Gr. 1-6

American Indian Games, American Indian Foods, etc., by J. Miller (True Books) Gr. 2-6

Buffalo Harvest, by Glen Rounds   Gr. 3-8
     Beloved author tells how several Plains Indian tribes hunted buffalo.

Indian Tribes of America, by Marion Gridley   Gr. 3-9

Indian Fishing and Camping, Indian Hunting, Indians at Home, Indian Games and Crafts, Indian Sign Language, The Indian and the Buffalo etc., by Robert Hofsinde   Gr. 3-12

Among the Plains Indians, by Lorenz Engel   Gr. 3-12
    Discusses the several tribes that inhabited the Great Plains.

Famous American Indians, by S. Carl Hirsch   Gr. 3-12
    Highlights several leaders of the various Plains tribes.

The Real Book about Indians, by Michael Gorham (Real Books)   Gr. 4-10

The Book of Indians, by Holling Clancy Holling   Gr. 4-12
    This is a rare, but beloved book.

The American Indian, by Sydney Fletcher   Gr. 4-12
    Nice illustrations.

The American Indian Story, by May McNeer   Gr. 4-12

Indian Chiefs of the West, by Felix Sutton (Messner)   Gr. 4-12

North American Indian, by Doug Murdoch (DK)   Gr. 4-12
    A display of Indian articles.

The Art of the Southwest Indians, by Shirley Glubok   Gr. 4-12

The Art of the Plains Indians, by Shirley Glubok   Gr. 4-12

Buffalo Hunt, by Russell Freedman   Gr. 5-12
An Indian Winter, by Russell Freedman   Gr. 5-12
Indian Chiefs, by Russell Freedman   Gr. 5-12
    Freedman's books always feature strong photographs and straightforward text. The first
    two listed reveal the life of various Plains tribes. *Indian Chiefs* covers the declining era
    of the Indians as faced by six important chiefs: Red Cloud, Satanta, Quanah Parker,
    Washakie, Chief Joseph, and Sitting Bull.

Indians on Horseback, by Alice Marriott   Gr. 5-12
    The life, culture, and foods, for example, of several Plains tribes.

Francis Parkman and the Plains Indians, edited by J. Shuter (Hist. Eyewitness)   Gr. 5-12
    This is an edited version of the journal made by Francis Parkman (a famous author of
    books on the Indians) when he traveled to the Plains to visit various Indians. You could
    read the full journal, if you have time. There are also various abridgements.

The American Indian, by Oliver LaFarge   Gr. 5-12

☞ Richard "Little Bear" Wheeler has done a video presentation/re-enactment, titled: *Origins of the Indians.*

> Want to read about some Indians who celebrated Resurrection Sunday?
>
> *Easter Fires,* by Wilma Pitchford Hays   Gr. 1-5

6b❧ Geographical listing

Great Plains Indians: (these are often described jointly as *Plains Indians*)

North & South Dakota–Sioux, Mandan   Texas–Comanche, Wichita
Iowa–Iowa   Montana–Crow, Blackfoot, Assiniboine
Missouri–Osage   Idaho–Nez Percé, Shoshone
Kansas–Kansas   Wyoming–Arapaho, Shoshone
Nebraska–Pawnee, Omaha, Oto (Otoe), Ponca   Colorado–Cheyenne, Arapaho
Oklahoma–Wichita

Great Southwest Indians:

Colorado (desert areas) & Utah–Ute
New Mexico & Arizona–Apache, Navajo, Pueblos (includes Hopi, Zuni, Taos, etc.)

Great Northwest & Coastal Indians:

The Indians of Washington, Oregon, and southern Alaska are usually grouped together as 'Northwest Indians' which includes such tribes as: Puyallap, Haida, Snohomish, Chinook, Tillamook, Suquamish, etc. California was populated by many small tribes, such as the Yokut, Pomo, Chumashan, Laguna, etc., which are often grouped as the 'Mission Indians,' since many were involved with the California missions.

6c Specific tribes

Apache Indians

The Value of Truth and Trust: Cochise, by Ann Johnson (ValueTales)   Gr. 1-5

*The Apache, by Andrew Santella (True Books)   Gr. 2-6

Geronimo: Fighting Apache, by Ronald Syme   Gr. 2-8

*The Story of Geronimo, by Zachary Kent (Cornerstones)   Gr. 3-8

Cochise: Apache Warrior and Statesman, by Edgar Wyatt   Gr. 3-8

Geronimo: The Last Apache War Chief, by Edgar Wyatt   Gr. 3-8

Cochise of Arizona, by Oliver LaFarge (Aladdin's American Heritage)   Gr. 3-9

The Story of Geronimo, by Jim Kjelgaard (Signature)   Gr. 3-9

The Apache Indians, by Sonia Bleeker   Gr. 3-12

Geronimo: Wolf of the Warpath, by Ralph Moody (Landmark)   Gr. 4-10

*The Apache Indians, by Nicole Claro (Junior Library of American Indians)   Gr. 4-12

Cochise: Apache Chief, by M. Schwartz (North American Indians of Achieve...) Gr. 4-12

Arapaho Indians

Friday, the Arapaho Indian., by A.M. Anderson (Am. Adventure, older series) Gr. 1-6

*The Arapaho Indians, by V. Haluska (Junior Library of American Indians)   Gr. 4-12

Blackfoot Indians

Legend of Scarface, by Robert San Souci   Gr. 1-6
    Nicely illustrated Blackfoot Legend. (Contains Indian religious beliefs.)

*The Blackfeet Indians, by Annemarie Hendrickson (Junior Library of...)   Gr. 4-12

❧ Cheyenne Indians

Three Little Indians, by George Stuart (National Geographic)   Gr. K-4
    One section reveals life of Cheyenne youngster.

The Cheyenne, by Andrew Santella (True Books)   Gr. 2-6

Fiction/Historical Fiction:

Lone Hunter and the Cheyennes, by Donald Worcester   Gr. 4-10
    Oglala Sioux boy is stolen by Cheyennes.

❧ Chumash Indians

Chumash Indians, by Bill Lund (Native Peoples)   Gr. 2-5

The Chumash Indians, by Martin Schwabacher   Gr. 4-12

❧ Comanche Indians

The Legend of the Bluebonnets, by Tomie de Paola   Gr. 1-3
    Comanche legend about Texas bluebonnets.

Quanah Parker: Indian Warrior for Peace, by LaVere Anderson (Garr. Am. All)   Gr. 3-8

The Comanche Indians, by Martin Mooney (Junior Library of American Ind.)   Gr. 4-12

Fiction/Historical Fiction:

Bigfoot Wallace and the Hickory Nut, by Helen Rushmore (Am. Folk Tales)   Gr. 1-4

❧ Crow Indians

The Crow Indians, by Sonia Bleeker   Gr. 3-12

The Crow, by E. Tarbescu (Watts Library: Indians of the Americas)   Gr. 4-12

❧ Kiowa Indians

The Kiowa Indians, by Terrance Dolan (Junior Library of American...)   Gr. 4-12

Indian Annie: Kiowa Captive, by Alice Marriott   Gr. 4-12
        Captured settler tries to adjust to Kiowa life.

❧ Mission (or California) Indians
We also mentioned the Mission Indians in an earlier guide, but you may want to study them here instead.

Ishi: The Last of His People, by David Petersen   Gr. 2-6
        Life of last known American Indian living natively.

*Life of the California Coast Nations, by Molly Aloian (Native Nations)   Gr. 4-9

The Missions Indians, by Sonia Bleeker   Gr. 4-12

Fiction/Historical Fiction:

Young Hawk, by Edna Walker Chandler   Gr. 2-7
        Story of Yokut Indian boy of early California.

*Island of the Blue Dolphins, **and**, **Zia*, by Scott O'Dell   Gr. 4-12
        Don't miss *Island of the Blue Dolphins!* This excellent novel is based on the real story of
        a young Indian girl stranded alone for years! (I didn't enjoy *Zia* quite as much.)

❧ Navajo (Navaho) Indians

Navaho Land, by Solveig Russell   Gr. 2-6

*The Navao, by Andrew Santella (True Books)   Gr. 2-6

Navajo: Herders, Weavers, and Silversmiths, by Sonia Bleeker   Gr. 3-10

*The Navajo, by Nancy Bonvillain   Gr. 5-12

Fiction/Historical Fiction:

Tall Boy and the Coyote, by Edna Walker Chandler   Gr. K-2
        Another in a series about fictional Indian children which gives insight into tribal life.

Indian Hill, by Clyde Robert Bulla   Gr. 1-6
        This book is actually about a modern Navajo boy who moves from his original home
        into the city, thereby facing a very different world.

Dancing Cloud, by Mary & Conrad Buff   Gr. 2-8
        Another one of the Buff's precious books, with their tender illustrations. This one tells
        the story of a Navajo boy and his sister.

Waterless Mountain, by Laura Armer — Gr. 3-12
   This Newbery Award winner vividly portrays the life of one Navajo boy.

Little Shepherds of Navajo Land, by Marian Schoolland — Gr. 3-12
   Rare Christian book by author of "Leading Little Ones to God."

Sing Down the Moon, by Scott O'Dell — Gr. 4-12
   Spanish slavers force the Navajo to make difficult move.

❧ Nez Percé Indians

Chief Joseph: Guardian of His People, by Elizabeth Montgomery (Garr. Am. Ind.) Gr. 1-5

Chief Joseph, by Olive Burt (Childhood) — Gr. 1-5

Nez Percé, by Alice Osinski (New True Book) — Gr. 1-6

Horsemen of the Western Plateaus, by Sonia Bleeker — Gr. 3-10

Chief Joseph of the Nez Percés, by Shannon Garst (Messner) — Gr. 4-12

The Nez Percé Indians, by Mark Rifkin (Junior Library of American Indians) — Gr. 4-12

Fiction/Historical Fiction:

Best Friends, by Loretta Krupinski — Gr. 1-5
   Nez Percé girl and pioneer girl make friends through hard times.

Thunder Rolling in the Mountains, by Scott O'Dell — Gr. 5-12
   The Nez Percé ordeal is told by the chief's daughter in this novel.

❧ Northwest Indians

Three Little Indians, by George Stuart (National Geographic) — Gr. K-4
   One section reveals the life of a Nootka youngster.

Chief Seattle: Great Statesman, by Elizabeth Montgomery (Garr. Am. Ind.) — Gr. 1-5

If You Lived with the Indians of the Northwest Coast, by Anne Kamma — Gr. 2-7

The Story of the Totem Pole, by Ruth Brindze — Gr. 3-9
   Tells religious meaning of Northwest Indians' totem poles, culture, beliefs, etc.

Nations of the Northwest Coast, by Kathryn Smithyman (Native Nations) — Gr. 4-9

The Sea Hunters, by Sonia Bleeker   Gr. 4-12

Sea and Cedar: How the Northwest Coast Indians Lived, by Lois McConkey   Unknown

Fiction/Historical Fiction:

Little Cedar's Tooth, by Edna Walker Chandler   Gr. 1-4

❧ Omaha Indians

*Omaha Indians, by M. Anderson (Watts Library: Indians of the Americas)   Gr. 4-12

❧ Papago Indians

Little Indian Basket Maker, by Ann Nolan Clark   Gr. K-4

❧ Pueblo Indians
(The ancient cliff-dwelling tribes, such as the Anasazi, were also covered in a much earlier *TruthQuest History* unit. Most resources which focus on that previous era are listed there.)

Ancient Skyscrapers, by Sherry Paul   Gr. 2-8

*The Pueblos, by Alice Flanagan (True Books)   Gr. 2-6

Cliff Dwellers of Walnut Canyon, by Carroll Fenton & Alice Epstein   Gr. 2-8

*Anasazi, by Leonard Everett Fisher   Gr. 3-9
    Fisher's powerful drawings evoke life of one tribe of ancient pueblo dwellers. Other books about the ancient tribes exist, but because they were also cited in earlier *TruthQuest History* guides, I'll only mention this one here.

The Pueblo Indians, by Sonia Bleeker   Gr. 3-12

*The Pueblo Indians, by Liza Burby (Junior Library of American Indians)   Gr. 4-12

Fiction/Historical Fiction:

Little Indian Pottery Maker, by Ann Nolan Clark   Gr. K-2
    Tender story of Pueblo girl as her mother teaches her to make pottery.

In My Mother's House, by Ann Nolan Clark   Gr. K-3
    Poetic look at Pueblo life.

Juanito Makes a Drum, by Edna Walker Chandler   Gr. 1-3

Hah-Nee of the Cliff Dwellers, by Mary & Conrad Buff   Gr. 3-8
  Another one of the Buff's precious books, with their tender illustrations. This one tells
  the story of a Navajo boy and his sister.

Stone Knife Boy, by Alida Malkus   Gr. 5-12
  Taos Indian boy of today still has many skills and adventures.

❧ Shoshone Indians

The Legend of Jimmy Spoon, by Kristiana Gregory (Great Episodes)   Gr. 4-10
  Exciting book (boys will love it!) is based on true story of boy who lives with Shoshone.

The Shoshone Indians, by Nathaniel Moss (Junior Library of American...)   Gr. 4-12

❧ Sioux Indians

Crazy Horse, by Glen Dines (See & Read)   Gr. 1-3

**If You Lived with the Sioux Indians*, by Ann McGovern   Gr. 1-4
  Kids' questions about Sioux life.

The Picture-Skin Story, by Alex Bealer III   Gr. 1-4
  Relates real pictorial history of the Sioux people painted on an animal skin.

Little Yellow Fur, by Wilma Pitchford Hays   Gr. 1-4
  Beloved author tells of her own childhood visits with the Sioux who lived nearby. Their
  affection was mutual, and the Indians named her for her blonde hair.

Crazy Horse: Sioux Warrior, by Enid Meadowcroft (Garr. Am. Indian)   Gr. 1-5

Red Cloud: Sioux War Chief, by Virginia Voight (Garr. Am. Indian)   Gr. 1-5

Sitting Bull: Great Sioux Chief, by LaVere Anderson (Garr. Am. Indian)   Gr. 1-5

The Story of Wounded Knee, by R. Conrad Stein (Cornerstones)   Gr. 1-5
  Sad story of a closing chapter in the battle between the Sioux and US troops.

**Sitting Bull*, by Augusta Stevenson (Childhood)   Gr. 1-6

**The Lakota Sioux*, by Andrew Santella (True Books)   Gr. 2-6

The Story of Crazy Horse, by Enid Meadowcroft (Signature)   Gr. 3-8

Sioux Indians: Hunters and Warriors, by Sonia Bleeker   Gr. 4-10

The Santee Sioux, by Terrance Dolan (Junior Library of American Indians)   Gr. 4-12

The Teton Sioux, by Nancy Bonvillain (Junior Library of American Indians)   Gr. 4-12

Sitting Bull, by B. Bernotas (North American Indians of Achievement)   Gr. 4-12

Indian Boyhood, by Ohiyesa (about Charles Eastman)   Gr. 5-12
    Real Sioux Indian tells of his childhood.

Sketchbook of Thomas Blue Eagle, **and**, *Ledgerbook of Thomas Blue Eagle*   Various
    by Gay Matthaei & Jewel Grutman
    I've not seen these books, but have read about them online.

Red Cloud, by Shannon Garst   Various
    Two books in one: an easier, illustrated biography, then a fuller biography.

Fiction/Historical Fiction:

Buffalo Boy, by Edna Walker Chandler   Gr. 2-6

Young Sioux Warrior, by Frances Kroll (Young Hero Library)   Gr. 2-7

Little Sioux Girl, by Lois Lenski   Gr. 2-9
    This story gives a glimpse of later Sioux life on a reservation in the 1940s.

Pony of the Sioux, by M.J. Pearson (Signal)   Gr. 3-9
    This series always offers high adventure!

Red Eagle, by Shannon Garst   Gr. 4-9
    Handicapped Sioux boy tries to prove his courage.

❧ Ute Indians

Indian Uprising, by George Cory Franklin   Gr. 4-9
    Early Colorado settler involved with the Utes.

6d✤ General fiction and picture books

Indian Two Feet series, by Margaret Friskey   Gr. K-2
    Several fun stories about young Indian boy.

*Little Chief, by Syd Hoff (I Can Read)   Gr. K-2

**Knots on a Counting Rope*, by Bill Martin, Jr.   Gr. 1-4
    Indian boy asks his grandfather for a story.

Broomtail: Brother of Lightning, by Miriam Mason   Gr. 1-5
    Indian boy catches wild pony.

Indians, Indians, Indians, by Phyllis Fenner   Gr. 3-12
    Collection of short stories.

Indian Paint, by Glen Balch   Gr. 4-12
    Story of Indian horse.

6e✤ Activity and art books
(Parents should determine suitability, safety, and interest levels.)

Let's Be Indians, by Peggy Parish   Various
    Fun activity book, especially for young students, by author of the *Amelia Bedelia* books.

The Indians Knew, by Tillie Pine   Various
    Fun look at Indian skills/knowledge with hands-on projects.

North American Indians, by Susan Purdy   Various

*Indian Crafts, by Keith Brandt   Gr. 1-6

Indian Harvests, by William Grimm   Gr. 4-12
    Interesting look at plants the Indians used. (Unclothed Indian in drawing on cover.)

The Red Man in Art, by Rena Coen   Gr. 4-12

Foods the Indian Gave Us, by Wilma Pitchford Hays   Adult needed
    How to plant, harvest, and cook the Indian way.

☞ Dover has coloring books available on many tribes.

7🍂 War in the West!

Now we can look at some very famous battles and warriors. Some of you may already have learned about these things in the last section, but I'm mentioning these topics here for those who didn't already learn about Custer's Last Stand, the Battle of Wounded Knee, Geronimo, and Chief Joseph. We'll end with a look at the Oklahoma Land Run; it's a good example of the struggle between Indians and settlers.

7a🍂 General and miscellaneous resources

Indian Fighter: Nelson A. Miles, by Ralph Bailey	Gr. 5-12
General Crook: Indian Fighter, by Fairfax Downey	Gr. 5-12

Fiction/Historical Fiction:

Portugee Phillips and the Fighting Sioux, by A.M. Anderson (Am. Adventures)	Gr. 2-8
Long Knife, by Glen Dines	Gr. 3-7
*Hope and Have, by Oliver Optic	Gr. 5-12

    This old classic–one in a series of four–is being reprinted now.

7b🍂 Custer's Last Stand

*Story of the Great Republic, by H.A. Guerber, Ch. LXI	Gr. 3-7

----

*The Story of the Little Bighorn, by R. Conrad Stein (Cornerstones)	Gr. 2-7
Custer's Last Stand, by Quentin Reynolds (Landmark)	Gr. 3-10
Little Bighorn, by Philip Steele (Great Battles and Sieges)	Gr. 5-10
Custer: Fighter of the Plains, by Shannon Garst (Messner)	Gr. 5-12
Once Upon the Little Big Horn, by Evelyn Lampman	Gr. 5-12
Chief Red Horse Tells about Custer, edited by Jessie McGraw	Various

    Very unusual book! Actual participant tells his story in real Indian sign language!

7c🍂 George Custer and family

George Custer (Childhood) by Augusta Stevenson	Gr. 1-6
Story of General Custer (Signature)	Gr. 3-8

> *Miranda's Last Stand*, by G. Whelan (Gr. 4-9)
> Mom & daughter left alone after Dad's death with Custer, work for Buffalo Bill; Mom deals with bitterness when Sitting Bull joins.

7d❧ Comanche (a US Cavalry horse, the only one to survive Custer's Last Stand)

Comanche and His Captain, by A.M. Anderson (Am. Adventure, older series)	Gr. 2-8
Comanche, by David Appel	Gr. 4-12

7e❧ Battle of Wounded Knee

The Story of Wounded Knee, by R. Conrad Stein (Cornerstones)	Gr. 3-8

7f❧ Geronimo

Geronimo: Young Warrior, by George Stanley (NEW *Childhood of...* series)	Gr. 2-6
Geronimo: Fighting Apache, by Ronald Syme	Gr. 2-8
The Story of Geronimo, by Zachary Kent (Cornerstones)	Gr. 3-8
Geronimo: The Last Apache War Chief, by Edgar Wyatt	Gr. 3-8
The Story of Geronimo, by Jim Kjelgaard (Signature)	Gr. 3-9
Geronimo: Wolf of the Warpath, by Ralph Moody (Landmark)	Gr. 4-10
Geronimo, by M. Schwarz (North American Indians of Achievement)	Gr. 4-12

7g❧ Chief Joseph

Chief Joseph: Guardian of His People, by Elizabeth Montgomery (Garr. Am. Ind.)	Gr. 1-5
Chief Joseph, by Olive Burt (Childhood)	Gr. 1-5
Chief Joseph, by M. Taylor (North American Indians of Achievement)	Gr. 4-10
Chief Joseph of the Nez Percés, by Shannon Garst (Messner)	Gr. 4-12

Fiction/Historical Fiction:

Thunder Rolling in the Mountains, by Scott O'Dell The Nez Percé ordeal is told by the chief's daughter in this novel.	Gr. 5-12

7b⚕ Oklahoma Land Run

Cherokee Strip: The Race for Land, by Aileen Fisher (Aladdin's Am. Heritage)   Gr. 3-8

The Story of Oklahoma, by Lon Tinkle (Landmark)   Gr. 3-10

Fiction/Historical Fiction:

*I Have Heard of a Land, by Joyce Thomas   Gr. 1-4
   Poignant picture book shows black woman gaining new life in Oklahoma.

*Beautiful Land, by Nancy Antle (Once Upon America)   Gr. 3-7

We Were There at the Oklahoma Land Run, by Jim Kjelgaard (We Were There)   Gr. 3-8

8⚕ Middle America...and New Ideas

Before moving on, let's check America's heartland and countryside, where there had been time for pioneer homesteads to blossom into comfortable farms, healthy businesses, and bustling communities...many of which were helped by the mighty Mississippi River and her steamboats.

Remember, though, that when times get easier, when folks have a little extra money, when life doesn't seem so risky...that's when people start forgetting about God! They start thinking they're the ones who made everything so nice! They forget that it's the blessings of the Lord they're enjoying. They forget that good things happen *only* when people obey God, because He loves us so much that His rules actually help us! So watch as you're learning about this time in history! Will 'Frank the Farmer' or 'Bob the Businessman' honor God and use his money to help others? Or will he think he's Superman and spend all his money on himself?!

Parents and older students! You will be blessed by something Abraham Lincoln said about this very issue! He made this powerful proclamation to all Americans asking them to pray and fast and humble themselves before God:

> *We have been the recipients of the choicest bounties of Heaven. We have been preserved, these many years, in peace and prosperity. We have grown in numbers, wealth, and power as no other nation has ever grown; but we have forgotten God. We have forgotten the gracious land, which preserved us in peace, and multiplied and enriched and strengthened us; and we have vainly imagined in the deceitfulness of our hearts, that all these blessings were produced by some superior wisdom and virtue of our own. Intoxicated with unbroken success, we have become too self-sufficient to feel the necessity of redeeming and preserving grace, too proud to pray to the God who made us.*

Or worse yet, will he start believing that new-fangled idea creeping about the land, the one we talked about earlier, the one that tried to knock God right off the throne of the universe! It said that it was a silly ol' idea to think God had created people; instead it said that people 'evolved' out of animals. *In other words, people sort of made themselves by always becoming better.* With this new belief, they didn't have to admit there was a God who had made them and was therefore bigger than them. They thought they were free of God! They thought they could be their own boss. They could do whatever felt good, whatever seemed right just for them!

Oh, my! I can't begin to tell you how much changed when people started believing this new idea called *evolution!* Life without God did *seem* pretty thrilling (just like I was feeling when I stormed out of my house the day I ran away). We understand that, don't we?! We know it's exciting to stomp our foot and say that no one is going to boss us around. But that thrill only lasts a little while! Pretty soon problems come. That's why I turned around that day and headed back home. But it can take longer for a whole country to turn around and 'head back home.'

Parents, for a quick insight into these key issues, you will enjoy:

History Through the Eyes of Faith by Ronald Wells, Ch. 13

Seven Men Who Rule the World from the Grave, by Dave Breese, Ch. 1-3

I'm hoping that one day soon, America will do just that. It is our great privilege to help people see how smart and right that decision would be! But in the meantime, you have to realize that evolution made a new way of thinking–new *Big 2 Beliefs*. And because evolution gives people the thrill of stomping their foot at God, these beliefs are very popular in our country right now. They are in almost every movie, TV show, public school, government decision, and more.

Oh, I know what you're thinking! You're saying to yourself that movies and shows and government decisions aren't about whether or not people came from monkeys. But guess what! That's not the main part of evolution! The main part is this–it's all about saying there is nothing higher than people. And if there is no God, there is no one to say what is right or wrong...and everyone can do what they feel like doing! Ack!

And think about this! God says that He is the same, yesterday, and forever! He *does not* change! That's why whatever God says is true is always true, and it's true for everybody; God and truth *do not* change. But evolution says there is one main force in the universe–*change!* Evolution says that nature has this power to change and it is making people better and better and better, until one day people will become perfect and they will finish making the world perfect! You can see, then, why people who believe in evolution think it's silly to learn history. They don't want to know what happened back when people were "less evolved." They only want to come up with new ideas (new "truths") they think will make a perfect tomorrow! Wow! People have made themselves into gods!

I hope you will take a minute or two to talk about these ideas with your parents. Though these ideas may seem too hard for you, if you ask God to give you wisdom, He promises that He will! You can ask God to help you understand the real truth about all this! Then you will understand the way many people in our world are thinking. And you will see why these people are making problems...for themselves and others. We know that God is the answer to these problems, and we need to help people understand that! What a big, important job we have! Wow!

Just think! As the American Revolution made such a big change in our country, so did this new belief of evolution! In fact, it made a revolution too, as you'll see, though the changes were so gradual that many people didn't realize what was happening! The sad thing is that many churches were teaching people to believe evolution! But where people loved God with all their heart, they refused to ignore the Bible and they refused to make themselves like gods! Yeah!

> *ThinkWrite 1: "What's the big deal?"*
>
> Though it may be hard, try to explain why it is so important that we know God created us and the whole world.

Anyway, can you please keep this 'big idea' in your mind while we learn about this time in America's history? (Do *ThinkWrite 1* now.)

8a❧ America's heartland and countryside

Story of the Great Republic, by H.A. Guerber   Gr. 3-7
    Ch. LXII-LXVI, LXVIII–LXXI

This Country of Ours, by H.A. Marshall, Ch. 94-95   Gr. 3-8

Mailing May, by Michael Tunnell   Gr. 1-4
    What happens when an Idaho girl wants to visit her grandmother? A true story!

> *A Time to Keep*, by Tasha Tudor, shows the lovely celebrations held by American families during this era.

The Way We Lived, by Martin Sandler   Gr. 5-12
    I don't know the tone of the text, but this book contains many actual photographs.

Christy, by Catherine Marshall   Gr. 5-12
    No girl should miss reading this fabulous, true story of life in Appalachia and one girl's attempt to help! I just learned that someone recently published an abridged version!

Little Britches, by Ralph Moody   Read-aloud
    I can't overstate the fondness this book (the first in a series) holds for many Americans. You might want to gather the whole family, and read this one aloud since it's too challenging for most young students to read independently.

Fiction/Historical Fiction:

Daniel's Duck, by Clyde Robert Bulla (I Can Read History)   Gr. K-2
    Dear story of Appalachian boy.

Fish Fry, by Susan Saunders   Gr. 1-3
    Texas townsfolk enjoy a festive summer day in 1912.

Lucy's Summer, by Donald Hall Gr. 1-4
Delightful picture book shows one summer in the life of a New Hampshire girl.

Copper-Toed Boots   Gr. 2-6
by Marguerite de Angeli
A Michigan boy longs for boots.

Time of the Wolves, **and**,   Gr. 2-6
Runaway Cattle, both by Verne Davis
Boys have rip-snorting adventure in post-Civil War Michigan.

Hannah, by Gloria Whelan   Gr. 2-8
Story of blind Michigan girl.

Mandie and the Secret Tunnel   Gr. 2-8
by Lois Gladys Leppard
First in Christian series about girl growing up in North Carolina.

Betsy-Tacy, by Maud Lovelace   Gr. 3-7
First in series.

Uncle Fonzo's Ford, by M. Miles   Gr. 3-8
Missouri family has adventures, especially with early auto.

In Grandma's Attic   Gr. 3-9
by Arleta Richardson
First of many in a series. An abridged collection of these homespun stories by a Christian author from Michigan can be found in: *Stories from Grandma's Attic.*

Pollyanna, by Eleanor Porter   Gr. 3-12
Classic tale of the great influence of one girl's cheerful attitude.

Understood Betsy, by Dorothy Canfield Fisher   Gr. 4-10
Beloved story of Vermont girl.

Rascal, by Sterling North   Gr. 4-12
Warm tale of boy & his raccoon.

Lumbering helped many states grow, as when Michigan forests rebuilt Chicago after her great fire. Let's meet these tough, ol' lumberjacks!

Lumberjacks of the North Woods   Gr. 3-8
    by L. Patterson (How They Lived)
Timber, by Walter Buehr   Gr. 3-10
Timber! by A. Fisher (Al. Am Her.)   Gr. 4-10
Early Loggers and the Sawmill, by Adams Gr. 4-12
Lumberjack, by W. Kurelek   Gr. 4-12
    Canadian lumbering.

Fiction/Historical Fiction:
Marven of the Great North Woods   Gr. 1-5
    by Kathryn Lasky
    True story of the author's father, who had to work in lumber camp as a boy.
Lumber Camp Library   Gr. 2-6
    by Natalie Kinsey-Warnock
Song of the Pines (Land of the Free) Gr. 4-12
    by Walter & Marion Havighurst
    Award-winning story of Norwegian settlers lumbering in Wisconsin.
Lumberjack, by Stephen Meader   Gr. 5-12

Tall tales of Paul Bunyan!

Paul Bunyan, by Steven Kellogg   Gr. K-4
    Kids love Kellogg's funny books.
Ol' Paul, the Mighty Logger, by Rounds Gr. 1-8
    Don't miss this laugh-till-you-cry book!

37

Rebecca of Sunnybrook Farm, by Kate Douglas Wiggin   Gr. 4-12
    There are abridged versions for younger readers. If you'd like, you can learn more about the author: *Kate Douglas Wiggin: Little Schoolteacher*, by Miriam Mason (Childhood; Gr. 1-6).

Elsie Dinsmore, by Martha Finley (first in a series of many about Elsie)   Gr. 4-12

Red Horse Hill, **and**, *The Buckboard Stranger*, by Stephen Meader   Gr. 5-12
    Stories set in small New Hampshire towns.

Films:

Rebecca of Sunnybrook Farm, starring Shirley Temple   All ages

Rascal   All ages

Pollyanna   All ages

Christy   Parental decision

8b⁂ Mississippi River, steamboats, and river culture

Steamboat! by Judith Gilliland   Gr. 1-5
    The true story of the first female steamboat captain, Blanche Leathers.

John Fitch: Steamboat Boy, by Augusta Stevenson (Childhood)   Gr. 1-6

Steamboats to the West, by Edith McCall (Frontiers of America)   Gr. 2-6
    Also titled, *Stories of American Steamboats*

Grant Marsh, Steamboat Captain   Gr. 2-6
by A.M. Anderson (Amer. Adventures)

Story of Mississippi Steamboats   Gr. 2-7
    by R. Conrad Stein (Cornerstone)

First Steamboat Down the   Gr. 3-7
Mississippi, by George Richter
    I've not seen this, so am not sure of the age recommendation.

Amazing Voyage of the New Orleans Gr. 3-8
    by Judith St. George

> How'd'ya like to meet the great songwriter of the Mississippi? He drew native sounds into his work, reflecting the increasing sense of *America!*
>
> *Stephen Foster: Boy Minstrel* (Childhood) Gr. 1-6
>   by Helen Higgins
> *Stephen Foster and His Little Dog Tray*   Gr. 2-6
>   by Opal Wheeler
> *The Story of Stephen Foster* (Signature)   Gr. 3-8
>   by Esther Douty
> *Stephen Foster*, by Catherine Peare   Gr. 4-9
> *He Heard America Sing*, by C. Purdy   Gr. 4-12
>   (Messner)

Mississippi Steamboat Days, by James McCague (How They Lived)   Gr. 3-8

First Steamboat on the Mississippi, by Sterling North (North Star)   Gr. 5-12

Fiction/Historical Fiction:

Down the Mississippi, by Clyde Robert Bulla   Gr. 1-6
    His stories are such favorites with young boys.

Mr. Yowder and the Steamboat, by Glen Rounds   Gr. 1-6

Many a tall tale's been told of Mike Fink, the legendary keelboatman!

*Mike Fink, by Steven Kellogg   Gr. 1-4
Pioneers on Early Waterways, Ch. 2   Gr. 2-6
    by Edith McCall (Frontiers of America)
Mike Fink: Best of the Keelboatmen   Gr. 5-12
    by Harold Felton

Willie Jasper's Golden Eagle   Gr. 2-10
    by F.N. Monjo
    Monjo writes wonderful books; this one
    tells of an exciting steamboat race!

Making the Mississippi Shout   Gr. 4-10
    by Mary Calhoun

*Swift Rivers, by Cornelia Meigs   Gr. 4-10

9🐚 Aloha!

It was during this time that important things were happening in beautiful Hawaii—which would later become a U.S. state!

*Story of the Great Republic, by H.A. Guerber, Ch. LXXVI-LXXVII   Gr. 3-7
    Some of this material is set at a later time, during Hawaii's statehood issues.

*This Country of Ours, by H.E. Marshall, Ch. 96b   Gr. 3-8
    Some of this material is set at a later time, during Hawaii's statehood issues.

Liliuokalani: Queen of Hawaii, by Mary Malone (Garrard)   Gr. 1-5

Liliuokalani: Young Hawaiian Queen, by S. Newman (Childhood)   Gr. 1-6

The Polynesians Knew, by Tillie Pine   Gr. 2-8
    Great series: the 'how-to' of Polynesian culture, with related hands-on activities.

*The Last Hawaiian Queen, by Paula Guzzetti   Gr. 3-6

*Last Princess, by Fay Stanley   Gr. 3-8

Hawaii: Gem of the Pacific, by Oscar Lewis (Landmark)   Gr. 3-9

Last Queen of Hawaii, by Hazel Wilson   Gr. 5-12

Fiction/Historical Fiction:

Kala's Pet, by Edna Chandler   Gr. 1-3

**Kaiulani,* by Ellen White (Royal Diaries)   Gr. 4-12

☞ I don't know if **Call It Courage,* by Armstrong Sperry, takes place precisely in Hawaii, but it's a great story! (Gr. 2-6)

10❧ Immigrants...and the 'Lady' Who Greeted Them!

Well, you can see from our long foray around the American west and heartland that it seemed life was nothing but blue skies! There *were* good things here in America. Why? Because many of the pilgrims and the founding fathers, for example, had tried hard to build this nation on the Lord and His truth. Good things always come from that! The problem was that some folks were saying that all the progress and opportunity were due to evolution! Waaaaay wrong! But people had a choice to make: honor and obey God, or go the path of pride. The godly path would ensure *true* freedom and progress; the path of pride would soon mean trouble. You'll see what happened!

Anyway, into this land of opportunity, where there was hope for a better future, came millions of immigrants! Do you realize that a new start in life was practically unheard of in past history?! People in other countries had always been utterly locked into their 'place,' their class, their lot in life. But in America, where people had originally been seen as special since they were made in the image of God, there was opportunity for almost everyone (with some very sad exceptions). Think of it! Except for the native Indians, every other American is descended from an immigrant! (What are *your* roots?) Our nation is called a 'melting pot' because so many different people from so many different places came to live together in the same land.

There are tons of yummy books to enjoy on this topic because many immigrants were amazing, longsuffering people. They often faced tremendous hardship on their journeys to this land and then faced the worst jobs and housing because they were usually poor and uneducated, but also because Americans and other immigrants had naughty attitudes about other races and nationalities. Some folks were just plain greedy and wanted to take advantage of the immigrants who were desperate for food and shelter. Too, many immigrants had to learn English before they could get good jobs. Still, they endured in order to make a better life for their children. Isn't that inspiring?!

There is another side to this story too, I must admit. Some of the immigrants came to America because they strongly believed in a new idea called *communism,* an idea which was partly based on evolution. The man who invented communism, Karl Marx, felt that he had the power to create a whole new way for nations, businesses, and families to live. His ideas–though they seemed good to many folks who were suffering–ignored God. Thus, everywhere communism went people were eventually treated like slaves. But at first, most supporters of communism didn't realize that. It all sounded so good. So, some of the immigrants came here to try communism in America. You can bet that the Americans who knew better than to fall for communism wanted those communist immigrants out of here!

Yes, there were many moments of virtue, and moments of pain, as you'll see...*if* I stop talking and let you read!

But I almost forgot! It was during this time that the Statue of Liberty was built and became an enduring symbol not only to the immigrants who first saw it on their way to Ellis Island, but to all Americans. Take a moment to ponder the famous lines written by Emma Lazarus, which are carved on Lady Liberty's pedestal:

> *Give me your tired, your poor,*
> *Your huddled masses yearning to*
> *breathe free,*
> *The wretched refuse of your teeming shore.*
> *Send these, the homeless, tempest-tost to me,*
> *I lift my lamp beside the golden door!*

~~~ ❀ ~~~

Statue of Liberty:
   (There are so many; I'll just mention a few.)

Story of the Statue of Liberty, by B. Maestro   Gr. K-3
Copper Lady, by Alice Ross (On My Own) Gr. 1-4
Story of the Statue of Liberty (Cornerstone)   Gr. 1-6
   by Natalie Miller
Child's History of Art, by Hillyer & Huey, (*Sculpture*
   section, Ch. 22) <u>OR</u>, *Young People's Story of*
   Sculpture, pp. 91-92   Gr. 2-8
Liberty, by Lynn Curlee   Gr. 4-9
Statue of Liberty, by Leonard E. Fisher   Gr. 6-12

Fiction/Historical Fiction:

Copper Lady (On My Own)   Gr. 1-3
   by Alice Ross
Apprentice to Liberty, by Mary Fox   Gr. 4-12
   Boy helps Bartholdi build the statue.
        ~~~~~~
Voice of Liberty: Emma Lazarus   Gr. 5-12
   by Eve Merriam

 **Immigrants:**

Dreaming of America, by Eve Bunting   Gr. 1-4
   True story of first immigrant through Ellis Island, a 15-year-old Irish girl, who was traveling with her two brothers.

Edward Bok: Young Editor, by Elisabeth Myers (Childhood)   Gr. 1-6
   Dutch immigrant became editor and met with many American leaders.

Streets of Gold, by Rosemary Wells   Gr. 2-5
   Beautiful picture-book biography of real Russian-Jewish girl who immigrates.

Coming to America, by Betsy Maestro   Gr. 2-5

The Story of Ellis Island, by R. Conrad Stein (Cornerstones)   Gr. 2-7

KIDS Discover magazine, April, 1998 issue: *Immigration*   Gr. 2-8

If Your Name was Changed at Ellis Island, by Ellen Levine   Gr. 3-8

Journey to Ellis Island, by Carol Bierman *et al*   Gr. 3-8

Immigrant Kids, by Russell Freedman   Gr. 4-12

They Sought a New World, by William Kurelek   Gr. 4-12
    Author/painter shows immigrants to Canada.

Sam Ellis's Island, by Beatrice Siegel   Gr. 5-10
    History of Ellis Island, from the beginning.

Fiction/Historical Fiction:

Molly's Pilgrim   Gr. 1-3
    by Barbara Cohen
    Excellent! Russian-Jewish girl
    teaches friends about freedom.

Watch the Stars Come Out   Gr. 1-3
    by Riki Levinson

Peppe the Lamplighter   Gr. 1-4
    by Elisa Bartone
    Nice picture book shows life
    of immigrant family.

A Picnic in October   Gr. 1-4
    by Eve Bunting
    Irish family goes back each
    year to the Statue of Liberty to
    remember immigration.

Annushka's Voyage   Gr. 1-4
    by Bruce Degen

Nils, by I. & E. d'Aulaire   Gr. 1-4

There is an entire series–*Land of the Free*–written by several good authors which highlights various immigrant and ethnic groups and their great contributions to America. (Gr. 4+) It's out-of-print, but many libraries still have copies. Here are several pertinent titles:

Beckoning Hills, by Gage (Italians in CA)
Blowing Wand, by Ziegler
    (Bohemian glassmakers in OH)
Chariot in the Sky, by Bontemps (Jubilee singers)
Climb a Lofty Ladder, by the Havighursts
    (Swedish in MN)
Deep Treasure, by Blackford
    (Greek sponge fishers in FL)
Desert Harvest, by Oakes (Japanese in CA)
Oak's Long Shadow, by Burt
    (Basque sheepherders in OH.)
Seek the Dark Gold, by Lundy (Scot furtraders)
Sign of the Golden Fish, by Robinson
    (Cornish fisherman in ME)
Sing in the Dark, by Thomas
    (Welsh coal miners in PA)
Tidewater Valley, by Lundy (Swiss settlers in OR)

(Thanks to Jan Bloom's **Who Should We Then Read?*)

Grandmother and the Runaway Shadow, by Liz Rosenberg   Gr. 1-4
   Russian-Jewish girl's voyage.

Mrs. Katz and Tush, by Patricia Polacco   Gr. 1-4
   African-American boys loves his Polish-American neighbor.

The Keeping Quilt, by Patricia Polacco   Gr. 1-5
   Jewish family (in Michigan) cherishes heirloom quilt.

The Hundred Dresses, by Eleanor Estes   Gr. 2-6
   Highly esteemed book about Polish-American girl who is harshly teased.

Land of Gray Gold, by August Derleth (Aladdin's American Heritage)   Gr. 3-8
   Cornish immigrants mine lead in Wisconsin.

One Bit of Land, by Edith Blackburn (Aladdin's American Heritage)   Gr. 3-8
   Mexican farmers thrive in California's Imperial Valley.

Pat and the Iron Horse, by Polly Angell (Aladdin's American Heritage)   Gr. 3-8

Michael's Victory: They Came from Ireland, by Clara Ingram Judson   Gr. 4-10
   Irish family settles in Ohio in the 1840s.

Lost Violin: They Came from Bohemia, by Clara Ingram Judson   Gr. 4-10
   Bohemian/Polish family settles in old Chicago.

Bruce Carries the Flag: They Came from Scotland, by Clara Ingram Judson Gr. 4-10
   Scottish family settles in Indianapolis.

The Green Ginger Jar, by Clara Ingram Judson   Gr. 4-10
   Story of Chinese immigrant family.

Mama's Bank Account, by Kathryn Forbes   Gr. 4-12
   The warm story of a loving immigrant family. There is a nice older film version, also.

The Runaways, by Glenn Balch   Gr. 5-10
   Latvian boy's adventure in Idaho.

11♣ Life in the Big City

The cities of America, especially in the north, were growing *so* fast! I can hear you New Yorkers, Bostonians, and Pittsburghers thinking, "Well, it's about time you noticed! We've only studied cowboys and sodbusters so far! How-za-bout us?!" Okay, I'll admit it: everyone was *very* impressed! What progress! Mark Twain, the famous author, teasingly called these years–when everything seemed golden–the Gilded Age. The cities were filled with inventors and immigrants, tycoons and tinkerers, wheeler-dealers and whiz kids! For example, Chicago was growing because it was close to the vast farmlands of the Great Plains. Grain poured into her train stations, then boarded ships on Lake Michigan for the trip out to eastern cities and beyond, and midwestern cattle were processed in Chicago's stockyards.

Now before you burst your buttons, don't forget that city life could be pretty rough too. There was some big-time corruption as people got too big for their britches and forgot about the God who wants justice done to all. Many cities had grown so quickly that people were double-cram-jammed; buildings were practically thrown together. So when the Great Fire swept through Chicago and an earthquake hit San Francisco, the damage was astonishing! Well, I think you'll have plenty to think about in the many books on these topics.

The Story of a Main Street, by John Goodall   Gr. PreK-8
  Unusual wordless book shows the development of an English city's main street, but can give an idea of the same process in American cities.

The Snow Walker, by Margaret Wetterer (On My Own)   Gr. 1-4
  Excitement, as boy braves Great Blizzard of 1888 in New York City.

This is New York, by Miroslav Sasek   Gr. 1-5

The Great Migration, by Walter Dean Myers   Gr. 1-6
  Prose picture-book about migration of ex-slave families into northern cities.

Child's History of Art, by Hillyer & Huey (*Architecture* section, Ch. 27-29) Gr. 2-8
<u>OR</u>, *Young People's Story of Architecture*, pp. 90-end

----

This may be a wacko suggestion, but I bet kids studying cities will enjoy a glimpse at all the subways and pipes and tunnels underneath!
  Underground   Gr. 3-12
    by David Macaulay

For city art: All ages
  Cities: Through the Eyes of Artists
    by Wendy & Jack Richards

If You Lived 100 Years Ago   Gr. 3-8
  by Ann McGovern

The Story of the Empire State Building   Gr. 3-10
  by Patrick Clinton (Cornerstones)

When Chicago Was Young   Gr. 3-10
  by James McCague (Garr. How They Lived)

The Way We Lived, by Martin Sandler   Gr. 5-12
  Contains many actual photographs.

Turn of the Century, by Robert Hoare   Gr. 5-12

The Art of the Gilded Age, by Shirley Glubok   Gr. 5-12
    This may be appreciated more after having met the business tycoons.

Fiction/Historical Fiction:

*The Little House, by Virginia Burton   Gr. 1-3
    This can help your littlest ones understand the growth of cities.

People on Long Ago Street, by Lillian Budd   Gr. 1-4

We Live in the City, by Lois Lenski   Gr. 1-6
    Set around the 1940s, but gives a sense of city life.

Anna, Grandpa, and the Big Storm, by Carla Stevens   Gr. 2-6
    Set during New York City's 'Great Blizzard' of 1888.

Lion in the Box, by Marguerite de Angeli   Gr. 2-6
    Poor New York family celebrates Christmas.

*Meet Samantha and others in the series, by Susan Adler (American Girls) Gr. 2-7
    If your family uses this series, the Samantha books are set during this time.

*All-of-a-Kind Family, by Sydney Taylor   Gr. 3-9
    The first in a series of very wonderful stories about a loving Jewish family of many
    daughters who live in New York City.

Big Fire in Baltimore, by Rosa Eichelberger   Gr. 3-9

*Roller Skates, by Ruth Sawyer   Gr. 3-10
    The story of a delightful, spunky NYC girl during the 1890s. (Newbery Award)

❧ Great Chicago Fire (1871)

There'll Be a Hot Time in the Old Town, by Robert Quackenbush   Gr. 1-6
     Illustrated version of folksong about the Great Chicago Fire.
The Story of the Chicago Fire, by R. Conrad Stein (Cornerstones)   Gr. 2-7
The Great Chicago Fire, by Mary Kay Phelan   Gr. 5-12

❧ San Francisco Earthquake (1906)

*If You Lived at the Time of the Great San Francisco Earthquake   Gr. 1-6
     by Ellen Levine
Story of the San Francisco Earthquake, by R. Conrad Stein (Cornerstone)   Gr. 2-6

Fiction/Historical Fiction:

The Pieces of Home, by Miska Miles   Gr. 1-5
     Boy and his family struggle after earthquake.
*Earthquake! by Kathleen Kudlinski (Once Upon America)   Gr. 3-8
     Boy cares for panicked horses during the earthquake.

12❧ Business is Booming!

Think back now. Do you remember we said that in order for people to think they could run the world, instead of God, they had to believe that God didn't create them? They had to believe instead that they evolved out of nature. Well, as always happens when people choose to believe something that is not true, problems quickly come. Can you think of what problems that wrong belief might bring?

I'll tell you one, and I think you older students can understand this: *If people were not made especially in God's image, if each person was not made uniquely by God because He wanted to love that person (as is really true), then each individual person didn't matter very much.* Of course, the first folks that jumped on the evolution bandwagon thought they'd be even *more* important if they said they weren't created by God; but just the opposite was true. Pretty soon, the philosophers of the world (the people who think about really big ideas) started noticing that with the new ideas there was no way to pretend that people were important. Now, that didn't make most of the turn back to God; instead they made *more* of their own new ideas about people. For example, they said that an individual was important because he was part of all the people in the country (<u>society</u>). There grew more new ideas, then, about making society more powerful. One of these ideas was called <u>socialism</u>. Do you see the same root word (*soc-*) in there?

This may sound complicated to you, since we're using all these fancy words, but actually you're about to grasp a very simple, but important idea. And this idea has to do with businessmen, which you may have noticed is the topic we were really going to talk about.

You see, when America was first being formed, its founders were mostly trying to build on God's ideas for how the world should be run. These early folks noticed in the Bible that people were important and that each person was given the privilege of growing like a strong young tree. Our founding fathers could see that God let people own their own land, their own tools, and their own businesses. They were supposed to use these good things to earn money to take care of their families and the poor folks around them.

Any 'good thing' which helps a person make money for their family is called *capital*. Thus, the American system of business allowed each person to own land and tools (such as hammers, or gold mines, or bulldozers, or bakeries) that would provide for each family. This is called *capitalism*. It gives people a lot of freedom. And because they have freedom and because they and their families benefit from their hard work, capitalism helps people be creative and motivated to do well.

While capitalism is not perfect[6] (and while it works well *only* when people *choose* to do the right thing even though they have freedom and could use that freedom to instead be greedy and hurtful), capitalism did help America become a very prosperous land! You're about to meet many great businessmen who understood this!

But that *socialism* we talked about is just the opposite. It is a body of ideas that says no one should own any land or any tools for themselves or their families. Instead, socialism says society should own everything. People should work for society–the whole nation–rather than themselves and their families. Since the 'whole nation' is run by the government, what this really means is that people would work for the government and the government would then give to each family whatever the government thinks that family should have. You can see there is no freedom here, no precious respect for the liberty of each person. The *communism* that Karl Marx started was a strong form of this socialism. Marx's ideas were becoming very powerful during the years we're studying now.

You may be wondering why I mention this now...when we're talking about business. Good question! I'll tell you why: because socialism has become so popular in America that almost every book written about a great businessman of the past will try to get you to believe that the businessman was wrong, evil, and selfish for being a great businessman. They will try to get you to believe that because he was not a socialist, that he was a bad person. I want to warn you about this before you read any books about the famous businessmen of the late 1800s and early 1900s.

That makes me feel very badly for several reasons, but I'll just mention one here. Businessmen deserve a lot of respect, when they're obeying God's laws as they ought. They are the ones that

---

[6] Ronald A. Wells, *History Through the Eyes of Faith* (San Francisco: Harper & Row, 1989) throughout Ch. 12.

take risks to start businesses so that they and the folks who work in their businesses can have the jobs we all must have to buy food and housing and clothing for our family. They are the ones who spend money to build us cars and computers and the many things we need, in hopes that we will buy them.

But as Americans moved away from thinking that God's rules should guide life, they started looking to the government (that great collection of the power of the people) to guide life. They wanted the government to decide how businesses should run.

Now, don't get me wrong! We do need government; God is the one who established it! (See Romans 13.) He wants government to punish anyone who does something wrong (including any naughty businessmen) and He wants the government to protect those folks who are obeying God's laws. It's only when government starts doing more jobs than God said for it to do that there are problems...and that is exactly what started happening! The founding fathers would be so sad!

I better just say one more thing about this! Do you remember that evolution taught people that rules were silly since the world is always changing. Yes, evolution said that a person could and should do *whatever* it takes to 'get ahead.' Well, to a lot of people, that meant they could be greedy and selfish and naughty. Think of it this way: can you imagine playing soccer with another team who changes the rules during the game?! What if they said, "Hey! We would be better at soccer if we carried the ball in our hands, so that's what we're going to do!"

Well, that is just what some businessmen started doing–making up their own rules as they went along. Then, when they hurt other people, the government *had* to control them...and that was much more limiting than God's laws! We can learn a real lesson from this, though! We can see that when we make ourselves do what is right we have more freedom than when someone else has to make us do what is right! So, in many books about these famous businessmen you might be told that *all* businessmen were wicked, so the government had to 'save' us all. Remember, though, that many folks in the government wanted to make America into a socialist nation, so they were just chomping at the bit to control businessmen...and that idea will be hidden in many of the books you read.

The good news is that many of the greatest businessmen of the Gilded Age (also called the Age of Enterprise) were really wonderful men who worked hard to make businesses that were good for themselves, their workers, and their customers! They labored over great new inventions and then hustled to get them to the people who could enjoy them. They had many ideas that made it possible for even poor people to buy things that made life so much easier. We should be thankful!

You can meet many great businessmen; just watch for their *Big 2 Beliefs*. They will show you which ones acted rightly and which acted wrongly. And remember that many of the most popular churches were mixing the ideas of evolution in with God's real truth; it must have been very confusing for people. But God expects each of us to look to the Bible to see what is really true. And there were businessmen who did that. For example, J.C. Penney, a great Christian, was very generous! In fact, he gave away 90% of his income! Wow!

☞ Remember! The more recent the book you're reading, the more likely it has an anti-business slant. Try to get the full truth.

Andrew Carnegie: Giant of Industry, by Mary Malone (Garrard Americans All)   Gr. 1-5

In the *Childhood of Famous Americans* series: Gr. 1-6
    Andrew *Carnegie*, by Joanne Henry; *A. P. Giannini*, by Marie Hammontree; *J.C. Penney*,
    by Wilma Hudson; *John D. Rockefeller*, by Elisabeth Myers; *John Wanamaker*, by Olive
    Burt; *F.W. Woolworth*, by Elisabeth Myers; *Harvey S. Firestone*, by Adrian Paradis

Andrew Carnegie and the Age of Steel, by Katherine Shippen (Landmark)   Gr. 3-9

Andrew Carnegie, by Clara Ingram Judson   Gr. 3-10

Nickels and Dimes, by Nina Brown Baker (biography of Woolworth)   Gr. 3-12

Mr. Penney, by Harry Albus   Gr. 4-10

From Rags to Riches; Better Mousetraps; **and**, *The Unsung Heroes*, by N. Aaseng   Gr. 5-12
    Short chapters highlight Mr's. Proctor & Gamble, Dow Jones, Mr's. Sears & Roebuck,
    Milton Hershey, J.C. Penney, Marriott, Hoover, the inventor of CocaCola, etc.

❧ **Circus Time!** See how much easier people's lives were?! They could buy circus tickets!

    Peter Spier's Circus, by Peter Spier   Gr. K-4
    The Ringling Brothers, by R. & S. Glendinning (Garrard Discovery)   Gr. 1-5
    P.T. Barnum: King of the Circus, by Lynn Groh (Garrard Discovery)   Gr. 1-5
    The Ringling Brothers: Circus Boys, by Olive Burt (Childhood)   Gr. 1-6
    P.T. Barnum: Circus Boy, by Augusta Stevenson (Childhood)   Gr. 1-6
    Circus Days Under the Big Top, by R. Glendinning (How They Lived)   Gr. 3-8
    World's Greatest Showman: P.T. Barnum, by Joe Bryan (Landmark)   Gr. 3-8
    The Real Tom Thumb, by Helen Cross   Gr. 3-12
        Real life of midget Charles Stratton, made famous as Tom Thumb.

Fiction/Historical Fiction:

    The Day the Circus Came to Lone Tree, by Glen Rounds   Gr. 2-6
        Zany adventure shows what a treat the circus was to those in remote areas.
    Toby Tyler, by James Otis   Gr. 4-10
        Waif boy lives with the circus people.

Want a general overview of the 1900s?

Ghosts of the 20ᵗʰ Century, by Cheryl Harness   Gr. 3-10
        Not really about ghosts; fun illustrations show the figures of the 1900s.

13❧ Technology!

Do you like technology? Then you're going to enjoy this section, because you are going to see where tons of good ideas got started! They sure did change life! Think of it! After thousands of years of traveling only on foot (whether it be the feet of people, horses, camels, or donkeys), there suddenly were automobiles and airplanes! After thousands of years of candles and oil lamps, now people could flip a switch for electric lighting! Try to imagine what it felt like to live through these changes! Radio! Telephones! Decent doctors! Movies! Oil wells! Dynamite! The earliest computers! And maybe most importantly...indoor plumbing! We'll just focus on American inventors and scientists here (except where it's necessary to meet others to understand the field), but folks were doing great things in other countries too!

Isn't it wonderful that God made people to be so creative and intelligent because we're in His image?! We love to solve problems and make more helpful inventions. Trouble comes only when people act like they are God and that all their great ideas come only from themselves. So once again, as you meet the great scientists and inventors of this era (just pick a few), try to look deeper for what they believed to be true. Then you'll have a better idea of how their work affected this world. Interesting! (Begin *ThinkWrite 2* now.)

> *ThinkWrite 2: "What do you make of it?!"*
>
> Why don't you pick one inventor and talk about something he/she made or discovered. But can you also dig a little deeper and find out what the person believed to be true about God and people? Then you can understand this person's life and work even better!

13a❧ General resources

Picture History of Great Inventors, by Gillian Clement   Gr. 2-7

Scientists Who Changed the World, by Philip Wilkinson *et al*   Gr. 3-7

Mathematicians are People, Too (Vol. 1 and 2), by L. & W. Reimer   Gr. 3-10

Famous Mathematicians, by Frances Stonaker   Gr. 3-10

*History Makers of the Scientific Revolution, by Nina Morgan (History Makers)   Gr. 4-9

*Men of Science, Men of God, by Henry Morris   Gr. 5-12
> Most of the biographical sketches in this book are too short to offer much insight.

Bright Design, by Katherine B. Shippen   Gr. 5-12
> This book is fascinating! It relates, in quite interesting narrative, the gradual discoveries made in the fields of electricity, atomic theory, general physical principles, etc., and how those discoveries built on each other. It includes chapters on many of the people listed above, such as John Dalton, about whom little else has been written for youth.

*Smithsonian Visual Timeline of Inventions, by Richard Platt   Gr. 5-12
> This book intrigues me.

*Invention, by Lionel Bender (Eyewitness)   Gr. 5-12
> This coffeetable-type book doesn't give a narrative history (needed for deep learning) but does offer fascinating photos of objects related to invention.

13b Specific discoveries and inventors

Anesthesia–this discovery (claimed by four different men) was so helpful!

Gift of Magic Sleep, by Irwin Shapiro   Gr. 4-8

Great Men of Medicine, by Ruth Hume (Landmark), Ch. 5   Gr. 4-9

Dr. Morton: Pioneer in the Use of Anesthesia, by Rachel Baker (Messner)   Gr. 5-12

*We Have Conquered Pain, by Dennis Fradin   Gr. 5-12

Automobiles (Henry Ford treated separately further below):

*Alice Ramsey's Grand Adventure, by Don Brown   Gr. 1-4
> An early cross-country trip.

Walter Chrysler: Boy Machinist, by Ethel Weddle (Childhood)   Gr. 1-6

*The Great Horse-less Carriage Race, by Michael Dooling   Gr. 2-6?
> This book is just about to be released, so I'm not sure of the age recommendation.

Eureka! It's an Automobile, by Jeanne Bendick   Gr. 3-8

Early Days of Automobiles, by Elizabeth Janeway (Landmark)   Gr. 3-10

Gasoline Buggy of the Duryea Brothers, by Robert Jackson   Gr. 3-12

Automobiles Past and Present, by Walter Buehr   Gr. 4-9

Karl Benz, by Brian Williams   Gr. 4-12

Look Out! Here Comes the Stanley Steamer, by K.C. Tessendorf   Gr. 4-12
    Story of steam-powered automobile.

Coast to Coast with Alice, by Patricia Hyatt   Gr. 5-10
    Early female motorist makes cross-country trip. May have feminist slant.

Berta Benz and the Motorwagen: The Story of the First Automobile Journey   Unknown
    by Mindy Bingham
    Mrs. Benz and her children set out on a trip across Germany to prove her husband's car.

Fiction/Historical Fiction:

Tin Lizzie, by Peter Spier   Gr. 3-6
    The fun adventures of an old Model T.

❧ Aviation (Wright Brothers treated separately further below)

Big Balloon Race, by Eleanor Coerr (I Can Read)   Gr. K-2

Pushers, Spads, Jennies, and Jets, by Leonard Everett Fisher   Gr. K-3
    Boys will look the strong illustrations which simply show the earlier aircraft.

Glorious Flight, by Alice & Martin Provensen   Gr. 1-4
    Lovely story of Louis Bleriot's attempt to fly over the English Channel.

The Story of Flight, by Mary Settle (Step-Up Books)   Gr. 1-5
    I love this older series, but chances of finding a copy aren't that great.

Pilot Jack Knight, by A.M. Anderson (American Adventure, older series)   Gr. 1-6
    One of the earliest pilots to fly US mail.

Glenn Martin: Boy Conqueror of the Air, by R.W. Harley (Childhood)   Gr. 1-6

Eureka! It's an Airplane, by Jeanne Bendick   Gr. 2-7

Brave Balloonists: America's First Airmen, by Esther Douty (How They Lived)   Gr. 3-8

When Men First Flew, by James McCague (How They Lived)   Gr. 3-8

Men of Flight: The Conquest of the Air, by Charles Verral (Al.'s Am. Heritage)   Gr. 3-8

Rider in the Sky: How an American Cowboy Built England's First Airplane   Gr. 4-12
      by John Hulls (This book will be published in Spring, 2003)

From Kite to Kittyhawk, by Richard Bishop   Gr. 5-12

❧ Alexander Graham Bell

Alexander Graham Bell: Man of Sound, by E. Montgomery (Garr. Discovery)   Gr. 1-4

Alexander Graham Bell, by Victoria Sherrow (On My Own)   Gr. 1-4

Aleck Bell, by Mabel Widdemer (Childhood)   Gr. 1-5

Ahoy! Ahoy! Are You There? by Robert Quackenbush   Gr. 2-6

Value of Self-Discipline: Alexander Graham Bell, by Ann Johnson (ValueTale)   Gr. 2-6

Mr. Bell Invents the Telephone, by Katherine Shippen (Landmark)   Gr. 3-9

Alexander Graham Bell and the Telephone, by Steve Parker (Science Discoveries) Gr. 4-8

Alexander Graham Bell, by Leonard Everett Fisher   Gr. 5-10

The Talking Wire, by O.J. Stevenson   Gr. 5-12

Films:

The Story of Alexander Graham Bell, starring Don Ameche & Henry Fonda   All ages

❧ Luther Burbank (plants/horticulture)

Luther Burbank: Partner of Nature, by Doris Faber (Garrard Discovery)   Gr. 1-5

53

Luther Burbank: Boy Wizard, by Olive Burt (Childhood)   Gr. 1-6

Here a Plant, There a Plant, by Robert Quackenbush   Gr. 2-6

Luther Burbank: Nature's Helper, by Lillian Bragdon (Makers of America)   Gr. 2-7

❧ Marie & Pierre Curie–who discovered radioactivity, and helped create our Nuclear Age

*Marie Curie: Brave Scientist, by Keith Brandt (Troll)   Gr. 1-3

*Marie Curie's Search for Radium, by Beverley Birch   Gr. 1-5
    So beautifully illustrated!

The Value of Learning: Marie Curie, by Ann Johnson (ValueTales)   Gr. 1-5

Marie Curie, by Robin McKown   Gr. 2-8

Marie Curie, by Edwina Conner (Great Lives)   Gr. 3-7

The Story of Madame Curie, by Alice Thorne (Signature)   Gr. 3-8

*Marie Curie and the Discovery of Radium, by Ann Steinke (Solutions)   Gr. 3-9

Marie Curie: Woman of Genius, by Adele de Leeuw   Gr. 3-12

*Marie Curie and Radium, by Steve Parker (Science Discoveries)   Gr. 4-8

Marie Curie, by Leonard Everett Fisher   Gr. 5-10
    This strongly-illustrated picture-biography would especially appeal to boys. It was
    recently in-print, so is probably in your public library still.

Films:

There is a **fantastic** film: **Madame Curie*, starring Greer Garson and Walter Pidgeon. You'll notice 'progressive' thinking in her philosophy given at the end of the film though. Also, there is a film on Curie in the "Inventors' Specials" series: **Marie Curie: More than Meets the Eye*.

❧ Lee DeForest, radio and television

Lee DeForest, by Lavinia Dobler (Childhood)   Gr. 1-6

❧ Drake's first oil well (in the US) and other stories of early oil

Drake Drills for Oil, by Louis Wolfe   Gr. 2-6

Fiction/Historical Fiction:

Gil Morgan, Oilman, by Ariane Dewey   Gr. 1-4
    Funny tall tale of legendary oilman!

Grandma Essie's Covered Wagon, by David Williams   Gr. 1-4
    Fact-based, family works in early oilfield.

Boom Town Boy, by Lois Lenski   Gr. 3-8

❧ George Eastman (photography)

George Eastman, by Joanne Henry (Childhood)   Gr. 1-6

Click! A Story about George Eastman, by Barbara Mitchell (Carolrhoda)   Gr. 1-5

George Eastman, by Lynda Pflueger   Unknown

❧ Thomas Edison (inventions; American children should definitely study Edison)

A Picture Book of Thomas Alva Edison, by David Adler   Gr. K-3

Thomas Alva Edison: Young Inventor, by Louis Sabin (Troll Easy Bio)   Gr. 1-3

The Wizard of Sound, by Barbara Mitchell (Creative Minds)   Gr. 1-5

Thomas Edison: Miracle Maker, by Mervyn Kaufman (Garrard Discovery)   Gr. 1-5

Tom Edison, by Sue Guthridge (Childhood)   Gr. 1-6

The Value of Creativity: Thomas Edison, by Ann Johnson (ValueTale)   Gr. 1-6

Thomas Alva Edison, Inventor, by R. Weir (Makers of America)   Gr. 2-7

Thomas Edison, by Nicholas Nirgiotis (Cornerstones)   Gr. 3-7
    This is one of the "Second Series" Cornerstones; I don't know if they've changed.

The Story of Thomas Alva Edison, by Enid Meadowcroft (Signature)   Gr. 3-8

*_Thomas Edison and Electricity_, by Steve Parker (Science Discoveries)   Gr. 3-9

*_The Story of Thomas Alva Edison_, by Margaret Cousins (Landmark)   Gr. 4-12

The Diary of Thomas A. Edison, by Thomas Edison, edited by K. McGuirk   Gr. 4-12
    Excerpts from Edison's own diary, along with family photos.

I Gave Thomas Edison My Sandwich, by Floyd Moore   Gr. 5-8
    True, illustrated story of boy who gave Edison a favorite sandwich.

☞ You might enjoy *Edison Experiments You Can Do*, by Marjorie VandeWater, for they are based on Edison's own notebooks! (Other authors have produced versions of his experiments, too.)

Films:

There are two truly fabulous films about Edison. Mickey Rooney plays Edison as a teen in *_Young Tom Edison_. The other is about his adulthood and stars Spencer Tracy–*_Edison, the Man_. There is also a video in the "Inventors' Specials" series: *_Edison: The Wizard of Light_.

⁂ Henry Ford (automobiles, assembly line method)

Henry Ford, by Adrian Paradis (See & Read)   Gr. 1-4

*_Henry Ford_, by Hazel Aird (Childhood)   Gr. 1-6

Along Came the Model T! by Robert Quackenbush   Gr. 2-6

*_We'll Race You, Henry_, by Barbara Mitchell (Creative Minds)   Gr. 2-6

The Story of Henry Ford and the Automobile, by Zachary Kent (Cornerstones)   Gr. 2-7

Henry Ford: Maker of the Model T, by Miriam Gilbert (Piper)   Gr. 2-8

*_Model T: How Henry Ford Built a Legend_, by David Weitzman   Gr. 3-8
    I have one of Weitzman's other books, and it's got a great feel to it.

*_Wheels of Time_, by Catherine Gourley   Gr. 3-8

John Holland (modern submarine)

Submarine Pioneer, by Frank Morriss   Gr. 5-12

Joseph Lister (surgery/health; now you know where 'Listerine' got its name!)

Scientists Who Changed the World, by Philip Wilkinson *et al*, pp. 44-47   Gr. 3-7

Great Men of Medicine, by Ruth Hume (Landmark), Ch. 7   Gr. 4-9

Marconi, and the development of radio

Marconi's Battle for Radio, by Beverley Birch   Gr. 1-5

Guglielmo Marconi and Radio, by Steve Parker (Science Discoveries)   Gr. 3-9

Guglielmo Marconi: Radio Pioneer, by Beverley Birch (Giants of Science)   Gr. 5-12

Fiction/Historical Fiction:

Radio Boy, by Sharon Denslow   Gr. 1-4
     This nice picture book relates the childhood of a real radio inventor, Stubblefield.

Jan Matzeliger, and his shoe-making machine

Shoes for Everyone, by Barbara Mitchell (Creative Minds)   Gr. 2-6

Matthew Maury—led by a Bible verse to a great discovery (navigation/oceanography)

Trail Blazer of the Seas, by Jean Lee Latham   Gr. 4-12
     This book is much-loved. I hope your library has a copy.

Panama Canal

Locks, Crocs, and Skeeters   Gr. 1-5
   by Nancy Winslow Parker

George W. Goethals: Panama Canal Engineer
   by Jean Latham (Disc.) Gr. 1-5

Story of the Panama Canal   Gr. 2-7
   by R.C. Stein (Cornerstones)

Mosquitoes in the Big Ditch   Gr. 3-8
   by R. Burlingame (Winston)

First Book of the Panama Canal   Gr. 3-8
   by Patricia Markun (First Books)

Panama Canal   Gr. 3-9
   by Bob Considine (Landmark)

> Believe it or not, two doctors were instrumental in building the Panama Canal! Walter Reed discovered yellow fever was carried by mosquitoes, and William Gorgas dealt directly with the yellow fever mowing down scads of the canal builders.
>
> *Walter Reed*, by H. Higgins (Childhood) Gr. 1-5
> *Walter Reed*, by L. Groh (Am. All)   Gr. 2-7
> *Doctors Who Conquered Yellow Fever*   Gr. 3-9
>   by Ralph N. Hill (Landmark)
> *Soldier Doctor* (about Gorgas)   Gr. 3-12
>   by Clara Ingram Judson
> *William Crawford Gorgas*   Gr. 5-12
>   by Beryl Williams & Sam Epstein
> *Walter Reed*, by L. Wood (Messner)   Gr. 5-12
> *Your Story Hour*, Vol. 6 (audio tapes) All ages

Panama Canal, by Elizabeth Mann (Wonders...)   Gr. 3-10

Louis Pasteur (health...and more!)

Louis Pasteur: Young Scientist, by Francene Sabin (Troll Easy Biography)   Gr. 1-3

Pasteur's Fight Against Microbes, by Beverley Birch   Gr. 1-5
   Beautifully illustrated!

Value of Believing in Yourself: Louis Pasteur, by Spencer Johnson (ValueTale)   Gr. 1-6

Louis Pastuer: Germ Killer, by John Mann   Gr. 2-5

The Quest of Louis Pasteur, by Patricia Lauber   Gr. 3-8

The Story of Louis Pasteur, by Alida Malkus (Signature)   Gr. 3-8

Louis Pasteur and Germs, by Steve Parker (Science Discoveries)   Gr. 3-9

Great Men of Medicine, by Ruth Hume (Landmark), Ch. 6   Gr. 4-9

Louis Pasteur, by Beverley Birch & Fiona Macdonald   Unknown

Films:

Louis Pasteur (Animated Hero Classics)   All ages

The Story of Louis Pasteur, starring Paul Muni   All ages

🖤 **Roebling family and the Brooklyn Bridge, one of the engineering marvels of the time!**

Story of the Brooklyn Bridge (Cornerstones)   Gr. 2-7
    by Zachary Kent

Brooklyn Bridge, by Lynn Curlee   Gr. 3-7

Big Bridge to Brooklyn (Alad.'s Am. Heritage) Gr. 3-8
    by Frances Browin

> Don't miss! How did the builders of a bridge over the Niagara get the first line across? You'll be surprised!
>
> *Flight of the Union*   Gr. 1-4
>   by Tekla White (On My Own)

Brooklyn Bridge, by Elizabeth Mann (Wonders of the World)   Gr. 3-10

☞ David Macaulay's new video series (*Big Buildings*) covers the marvels of the Brooklyn Bridge in the episode devoted to bridges. It's fascinating!

🖤 **Röntgen/Roentgen–discoverer of x-rays!**

The Mysterious Rays of Dr. Röntgen, by Beverly Gherman   Gr. 3-8

🖤 **Steinmetz (electrical engineer/inventor who fostered GE)**

Steinmetz: Wizard of Light, by Anne Guy   Gr. 3-8

🖤 **Transatlantic Cable, headed by Cyrus Field against incredible odds!**

Story of the Great Republic, by H.A. Guerber, Ch. LIX   Gr. 3-7

The First Transatlantic Cable, by Adele Gutman (Landmark)   Gr. 3-9

Young Man in a Hurry, by Jean Lee Latham   Gr. 4-12

❧ Westinghouse (inventions, especially related to trains)

George Westinghouse, by Montrew Dunham (Childhood)	Gr. 1-6
*George Westinghouse: A Genius for Invention, by B. Ravage (Innovative Minds)	Unknown

❧ Wright Brothers (aviation)

*Young Orville and Wilbur Wright, by Andrew Woods (Troll First-Start) — Gr. K-2

*Will and Orv, by Walter Schulz (Carolrhoda's On My Own) — Gr. 1-3

*Taking Flight, by Stephen Krensky (Ready-to-Read) — Gr. 1-3

*Wilbur & Orville Wright, by Louis Sabin (Troll Easy Biographies) — Gr. 1-4

Wright Brothers: Kings of the Air, by Mervyn Kaufman (Garrard Discovery) — Gr. 1-5

*Wilbur and Orville Wright, by Augusta Stevenson (Childhood) — Gr. 1-6

Wright Brothers: First to Fly, by Madge Haines (Makers of America) — Gr. 1-6

*First Flight, by George Shea (I Can Read) — Gr. 2-4
Tells of Tom Tate, who made in early solo flight in the Wrights' glider.

*To Fly, by Wendie Old — Gr. 2-5

Take Me Out to the Airfield! by Robert Quackenbush — Gr. 2-6

The Value of Patience: The Wright Brothers, by Spencer Johnson (ValueTale) — Gr. 2-6

*The Story of the Flight at Kitty Hawk, by R. Conrad Stein (Cornerstones) — Gr. 2-7

*Wright Brothers, by Quentin Reynolds (Landmark) — Gr. 3-9

Three Together, by Lois Mills — Gr. 3-9
Shows the help of their sister!

*The Wright Brothers and Aviation, by Steve Parker (Science Discoveries) — Gr. 3-9

Wright Brothers at Kitty Hawk, by Donald Sobol — Gr. 4-9

Into the Air, by Robert Burleigh   Gr. 5-8
> I don't know about this one. Different format. Different style. Maybe check it for your very reluctant readers.

Fiction/Historical Fiction:

We Were There at the First Airplane Flight, by Felix Sutton (We Were There)   Gr. 3-8

> What a time of great confidence and energy! America bought Alaska from the Russians (1867), the French built the Eiffel Tower (1889), and the world held the first modern Olympics (1896)!
>
> *The Story of Seward's Folly*, by Susan Clinton (Cornerstones)   Gr. 2-6
>   This is the original Cornerstones of Freedom book on the topic.
> *Seward's Folly*, by Melissa Whitcraft (Cornerstones)   Gr. 3-8
>
> Any books on the world's great buildings will cover the Eiffel Tower, and there are many books on the history of the modern Olympics.

14❧ Achieve-A-Rama!

Well, with all the excitement in the world at this time, people felt they could accomplish the impossible! A man named Blondin walked a tightrope over Niagara Falls! Brave men clawed their way to the North and South Poles! Everywhere, there was a new feeling in the air. A woman walked into a medical school and said she wanted to be a doctor! Such a thing had never been allowed before! George Washington Carver made brilliant discoveries, and that forced some Americans with wrong attitudes to admit that black folks were just as smart as any other folks, something they should have known all along! Alexander Graham Bell's work with the deaf—a key factor in him developing the telephone—led to his friendship with Helen Keller, and her story showed how much handicapped people could accomplish! (Parents: Many of these issues would later be politicized, and so may be the books you read about them; be careful!)

14a❧ Arctic explorers (listed specifically immediately below)

Into the Ice, by Lynn Curlee   Gr. 2-6

The Race to the South Pole, by Rupert Matthews (Great Journeys)   Gr. 3-8

Conquest of the North and South Poles, by Russell Owen (Landmark)   Gr. 3-10

❧ Richard Byrd

Richard E. Byrd: Adventurer to the Poles, by Adele de Leeuw (Garr. Discovery)   Gr. 1-5

*Richard Byrd, by Guernsey Van Riper, Jr. (Childhood)   Gr. 1-6

*Black Whiteness: Admiral Byrd Alone in the Antarctic
   by Robert Burleigh   Gr. 4-9
   I've heard wonderful things about this.

Admiral Byrd of Antarctica (Messner)   Gr. 5-12
   by Michael Gladych

> **Historical Fiction:**
>
> *We Were There with Byrd at the South Pole*, by Charles Strong   Gr. 3-8

❧ Matthew Henson, an African-American explorer of the Arctic

Matthew A. Henson, by Charles Graves (See & Read)   Gr. K-2

Matthew Henson & Robert Peary, by Laurie Rozakis (Partners)   Gr. 2-5

*Arctic Explorer, by Jeri Ferris (Carolrhoda)   Gr. 3-6

Matthew Henson: Arctic Hero, by Sheldon Ripley (Piper)   Gr. 3-8

*Matthew Henson and the North Pole Expedition, by A. Gaines (Journey to Free...) Unknown

Films:

*Glory & Honor   Parental decision
   I KNOW NOTHING about this film and have no idea of it's moral content, but simply
   read that it's about Henson's key role in the expedition with Peary.

❧ Robert Peary

Robert E. Peary: North Pole Conqueror, by Erick Berry (Garrard Discovery)   Gr. 1-5

Robert Peary, by Electa Clark (Childhood)   Gr. 1-6

*Story of Admiral Peary at the North Pole, by Zachary Kent (Cornerstones)   Gr. 2-8

Peary to the Pole, by Walter Lord   Gr. 4-10

Fiction/Historical Fiction:

*Call Me Ahnighito, by Pam Conrad   Gr. 1-5
        True; Peary retrieves meteorite that fell on Greenland. Story is told *by* the meteorite!

14b✿❧ Daredevils

Blondin: Hero of Niagara, by R. Boning Gr. 1-6

☞ The *Mirette* books (*Mirette on the High Wire, Starring Mirette & Bellini*, and, *Mirette & Bellini Cross Niagara Falls* (Gr. 1-4), all by Emily McCully, feature daring challenges.

> To capture the spirit of the age, read:
>
> *Around the World in Eighty Days*
>   by Jules Verne
> Unabridged and abridged, so all students may enjoy!

14c❧ Achievements of women

❧ Elizabeth Blackwell, first (modern) female doctor

Elizabeth Blackwell, by Francene Sabin (Troll)   Gr. 1-3

Elizabeth Blackwell: First Woman Doctor, by Carol Greene (Rookie)   Gr. 1-3

Elizabeth Blackwell, by Jean Lee Latham (Garrard Discovery)   Gr. 1-4

Elizabeth Blackwell, by Joanne Henry (Childhood)   Gr. 1-5

Elizabeth Blackwell, by Matthew Grant Gr. 1-5

Dr. Elizabeth, by Patricia Clapp   Gr. 4-12

First Woman Doctor, by Rachel Baker Gr. 5-10

> Both *Native American Doctor*, by Jeri Ferris (Carolrhoda; Gr. 2-5), and *Homeward the Arrow's Flight*, by Marion Marsh Brown (Gr. 5-12), tell of Susan LaFlesche, first American Indian woman doctor!

❧ Maria Mitchell, astronomer

Maria's Comet, by Deborah Hopkinson   Gr. 1-4

Maria Mitchell: Stargazer, by Katharine Wilkie (Garrard Discovery)   Gr. 1-4

Maria Mitchell: Girl Astronomer, by Grace Melin (Childhood)   Gr. 1-6

Rooftop Astronomer, by Stephanie McPherson (Creative Minds)   Gr. 1-6

❧ Nellie Bly, journalist

Nellie Bly: Reporter for the World, by C. Graves (Garr. Americans All)   Gr. 1-4

Around the World with Nellie Bly, by Emily Hahn (North Star)   Gr. 5-12

Fiction/Historical Fiction:

*Nellie Bly's Monkey, by Joan Blos   Gr. 2-5

❧ Ruth Law and Jacqueline Cochran, aviators

*Ruth Law Thrills a Nation, by Don Brown   Gr. K-3

Jacqueline Cochran (Garrard Americans All)   Gr. 1-8
by Marquita Fisher

> **The Big Balloon Race*, by Eleanor Coerr (I Can Read, Gr. K-3) is the true story of an early female balloonist!

❧ Ellen Richards, chemist

*Adventurous Spirit, by Ethlie Vare (Creative Minds)   Gr. 2-6

America's First Woman Chemist, by Esther Douty (Messner)   Gr. 8-12

❧ Linda Richards, nurse

Linda Richards: First Trained...., by David Collins (Garr. Discovery)   Gr. 1-4

America's First Trained Nurse, by Rachel Baker (Messner)   Gr. 6-12

❧ Blanche Leathers, steamboat captain!

*Steamboat! by Judith Gilliland   Gr. 1-5

14d❧ Achievements of blacks/African-Americans

❧ George Washington Carver

George Washington Carver, by Peter Towne (Crowell Biography)   Gr. 1-3

George Washington Carver, by Andy Carter (On My Own)   Gr. 1-3

A Picture Book of George Washington Carver, by David Adler   Gr. 1-3

George Washington Carver, by S. & B. Epstein (Garr. Discovery)   Gr. 1-4

George Washington Carver, by Carol Greene (Rookie)   Gr. 1-5

George Carver, by Augusta Stevenson (Childhood)   Gr. 1-6

The Story of George Washington Carver, by Eva Moore (Scholastic)   Gr. 1-6

A Pocketful of Goobers, by Barbara Mitchell (Creative Minds)   Gr. 2-8

George Washington Carver, What do You See? by J. Benge (Another...)   Gr. 3-4
    Christian author, but I've heard it has comic book-like illustrations.

A Weed is Not a Flower, by Aliki   Gr. 3-6

Carvers' George, by Florence Means   Gr. 3-7

Hero Tales—Vol. III, by Dave & Neta Jackson, pp. 44-55   Gr. 3-7

The Story of George Washington Carver, by Arna Bontemps (Signature)   Gr. 3-8

George Washington Carver, by Ann White (Landmark)   Gr. 3-10

George Washington Carver, by Janet & Geoff Benge (Christian Heroes) Gr. 4-10

George Washington Carver, by David Collins (Sower, shows his faith)   Gr. 5-12

George Washington Carver, by Sam Wellman (Heroes of the Faith)   Gr. 5-12

☞ You'll find a wonderful story of Carver's faith in: *Your Story Hour (Vol. 7)*.

Fiction/Historical Fiction:

Forty-Acre Swindle, by Dave & Neta Jackson (Trailblazer)   Gr. 3-9

❧ Booker T. Washington

Story of the Great Republic, by H.A. Guerber, Ch. LXVII   Gr. 3-7

Booker T. Washington, by Thomas Amper (On My Own)   Gr. 1-3

Booker T. Washington, by William Wise (See & Read)   Gr. 1-3

More than Anything Else, by Marie Bradby   Gr. 1-4
> I've heard this is beautifully illustrated; it tells of young Booker's desire to read.

Booker T. Washington, by Lillie Patterson (Garrard Discovery)   Gr. 1-5

Booker T. Washington, by Augusta Stevenson (Childhood)   Gr. 1-6

Story of Booker T. Washington, by P. & F. McKissack (Cornerstones)   Gr. 3-8

Around 1900, blacks (African-Americans) began to fight harder for the respect they were due; folks, such as W.E.B. DuBois, organized active groups. Paul Dunbar and Langston Hughes expressed the feelings of many blacks in their poetry. Black ragtime, blues, and jazz music began to be appreciated. (Jazz will be covered later.)

Raggin': A Story about Scott Joplin, by Barbara Mitchell (Creative Minds) Gr. 2-7

William C. Handy: Father of the Blues, by E. Montgomery (Gar. Am. All) Gr. 2-8

✎ Mary McLeod Bethune

Mary McLeod Bethune, by Ruby Radford (See & Read)   Gr. 1-4

Mary McLeod Bethune, by Eloise Greenfield (Crowell Biography)   Gr. 1-5

Mary McLeod Bethune, by Olive Burt (Childhood)   Gr. 1-5

Hero Tales–Vol. III, by Dave & Neta Jackson, pp. 8-19   Gr. 3-7

Story of Mary McLeod Bethune, by P. & F. McKissack (Cornerstones)   Gr. 3-8

Mary McLeod Bethune, by Emma Gelder Sterne   Gr. 5-12

Fiction/Historical Fiction:

Defeat of the Ghost Riders, by Dave & Neta Jackson (Trailblazer)   Gr. 3-9

14e⚜ Achievements of the handicapped

⚜ Helen Keller

Young Helen Keller, by Anne Benjamin (Troll First-Start)   Gr. K-2

Helen Keller and the Big Storm, by Pat Lakin (Ready to Read 2)   Gr. 1-2

Helen Keller, by Jane Sucliffe (Carolrhoda's On My Own)   Gr. 1-3

A Picture Book of Helen Keller, by David Adler   Gr. 1-3

Helen Keller: Toward the Light, by Stewart & Polly Graff (Garr. Disc.)   Gr. 1-4
    This book may have been issued as: *Helen Keller: Crusader for the Deaf and Blind*.

Helen Keller: Courage in the Dark, by J. Hurwitz (Step Into Reading 3)   Gr. 1-4

Helen Keller, by Katharine Wilkie (Childhood)   Gr. 1-5

Helen Keller, by Margaret Davidson (Scholastic Biography)   Gr. 1-6

Helen Keller, by Janet Benge Gr. 3-7
    (Another Great Achiever)

Story of Helen Keller, by Lorena Hickok
    (Signature)   Gr. 3-8

☞ You might enjoy the film about Keller and Sullivan: *Miracle Worker*, starring Ann Bancroft and Patty Duke. I've not seen it, so cannot comment on age-appropriateness.

You'll also enjoy the story of Helen Keller's teacher, Ann Sullivan:

Annie Sullivan (See & Read)   Gr. K-3
    by Mary Malone
Story of Annie Sullivan (Dell)   Gr. 3-7
    by Bernice Selden
Helen Keller's Teacher   Gr. 3-10
    by Margaret Davidson

⚜ Thomas Gallaudet (who lived just before this time, but fits here best, since he was the first to really help the deaf and was thus studied by Alexander Graham Bell)

World of Knowing, by Andy Bowen (Creative Minds)   Gr. 3-10

Gallaudet: Friend of the Deaf, by Etta De Gering   Gr. 4-12

15🝔 Battle of Beliefs

Remember! We are saying there *was* a lot of progress during this time in history: there were great inventions, better doctors, easier travel, faster communication, and folks were even starting to work on some problems in American society. *But here's the issue:* some folks were rightly seeing the Lord and His wise laws as the source of all that was good in America, and they were trying to solve America's problems by looking more closely at God's teachings. That means they were also trying to be honest about people's sinful natures (and how they should be dealt with). Other folks believed that all the progress was because people had 'evolved' so much that sin was just an old-fashioned idea, and that if people banded together in groups (as in the power of government), they could solve America's problems using their own ideas and ignoring what the Bible said. How could they ignore the Lord? Because they didn't believe He was the Creator; and that meant they also didn't believe He was the Lord Who could alone say what was right and wrong. They thought they could make the world just how *they* wanted it to be. That is the issue of this time in history. Do you see?

When you're older, you can learn about this battle of beliefs. You'll see how many folks tried to tackle real problems in American society (such as the way certain groups of people were treated) in both wrong ways and right ways; they changed government and education and laws and lots of other things, but we can't get into that while you're still young because we can't fairly show you all parts of the issues in a way that would help you see the whole truth. Just know that pretty soon almost everyone started believing that only the government could take care of them, educate them, and a whole lot more. When people started believing that, they let go of something very special in the way that God made people. (Parents: if you want to dig into these topics, read *TruthQuest History: Age of Revolution III* and *History Through the Eyes of Faith*, by Ronald Wells, Ch. 14.)

You homeschool parents may be interested in this quote, a topic we address in the *TruthQuest History: Age of Revolution IV* guide for older children. It shows some of the major belief battles going on in America at the time:

The public school movement was always more than simply an effort to have schools provided at taxpayer expense. Nor was it simply an effort to have an educated electorate as the franchise [right to vote] was extended to more people, as is sometimes alleged. The most zealous of reformers were determined to use the power of the state by way of the schools to break the hold of religious tradition and the inherited culture and to change society through the child's training.

Clarence Carson, *Basic History of the United States–Vol. 3*, pp. 90-91.

Phew! I just have to stop right now and just praise God's name! Wow! It just amazes me how real He is, how true He is, that He IS! His way is the only way, and it's such a good way. To whatever degree mankind gets on His track, there is just greatness ahead! He is sooooo good! We are incredibly privileged to KNOW Him! Praise His Name! Phew! Sorry, but if I didn't praise Him, the very rocks would cry out, ya' know?!

16⚜ Teddy Roosevelt

You're about to meet an amazing man! He did *so much* during his very adventurous life! He spoke openly about his Christian faith, but you older students also may notice that some of the 'human progress' (progressive) thinking of his day seems to have seeped into his mind. We have to be careful about the same thing; it can happen so easily! Yes, it's simple to understand how Mr. Roosevelt could get a little confused when so many churches were teaching a strange blend of Bible truth and the new-fangled ideas about human progress. On the other hand, each of us must work to learn what God says is right. Anyway, Teddy Roosevelt seemed to think that it was good for the American government to use its power to forcefully spread 'progress' to other countries in the world, and that motivated some of his deeds. I can't explain it all to you now when you're young; it's even hard for us parents to understand because our schools taught *us* lots of progressive ideas about presidents and governments and people and wars. Well, we get into all this more deeply in the *TruthQuest History* guide for older students (Age of Revolution III). But now we *can* enjoy meeting this famous man!

☞ Remember, most children's books will only praise his brave deeds, not honestly discuss his progressive beliefs.

This Country of Ours, by H.E. Marshall, Ch. 97	Gr. 3-8

Theodore Roosevelt, by Sibyl Hancock (See and Read)	Gr. 1-3
Teddy Roosevelt: Rough Rider, by Louis Sabin (Troll Easy Biography)	Gr. 1-3
Meet Theodore Roosevelt, by Ormonde de Kay (Step-Up Books)	Gr. 1-4
Legend of the Teddy Bear, by Frank Murphy	Gr. 1-5
Beautiful book relates incident in Teddy Roosevelt's life that gave rise to 'teddy bear.'	
The One Bad Thing about Father, by F.N. Monjo (History I Can Read)	Gr. 1-5
Theodore Roosevelt: Man of Action, by James Beach (Garrard Discovery)	Gr. 1-5
Theodore Roosevelt's Boys, by Stewart Graff	Gr. 1-5
Teddy Roosevelt, by Edd Parks (Childhood)	Gr. 1-6
Don't You Dare Shoot that Bear! by Robert Quackenbush	Gr. 1-6
Holt and the Teddy Bear, by Jim McCafferty	Gr. 2-6
Meet Teddy Roosevelt's hunting guide involved in episode that yielded 'teddy bear.'	
Theodore Roosevelt: An Initial Biography, by Genevieve Foster	Gr. 3-8
Adventure in Courage, by Frances Cavanah	Gr. 3-8

The Story of Theodore Roosevelt, by Winthrop Neilson (Signature)	Gr. 3-8
*Young Teddy Roosevelt, by Cheryl Harness	Gr. 3-8
*Theodore Roosevelt, by Zachary Kent (Encyclopedia of Presidents)	Gr. 5-12
Theodore Roosevelt, by Clara Ingram Judson	Gr. 5-12

Fiction/Historical Fiction:

*A Christmas Tree in the White House, by Gary Hines What happens when Roosevelt's sons sneak in a Christmas tree?	Gr. 1-4

17🍂 Spanish-American War

When you were reading about Teddy Roosevelt in the last section, you probably noticed that he got involved in the Spanish-American War while he was the Secretary of the Navy and when he led the Rough Riders into Cuba. Well, we can learn more about that war now, though we'll wait until you're older to talk about the way 'human progress' (progressive) ideas led to some very bad American decisions. But you can learn about some of the heroic men while you're young. They give us a good example of bravery!

*Story of the Great Republic, by H.A. Guerber Ch. LXXII-LXXV, LXXVIII-LXXIX	Gr. 3-7
*This Country of Ours, by H.E. Marshall, Ch. 96a --------	Gr. 3-8
George Dewey, by Laura Long (Childhood)	Gr. 1-6
The Story of the Sinking of the Battleship <u>Maine</u>, by Zachary Kent (Cornerstones)	Gr. 2-7
The Story of the Rough Riders, by Zachary Kent (Cornerstones)	Gr. 2-7
*The Spanish-American War, by Mary Collins (Cornerstones)	Gr. 2-7
Teddy Roosevelt and the Rough Riders, by Henry Castor (Landmark)	Gr. 3-9
*The Spanish-American War, by Edward Dolan	Gr. 5-8
*The Spanish-American War, by Kathlyn & Marvin Gay	Gr. 5-9
George Dewey: Admiral of the Navy, by Fredrika Smith	Gr. 5-12

18 ☙ Ideas in Art, Books, and More!

Well, let's explore a little bit. Let's look at the many paintings, sculptures, books, and songs created during this time in America. These things always show what the folks who created them are believing. Remember, history is not first about what people do, it's about what God says and whether people believe it to be true. And in American art, you'll see this mixing of beliefs I have been talking about. Some artists, composers, and writers were still holding to the basic truths of the Christian faith (whether or not they were personally Christians): they created solid, wholesome works which saw human life as valuable and which presented a world that made sense because there was a loving God in charge. Other artists and writers no longer believed in a real God Who cared for the world, Who gave meaning to all people and all things, and Who gave solid truths that were the only right basis for living. (Remember, if one doesn't believe that God created people in His image, the specialness of people is gone. If one doesn't believe that God is the Judge and Lawmaker, then there is no way to say that one thing is right and another thing is wrong. If one doesn't believe that God is the King, there is no hope that things are under His control.) And then there were artists who had a foot in both worlds because they were confused, or were moving away from one belief toward the other. You can see there is a lot to think about when you're looking at paintings or meeting famous artists!

<u>Oh, first I must share the usual art-study disclaimer!</u>

1) Parents, you <u>*must*</u> determine the suitability of the artworks your children will be viewing, reading, and hearing. The artists, and some of their works, can be inappropriate for children (and adults), and that means books about them will be too. Many books contain nudes, even some of those listed here. I've 'dressed up' some of my books, but you may be using borrowed books. Of course, families vary on this issue. Use discretion!

2) Please don't try to study them all! Just pick a few and get to know them. Listen to their music. Gaze at their art. Read their poems and books. Now's the chance to absorb it all in context, not under the microscope of a textbook's analysis! Once you've selected a few for study, get to know their *Big 2 Beliefs*, and you'll be able to guess if their life and career ended in confident peace or discouraged hopelessness.

3) It's not easy to place artists, composers, and writers accurately in a single 'ism' because the terminology is inexact, sources disagree, and because artists moved through various phases in their career. Keep this in mind, if your sources differ.

4) Specific biographies, written at a youth level, will of course be listed here. Otherwise, you'll certainly find info in your favorite art/music/literature history books, such as: *Story of Painting for Young People*, by the Jansons, *Looking at Pictures*, by Joy Richardson, *Lives of the Artists*, by Kathleen Krull, *Famous Paintings*, by Chase, and *Sister Wendy's many art books; The Book of Music*, edited by Gill Rowley (pp. 48-53), *Story-Lives of Great Composers* and *Story-Lives of American Composers*, both by Katherine Bakeless; *Famous Authors*, by Ramon Coffmann, and *Lives of the Writers*, by Kathleen Krull; etc.

Part I: Visual Arts

❧ Mary Cassatt, an American Impressionist who worked during the time of Monet, Manet, Renoir, Degas, & Morisot

For hands-on projects based on the work of many artists:

Discovering Great Artists by MaryAnn Kohl

Mary Cassatt, by M. Venezia (Getting to Know...)   Gr. 1-5

Lives of the Artists, by Kathleen Krull, pp. 36-39   Gr. 3-7

Mary Cassatt, by Thomas Streissguth   Gr. 5-10

What Makes a Cassatt a Cassatt, by Richard Muhlberger   Gr. 5-12

Fiction/Historical Fiction:

Suzette and the Puppy: A Story of Mary Cassatt, by Joan Sweeney   Gr. 1-4
 Fictional tale of girl who posed in real Cassatt painting.

Films:

Mary Cassatt: American Impressionist (Artists' Specials)   Parental decision

For general information on Impressionism:

Child's History of Art, by Hillyer & Huey, (*Painting* section, Ch. 26)   Gr. 2-8
OR, *Young People's Story of Fine Art: Last Two Hundred Years*, pp. 52-59

Katie Meets the Impressionists, by James Mayhew   Gr. 1-4
 Sounds wonderful; a girl at an art museum 'slips' in and out of
 various paintings collection flowers for her grandmother, and meets
 Impressionist masters along the way.

❧ Winslow Homer, George Inness, Thomas Eakins, Whistler, and John Singer Sargent, artists who seemed to focus on capturing 'real life'

Child's History of Art, by Hillyer & Huey, (*Painting* section, Ch. 29b & 30)   Gr. 2-8
OR, *Young People's Story of Fine Art: Last Two Hundred Years*, pp. 79-95

A Weekend with Winslow Homer, by Ann Beneduce   Gr. 4-9

John Singer Sargent: The Life of an Artist, by Eshel Kreiter   Unknown

Films:

Winslow Homer: An American Original (Artists' Specials)   Parental decision

❧ Sculpture

Child's History of Art, by Hillyer & Huey, (*Sculpture* section, Ch. 23, 25-27)   Gr. 2-8
<u>OR</u>, *Young People's Story of Sculpture*, pp. 93-95, 102-114

Part II: Music

❧ Aaron Copland and John Philip Sousa, who tried to compose music that captured the feeling of grassroots America

Aaron Copland, by Mike Venezia (Getting to Know the World's...)   Gr. 1-5

John Philip Sousa, by A. Weil (Childhood)   Gr. 1-6

❧ Edward MacDowell

Edward MacDowell and His Cabin In the Pines, by Opal Wheeler & Sybil Deucher Gr. 1-6

Part III: Literature

As America blossomed as a nation, Americans longed for their own literature—stories of their own people and land—written by their own authors.[7] Wonderful writers soon filled this need. These American writers seemed to focus on the things that made America tick; they brought to life their various home regions; they showed real living and individuality; some even waxed nostalgic about the 'good ol' days' now that America seemed so advanced. Be sure to look at the Mark Twain; he really tried to capture the feeling of America.

---

[7] Carson 3:68-69.

Parents: You should carefully decide which authors to study based on available time, the suitability of the authors and their works (though I've tried to list only those that come closest to being appropriate for young children; others are covered in the guide for older children). Please know that I'm certainly not endorsing all these authors and books; let the Lord's standards be applied as seen fit by your family.

❧ Louisa May Alcott (_Little Women_, _Little Men_, etc.)

*_Louisa May Alcott_, by Laurence Santrey (Troll Easy Biography)	Gr. 1-3
*_Louisa Alcott_, by Jean Wagoner (Childhood)	Gr. 1-5
*_An Alcott Family Christmas_, by Alexandra Wallner	Gr. 1-5
*_Louisa May Alcott: Girlhood Diary_, by Alcott, edited by Cary Ryan See excerpts from Alcott's diary in this pretty book.	Gr. 2-12
The Story of Louisa May Alcott, by Joan Howard (Signature)	Gr. 3-8
*_Lives of the Writers_, by Kathleen Krull, pp. 52-55 This book features humorous, brief biographical chapters.	Gr. 3-8
*_The Little Women Book_, by Lucille Penner You'll love this collection of crafts, recipes, etc., from the book. You also might like _The Louisa May Alcott Cookbook_, by Gretchen Anderson.	Gr. 3-12
Louisa May Alcott, by Helen Papashvily (North Star)	Gr. 4-10
Invincible Louisa, by Cornelia Meigs This beloved biography won the Newbery Award in 1934.	Gr. 4-12
Louisa May Alcott: Her Life, by Catherine Owens Peare	Gr. 4-12

❧ Emily Dickinson–reclusive poet

*_Emily_, by Michael Bedard In this beautiful picture book, a young girl meets Miss Dickinson.	Gr. 1-4
*_Emily Dickinson_, by Carol Greene (Rookie)	Gr. 1-5
*_Emily Dickinson's Letters to the World_, by Jeanette Winter	Gr. 2-5

Emily Dickinson, edited by Frances Bolin (Poetry for Young People)   Gr. 2-7
    There's a brief biographical intro, then illustrated selections of her poetry.

Fiction/Historical Fiction:

The Mouse of Amherst, by Elizabeth Spires   Gr. 3-6
    A mouse living in Ms. Dickinson's room 'reads' and 'writes back' to her poems.

✌ Mary Mapes Dodge (*Hans Brinker, or the Silver Skates*)

Mary Mapes Dodge: Jolly Girl, by Miriam Mason (Childhood)   Gr. 1-6

✌ Thomas Nelson Page (an especially Southern writer–*Two Little Confederates*, etc.)

✌ Mark Twain–such an important American writer! (*Tom Sawyer, Huckleberry Finn*, etc.)

Young Mark Twain, by Louis Sabin (Troll Easy Biographies)   Gr. 1-4

Samuel Clemens, by Charles Daughtery (Crowell Biography)   Gr. 1-4

Mark Twain, by Carol Greene (Rookie)   Gr. 1-5

Mark Twain, by Miriam Mason (Childhood)   Gr. 1-6

Mark Twain and the Queens of the Mississippi, by Cheryl Harness   Gr. 1-6

Mark Twain? What Kind of Name is That? by Robert Quackenbush   Gr. 2-7

Mark T-W-A-I-N! by David Collins (Creative Minds)   Gr. 3-7

Mark Twain: His Life, by Catherine Owens Peare   Gr. 3-7

Young Mark Twain and the Mississippi, by Harnett Kane (Landmark)   Gr. 3-8

Story of Mark Twain, by Joan Howard (Signature)   Gr. 3-8

A Brilliant Streak, by Kathryn Lasky   Gr. 4-8

River-Boy: The Story of Mark Twain, by Isabel Proudfit (Messner)   Gr. 5-12

Mark Twain and the River, by Sterling North (North Star)   Gr. 5-12

America's Own Mark Twain, by Jeanette Eaton   Gr. 5-12

Films:

*The Adventures of Mark Twain, starring Frederic March   Parental decision

*Mark Twain, a documentary film by Ken Burns   Parental decision

❧ **Cautionary note for parents regarding the Transcendentalists**

There are a handful of American writers–Ralph Waldo Emerson, Henry David Thoreau, Bronson Alcott (father to Louisa May Alcott), and Walt Whitman, for example–who are called *Transcendentalists*. They urged Americans to embrace the ideas of 'human progress' we've been talking about; they said truth could be found in nature and in the human heart, rather than coming only from God. There are several lovely children's books on these writers (since they are highly esteemed by current humanists and because their writings are very beautiful). But because we can't adequately explain the real nature and impact of their beliefs to young children, I'll only introduce them in the guide covering this era for older children–*TruthQuest History: Age of Revolution IV*.

> **FYI** Some European authors writing at the same time were: Jules Verne (*Around the World in Eighty Days, 20,000 Leagues Under the Sea*), James Barrie (*Peter Pan*), R.D. Blackmore (*Lorna Doone*), Frances Hodgson Burnett (*Little Lord Fauntleroy, Secret Garden, Little Princess*), Lewis Carroll (*Alice in Wonderland*), Charles Kingsley (*Water-babies*), George MacDonald (so many!), Beatrix Potter (*Peter Rabbit*), etc. It was a famous era in children's literature!

19❧ More Heroes!

Now, don't you dare think for one minute that *all* churches were mixing in the lie about 'human progress.' No! America still had many people and churches who loved the Lord, who knew He was the truth, and who wanted to obey Him. Yeah! Remember when Elijah, the Old Testament prophet, was discouraged? He thought he was the only one in Israel who still loved the Lord! But the Lord told him there were many who still served Him!

And this is *so* important because the Lord wants His followers to help others in this world understand Who He is–the Lord and Savior of our souls, if we will repent and ask Him–and to see that the Lord's way is the best way! In fact, during these years we've been studying there were some folks who were used by God to do wonderful things! Let's meet them!

But don't forget that you need to ask the Lord what He wants to do in *your* life! He may want you to bring good truth not only to your children, but also to government, a courtroom, a school, a hospital, a business, a neighborhood, a church, a film studio, a music studio, an art studio, or to a foreign country! How exciting! That's why you're learning right now...so you can keep discovering that God is much more loving, and more intelligent, and more powerful than you know today...and so that you can serve Him well now *and* when you're grown up! Use this time wisely! Get ready! God has great things in store for you, whether it be a fancy role or the almost invisible role of praying and raising strong families...though God is surely pleased with those good works! There are many needs in this world, and the Lord would like His people to be the first to respond, not the last, since we best understand that the most important needs are spiritual at their root! (You may want to cover only American missionaries at this time, though.)

*In the *Young Reader's Christian Library* series   Gr. 1-4
       D.L. Moody; David Livingstone; "In His Steps;" Samuel Morris

Hero Tales–Vol. I-IV, by Dave & Neta Jackson   Gr. 3-7
       There are units on: Amy Carmichael, Dwight L. Moody, Samuel Morris, Amanda Smith, Cameron Townsend, Eliza George, William Seymour, Charles Tindley, and Lottie Moon.

*In the *Christian Heroes, Then and Now* series, by Janet & Geoff Benge   Gr. 4-10
       Amy Carmichael

Fanny Crosby, by Sandy Dengler   Gr. 4-12

**With Daring Faith*, by R. Davis   Gr. 5-10
       A biography of Amy Carmichael.

*In the *Heroes of the Faith* series: Gr. 5-12
       Amy Carmichael, by Sam Wellman; *Fanny Crosby*, by Bernard Ruffin; *Samuel Morris*, by Terry Whalin; **Charles Sheldon*, by Ellen Caughey; **D.L. Moody*, by Bonnie Harvey; **Billy Sunday*, by Rachael Phillips

**Billy Sunday*, by Robert Allen (Sower series)   Gr. 5-12

Fiction/Historical Fiction:

*In the *Trailblazer* series, by Dave & Neta Jackson   Gr. 3-9
       Danger on the Flying Trapeze* (Moody) **and **Drawn by a China Moon* (Lottie Moon)

There was also a temperance (anti-drunkenness) movement. I don't know its spiritual base. An example can be seen in: *Frances Willard*, by M. Mason (Childhood) Gr. 1-5

Audio:

*Your Story Hour, Volume 7 (Moody)

A sad event in American history occurred when the great athlete, Jim Thorpe, was stripped of his gold medals and records after a wonderful performance at the 1912 Olympics. It seems that some were opposed to his Indian ancestry.

*Jim Thorpe, by Guernsey Van Riper, Jr. (Childhood)	Gr. 1-6
Jim Thorpe: Young Athlete, by Laurence Santrey (Troll)	Gr. 2-5
Jim Thorpe: All-Around Athlete, by George Sullivan (Americans All)	Gr. 2-7

Oh, my! We must mention one other disaster that was not only terribly sad, but was rather disturbing to everyone's confidence in their ability to run the world perfectly. Engineers had promised an "unsinkable" ship, but it didn't even survive its first voyage in 1912. *Titanic!* You'll find many *Titanic* books in your library, so I'll just mention a few here.

*Titanic: Lost...and Found, by Judy Donnelly (Step...3)	Gr. K-4
*Polar the Titanic Bear, by D. Spedden	Gr. 1-4
True story of boy & teddy bear on Titanic.	
*Heroine of the Titanic, by Joan Blos	Gr. 2-8
Story of "Unsinkable Molly Brown."	
*Hero Tales–Vol. III, pp. 44-55	Gr. 3-7
Story of John Harper, a Christian aboard.	
*Exploring the Titanic, by Robert Ballard (Time Quest)	Gr. 3-12
Story of Ballard's later discovery of the sunken ship	
*On Board the Titanic, by S. Tanaka	Gr. 4-9
*Inside the Titanic, by K. Marschall	Gr. 4-10
*Discover the Titanic, by Eric Kentley	Gr. 4-12

Fiction/Historical Fiction:

*Voyage on the Great Titanic, by Ellen White (Dear America)	Gr. 3-9
Fictional diary, for those who like this series.	

Films/Videos:

*A Night to Remember	Parental decision
This is an older film that is truly excellent.	
*Titanic's Last Hero	Parental decision
Christian film about hero on board.	

20 🍃 *Peace? No! World War One!*

Okay, guys. We're about to tackle a big subject. You'll need to settle down and think hard for a few minutes! You have to remember that there were many folks who believed people had evolved so far that they could handle the world all by themselves. They didn't agree with God that all were sinful and needed laws to keep them behaving well. They thought they could solve all the world's problems! They thought there would never be another war since people were so nice and so smart now! They thought there would always be peace...without obeying Christ, the Prince of Peace!

Well, no matter what they believed, the truth was still the same. People were still sometimes greedy, and that means that nations were still sometimes greedy too. In fact, during the 1910s, some of the nations in Europe were especially feisty. They ended up fighting each other in a big war.

Some Americans thought we should get involved in the war too. They thought we ought to help our old friends, the English, against the Germans. Now, this story gets very complicated because the founding fathers of our country had not wanted us to get involved in Europe's wars because those countries were always fighting each other. Any time one European country would get more powerful than the rest, the others would gather together and try to knock the stronger country down to size. They tried to keep their power equal. Big people call that a 'balance of power.' Too, countries in Europe always teamed up: if one country got in a fight, the other team-countries would help. (Of course, the teams were always changing.)[8]

Anyway, when an important Austrian man was killed one day in August, 1914 by a Serbian man, and Austria decided to make war on Serbia, all the friends of Austria and Serbia were instantly at war too because of their 'team' promises. Then, enemies of the countries at war were worried because these enemy armies were on the move; they didn't know what would happen to them.

Added to that, the English had been getting extra, extra powerful. They had been the first to have the Industrial Revolution we talked about in the last guide; this means they were the first to have powerful machines. These machines helped them get wealthy because they could do so much more work and produce so many more things in a faster time. They also figured out how to make stronger weapons. This allowed England, under Queen Victoria, to control many parts of the world. The English Empire was absolutely huge; it included much of Africa, Asia, Australia, and more! This worried less-powerful countries in Europe, like Germany, who wanted to be powerful and control other lands too, and who didn't want to worry that a strong England might take over all Europe!

---

[8] Richard Maybury, *World War I* (Placerville, CA: Bluestocking Press, 2002) Ch. 36.

Phew! What a mess! And there were more reasons that I won't even bother to tell you about since you're young yet, but you can surely see why a big war started! It would be called the Great War! (Later, in the 1940s, when another huge war started, folks started calling this 'Great War' by another name–*World War I*–so they could call the second 'great war' *World War II*.)

Well, many Americans didn't want to get involved in a war like that. I remembered learning that in school, but I didn't realize until just recently that there were some really good reasons for being careful about getting into World War I. I always just assumed that *all* the folks who didn't want to get in were sissies or something worse! I guess that shows that we always need to be learning no matter how old we are! Yes, there were many folks who *did* want to stay out of the war because they were still dreaming we had evolved so far that we could have peace easily. But there were also some good reasons for caution.

Anyway, the war had been going on for a while and still we Americans weren't in it. Many Englishmen, Frenchmen, Germans, and Russians had already been hurt in the fighting; the war was 'tied,' it was at a stalemate. Neither side could budge the other, so the men were stuck in the same muddy trenches. The conditions were awful; many got very sick. And many more citizens would be lost to influenza because so many houses and farms had been wiped out in the fighting and people were cold and hungry. Some of the fighting countries started talking about ending the war.

Still, America was deciding whether or not to send soldiers to the war. One decision *had* been made: we were sending supplies to the English, even on ships carrying passengers, such as the *Lusitania*. Well, the Germans didn't want their English enemies to get those supplies, so they tried to sink those ships after warning the American people not to get on ships carrying supplies. Even so, this made a lot of Americans angry because passengers were being lost at sea (and most Americans didn't know everything that was happening behind the scenes, as is often the case during war).[9]

But there is just one other thing we should also mention about America in this war: our president at the time, Woodrow Wilson, really believed that people had progressed so far that we could all have peace. Wilson wanted to make a 'League of Nations' where everyone would work out their problems in a human-only way. He seems to have thought that if America entered the war and helped win it, then he might get to set up his League of Nations.[10] Well, in the end, with all the factors swirled together, that's exactly what he decided to do. Brave young men, who were courageously going when the call was given, went into World War I.

---

[9] Clarence Carson, *A Basic History of the United States—Volume 4* (Wadley, AL: American Textbook Committee, 1985) 188.

[10] Carson 4:190. "His reformist zeal was moving out on the world stage, and victory for the allies in the war might offer the prospect of remaking Europe. The surest way to be a participant in the peace conferences was to become involved in the war."

As you know, America's arrival helped the Allies (England and France, mostly) quickly crush Germany and Austria. It was such a huge defeat that the Germans were forced to accept very hard terms of surrender. But the top French marshal was quite worried about the humiliating surrender put on the Germans; he knew they would resent it and would try to get free of Allied control as soon as they were strong enough to do so. Here's what he said:

> *This is not peace; it is an armistice* [a truce] *for twenty years.*[11]

Ooh, he was so right. Exactly twenty years later, a resentful Germany would set out to conquer those old Allies and show its power in Europe, which would help start World War II! But we'll focus now on World War I. Remember that we thank the soldiers who fought heroically because they wanted to protect America and others.

(Parents: You'll need to decide the age-appropriateness of these topics and resources for your children. Remember, not all books, even those listed here, will be honest about the 'progressive' element in Wilson's thinking. It's not easy to explain all to young children; you'll have to look carefully for the right resources.)

Parents, if you're following along:
Basic History of the United States–Vol. 4, by Clarence Carson, Ch. 8

20a❧ General resources

This Country of Ours, by H.E. Marshall, Ch. 98-99	Gr. 3-8
Chapter 98 is actually about Wilson's role in the Mexican conflict.	
World War I Tommy, by Martin Windrow (Soldier Through the Ages)	Gr. 3-12
America's First World War, by Henry Castor (Landmark)	Gr. 4-9
The First World War, edited by John Clare (Living History)	Gr. 4-9
Flying Aces of World War I, by Gene Gurney (Landmark)	Gr. 4-12
The Story of World War I, by Robert Leckie (Landmark Giant)	Gr. 4-12
World War I, by Tom McGowen	Gr. 4-11

20b❧ Specific battles, events, and squadrons

The Story of the Lafayette Escadrille, by R. Conrad Stein (Cornerstones)	Gr. 2-6
Spies with Wings, by Arch Whitehouse	Gr. 4-12
A tale based on real stories of the Lafayette Escadrille.	

---

[11]Marshal Foch, quoted in Carson 4:200.

The Lost Battalion, by Irving Werstein   Gr. 5-12
    Troops' whereabouts unknown for several days during the Battle of the Argonne.

20c☙ Individuals, dogs, and *pigeons* of note!

Eddie Rickenbacker, by Cathrine Cleven (Childhood)   Gr. 1-6

Alvin C. York, by Ethel Weddle (Childhood)   Gr. 1-6

Stubby: Brave Soldier Dog, by Richard & Sally Glendinning   Gr. 1-6

Sergeant York: Reluctant Hero, by Peter Andrews   Gr. 3-6

Richthofen, the Red Baron, by Nicholas Fisk   Gr. 3-8

The Story of Edith Cavell, by Iris Vinton (Signature)   Gr. 3-8

Medal of Honor Heroes, by Col. Red Reeder (Landmark)   Gr. 3-9
    Includes some World War I heroes.

Edith Cavell, by Adele de Leeuw (Spies of the World)   Gr. 3-10

Edith Cavell: Heroic Nurse, by Juliette Elkon (Messner)   Gr. 4-12

Heroic Pigeons, by Arch Whitehouse   Gr. 5-12

John J. Pershing, by Arch Whitehouse   Gr. 5-12

> The 1928 Newbery Medal winner is about a World War I pigeon trained in India.
>
> *Gay-Neck*, by Dhan Mukerji Gr. 5+

Films:

There is a *wonderful* old film, *Sergeant York*, in which Gary Cooper's role reveals York's heart.

20d☙ Fiction/Historical Fiction

Casey Over There, by Staton Rabin   Gr. 1-3
    Boy pines for his older brother fighting in World War I; poignant picture book.

The Language of Doves, by Rosemary Wells   Gr. 1-4
    Girl learns about homing pigeons/doves from grandfather who worked with them during World War I. (Note: this poignant story ends with a comment that could be construed to misrepresent the biblical view of death. Parents, please pre-read!)

We Were There with the Lafayette Escadrille, by Clayton Knight (We Were There) Gr. 3-8

*Hero Over Here, by Kathleen Kudlinski (Once Upon America)　　Gr. 3-8
　　　　Boy cares for influenza-sickened family during World War I.

**When Christmas Comes Again*, by Beth Levine (Dear America)　　Gr. 3-8

*The Singing Tree, by Kate Seredy　　　　　　　　　　　　　Gr. 4-12
　　　　Hungarian children live through World War I. Good author, but greatly heroicizes
　　　　Woodrow Wilson.

*Over the Waves, by Marianne Olson　　　　　　　　　　　　Gr. 4-12
　　　　Swedish-American mother and son are trapped in Sweden when war breaks out.

Jacqueline of the Carrier Pigeons, by Augusta Seaman　　　　　　Gr. 4-12
　　　　I think this story of a French girl who helps with her pigeons is actually true.

No Hero for the Kaiser, by Rudolf Frank　　　　　　　　　　　Gr. 5-12
　　　　A Polish boy traveling with the German army lives through World War I.

Over There! Stories of World War I, edited by Phyllis Fenner　　　Gr. 5-12
　　　　Fenner is renowned for her good story collections.

> Two lovely stories are set during 1918, but are
> not related to the war:
>
> *Old Bones the Wonder Horse*, by M. Pace Gr. 3-10
> *Rascal, by Sterling North　　　　Gr. 4-12

21🕮 After the War...and How 'Art' America?

Phew! What can I say after all that about World War I?! You'd like to think the war made people more honest about their need for God and His truths. But that's not what happened. Folks were more determined than ever to have their own way; they were still feeling like I felt the day I stomped out the door and ran away from home. They *still* thought they could take care of themselves—and the whole world—and they didn't want anyone else telling them what to do! All they needed, they thought, was *more* time and *more* change in order to 'fix' the whole world.

Well, change did come—fast and furious—around the world and in America. The belief in *socialism* we've been talking about (the idea that people have evolved or progressed to a peaceful state where it's okay to have the government own all land, tools, resources, etc.) had seeped into many governments in Europe. And socialists were working hard here in America too, but they usually didn't call themselves 'socialists' because most Americans were put off by that word. Instead, they just said they were working toward a stronger *democracy* in America—which means that whatever 51% (or, the bigger half) of the people want they can have. That sounded good...to folks who didn't know better. But the founding fathers *did* know better. They made America to be a republic, not a democracy. They made a system of representation (a *republic*) that tried to sift out whims and fads and silliness and greediness...in the common people, and in those who had the power of government. Even then, socialism only *said* it wanted people to have more power; but it meant something different than the founding fathers did when they said that. Socialists wanted the people to have 'power' to be taken care of by the government, which actually gives the government power over the people.

Anyway, this was the huge 'idea struggle' happening just after World War I. Think about it! During the war, the government had controlled important goods, such as steel, food, etc., and it had transported them to the troops. Many government workers felt that it would 'safer' for America if they went right on controlling these goods and their transportation.[12] It was hard for these government folks to let go of the control they had enjoyed during the war. But now the war was over. You can see that there was some tension there.

And then, there were two different presidents after World War I (during the 1920s): Warren Harding and Calvin Coolidge. They tried to fight this slide toward socialism,[13] and that made for more tension. Soon, there were riots and strikes and all sorts of things you don't have to think about until you're older. I just want you to know there was a real struggle going on; two completely different ways of looking at life were in battle! It shows you one thing: peace comes only from obeying God's ways! Actually, it shows you something else! It shows how much our life is affected by what we believe!

You will see some of this belief-struggle in the modern art that was coming out at this time, because art always shows what people were thinking, feeling, and believing when they made their art. Things had gone so far toward *God*less evolution in Europe that artists like Picasso, Matisse, and Klee were making *really* different pictures that didn't show whole, lifelike people.[14] Instead, people were shown in funny, boxy shapes, or with just certain pieces of them being painted here and there. We can't discuss all this now; there's a lot more to it than I can explain here, both good and bad, so we'll get into it when you're older.

---

[12] Carson 4:192-198.

[13] Harding, quoted by Carson 4:235. "The world needs to be reminded that all human ills are not curable by legislation, and that quantity of statutory enactment and excess of government offer no substitute for quality of citizenship."

[14] David Duncan, quoted by Francis A. Schaeffer, *How Should We Then Live?* (Old Tappan, NJ: Fleming H. Revell, 1976) 187.

But you *can* meet some of the American painters who were working at this time. You'll see that some artists had a peace that the world and life and people were precious. You'll also see art that shows ideas of evolution: people look lifeless, or their bodies are shown to be boxy, machine-like pieces, because the painters

Parents: You may want to explore this more deeply. *How Should We Then Live?* by Francis Schaeffer, Ch. 10 (or view Video Episode # 8).

thought mankind made himself out of the goop of the earth...instead of being made a spiritual being by God.[15] Then there were the ultra-ultra-realistic painters; I wonder if *some* were trying to give importance, in this way, to things in this world, because without a loving Creator things *don't* have any real meaning. Too, evolution said that everything happened by chance.[16] One American painter, named Jackson Pollock, tried to paint 'by chance!' He just swung buckets of paint over paper to see what would happen. In the same way, there were some composers who started writing music by flipping a coin to decide the next note.

So keep your eyes and ears open. Art at this time was quite a mixed bag! Hey! I don't always understand all of this either; it can be confusing. And I can't fully see into the heart of a painter or composer, but I know Who *does* know it all–the Lord! He knows which artists were rebelling against Him and which were seeking truth through their art. And He says we can ask Him for wisdom! Yeah!

21a❧ General Resources

☞ *PARENTS! Remember to read the <u>cautionary notes</u> about studying art which were included in our last listing of artists (Section 18). Many of these painters produced works that are inappropriate, in my opinion!*

Discovering Great Artists, by MaryAnn Kohl   Various
    Provides hands-on projects related to the styles of many artists.

Art of American in the Early Twentieth Century, by Shirley Glubok   Gr. 5-12

---

[15] Schaeffer 164. During a session with Francis Schaeffer, a Harvard professor claimed that "four hundred years ago there was a collection of molecules named Shakespeare...." Mankind had, unwittingly, given up his claim to specialness, and had instead made himself only a chemical and mechanical being. "Man beginning with his proud, proud humanism, tried to make himself autonomous, but rather than becoming great, he found himself ending up as only a collection of molecules–and nothing more," Mr Schaeffer says.

[16] Schaeffer 188. Mr. Schaeffer quotes a writer speaking of Picasso: "Of course, not one of these pictures was actually a portrait but was his prophecy of a ruined world."

21b❧ Abstract painters, including a few Americans: Jackson Pollock (though slightly later), Marcel Duchamp (French-born), John Marin, etc.

Child's History of Art, by Hillyer & Huey, (*Architecture* section, Ch. 30) Gr. 2-8
(Later editions tack an additional painting topic onto the *Architecture* section.)
OR, *Young People's Story of Fine Art: Last Two Hundred Years*, pp. 104-112

Child's History of Art, by Hillyer & Huey, (*Architecture* section, Ch. 32) Gr. 2-8
(Later editions tack an additional sculpture topic onto the *Architecture* section.)
OR, *Young People's Story of Sculpture*, pp. 115-117

Jackson Pollock, by Mike Venezia (Getting to Know....) Gr. 1-6

**Lives of the Artists*, by Kathleen Krull, pp. 64-67 Gr. 3-7

21c❧ Realistic/naturalistic artists (some of it *extreme* realism)

Child's History of Art, by Hillyer & Huey, (*Architecture* section, Ch. 31) Gr. 2-8
(Later editions tack an additional painting topic onto the *Architecture* section.)
Young People's Story of Fine Art: Last Two Hundred Years, pp. 104-123

Child's History of Art, by Hillyer & Huey, (*Sculpture* section, Ch. 28) Gr. 2-8
***OR**, Young People's Story of Sculpture*, pp. 118-123

❧ George Bellows

Child's History of Art, by Hillyer & Huey, (*Painting* section, Ch. 31b) Gr. 2-8
***OR**, Young People's Story of Fine Art: Last Two Hundred Years*, pp. 100-103

❧ Edward Hopper

Edward Hopper, by Mike Venezia (Getting to Know the World's Greatest...) Gr. 1-5

❧ Grant Wood

**Grant Wood*, by Mike Venezia (Getting to Know the World's Greatest...) Gr. 1-5

**Artist in Overalls: The Life of Grant Wood*, by John Duggleby Gr. 5-10

Lives of Poor Boys Who Became Famous, by Sarah Bolton, Ch. 23 Gr. 5-12

• Thomas Hart Benton

• Georgia O'Keeffe (who has done various styles, but if best known for her flowers)

Georgia O'Keeffe, by Mike Venezia (Getting to Know the World's Greatest...) Gr. 1-5

Georgia O'Keeffe, by Linda Lowery (On My Own)   Gr. 1-5

My Name is Georgia, by Jeanette Winter   Gr. 2-6

Lives of the Artists, by Kathleen Krull, pp. 68-71   Gr. 3-7

Georgia O'Keeffe: The 'Wideness and Wonder' of Her World, by B. Gherman   Gr. 4-12

• Andrew Wyeth (caution!)

22• The Roaring '20s

If you're like me, the *Roaring '20s* makes me think of 'flapper' outfits, the Charleston dance, excitement over newfangled radios and cars, baseball and Babe Ruth, crazy fads, the daring flight of Charles Lindbergh, the feats of Houdini, and silent movies. By the end of the 1920s, television had been invented and the first primitive TV shows were being made; Mickey Mouse had even made his debut. But one good historian, Mr. Carson, reminds us that many Americans still lived a very simple life: they used horses and buggies, had no electricity, and loved the Constitution, hard work, and their neighbors. I'm glad for that solidness, because many of the big churches were still teaching people a mix of truth and wrong 'human progress' ideas. Well, let's look at these *Roaring 20s*!

22a• General Resources

The Roaring Twenties, by R. Conrad Stein (Cornerstones)   Gr. 3-7

Ticket to the Twenties, by Mary Blocksma   Gr. 3-9
       Fun! A look at real life for kids in the 20s.

Warren Harding, by Linda Wade (Encyclopedia of Presidents)   Gr. 5-12

Calvin Coolidge, by Zachary Kent (Encyclopedia of Presidents)   Gr. 5-12

Lives of Poor Boys Who Became Famous, by Sarah Bolton, Ch. 21   Gr. 5-12
This chapter covers Calvin Coolidge.

Fiction/Historical Fiction:

Ike & Mama and the Once-in-a-Lifetime Movie, by Carol Snyder   Gr. 2-6
New York City boy gets to participate in the making of an early D.W. Griffith movie.
There are five titles in this series, if you decide to sample more.

22b꙳ Baseball and Babe Ruth

> Harry Houdini and Walt Disney both worked in the 1920s. Many families may not want to pursue these topics, but if you do, there are books in all the main series: Childhood, Americans All, etc.

Babe Ruth: Home Run Hero   Gr. 1-5
by Keith Brandt (Troll Easy Bio)

Babe Ruth (Childhood)   Gr. 1-6
by Guernsey Van Riper, Jr.

Baseball's Best: Five True Stories, by A. Gutelle, Ch. 1 (Step Into Reading 4)   Gr. 2-5

The Girl Who Struck Out Babe Ruth, by Jean Patrick (On My Own)   Gr. 2-5

Home Run: The Story of Babe Ruth, by Robert Burleigh   Gr. 2-6

The Babe Ruth Ballet School, by Tim Shortt   Gr. 3-8
Almost unbelievable story of 9-year-old girl who was a friend of Babe Ruth's and who actually pitched to some of babeball's greats...and struck them out!

The Story of Babe Ruth, by Lisa Eisenberg   Gr. 3-10

Fiction/Historical Fiction:

When Willard Met Babe Ruth, by Donald Hall   Gr. 2-6
I hope you find this poignant revealing of the life of a typical early-1900s American boy.

22c꙳ Charles Lindbergh, and his wife, Anne

Flight, by Robert Burleigh   Gr. 1-3

Charles Lindbergh: Hero Pilot, by David Collins (Garrard Discovery)   Gr. 1-5

Good-bye, Charles Lindbergh, by Louise Borden   Gr. 1-5
Fact-based, a young Mississippi boy gets to meet Lindbergh!

Ride on the Wind, by Alice Dalgliesh   Gr. 2-6

Story of the Spirit of St. Louis, by R. Conrad Stein (Cornerstones)   Gr. 2-6

*Anne Morrow Lindbergh: Pilot and Poet, by Roxanne Chadwick (Carolrhoda)   Gr. 3-6

Film and Audio:

Your Story Hour, Volume 6 (audio series)

*The Spirit of St. Louis, starring Jimmy Stewart   All ages
        This is one of my absolute favorite films, especially how he cries to God at the end.

22d⁊ Bessie Coleman–first black female pilot!

*Fly High! The Story of Bessie Coleman, by Louise Borden   Gr. 1-5

*Up in the Air: The Story of Bessie Coleman, by Philip Hart (Carolrhoda)   Gr. 3-6

22e⁊ Authors: There are a few who wrote certain pieces which might interest young children: Robert Frost, Carl Sandburg, Vachel Lindsay, Booth Tarkington, and Edna St. Vincent Millay.

Robert Frost, by Ellen Wilson (Childhood)   Gr. 1-6

Carl Sandburg, by Grace Melin (Childhood)   Gr. 1-6

*Good Morning, Mr. President: A Story about Carl Sandburg (Carolrhoda)   Gr. 2-6
        by Barbara Mitchell

Robert Frost: America's Poet, by Doris Faber   Gr. 2-7

Carl Sandburg: Voice of the People, by Ruth Franchere   Gr. 3-8

Robert Frost (Poetry for Young People)   Gr. 3-12
        An illustrated collection of Frost's poetry.

Carl Sandburg (Poetry for Young People)   Gr. 3-12
        An illustrated collection of Sandburg's poetry. Kids like his "Arithmetic" poem.

Edna St. Vincent Millay (Poetry for Young People)   Gr. 3-12
        An illustrated collection of Millay's poetry.

*Prairie-Town Boy, by Carl Sandburg (Odyssey Classic)   Gr. 5-12
        Sandburg tells of his youth in a prairie town.

22f• Scientists–There are a few that some students may be ready to meet: Albert Einstein (physics); Geiger and his Geiger Counter; J.J. Thomson (physics); Niels Bohr (physics); Robert Goddard (rocketry); Edwin Hubble (astronomy); Baird (TV); Banting (insulin); Alexander Fleming (penicillin); and Clyde Tombaugh (discovered Pluto). Much research was also being done on specific diseases, and more vitamins were being discovered.

Clyde Tombaugh and the Search for Planet X, by M. Wetterer (On My Own)　　Gr. 1-4

Young Albert Einstein, by Laurence Santrey (Troll)　　Gr. 1-4

Robert Goddard: Space Pioneer, by Milton Lomask (Garrard Discovery)　　Gr. 1-5

**Albert Einstein*, by Marie Hammontree (Childhood)　　Gr. 1-6

Robert Goddard, by Clyde Moore (Childhood)　　Gr. 1-6

**Albert Einstein*, by Saviour Pirotta (Scientists Who Made History)　　Gr. 2-6
　　I've not seen this book, so am not real sure of the age recommendation.

Scientists Who Changed the World, by P. Wilkinson & M. Pollard, pp. 69-71　　Gr. 2-6
　　Describes the Baird's work to develop television.

Robert Goddard: Trail Blazer to the Stars, by Charles Daugherty　　Gr. 2-6

**Robert Goddard*, by Lola Schaefer (Famous People in Transportation)　　Gr. 3-6
　　I've not seen this, so am not sure about the age recommendation.

**Who was Albert Einstein?* by Jess Braillier　　Gr. 3-5

**Ordinary Genius: The Story of Albert Einstein*, by S. McPherson (Carolrhoda)　　Gr. 3-6

Rocket Pioneer, by Charles Coombs (American Adventure, older series)　　Gr. 3-7

**Mathematicians are People Too*, Vol. 2, by L. & W. Reimer, pp. 119-125　　Gr. 3-8
　　These pages cover Einstein.

Great Men of Medicine, by Ruth Hume (Landmark)　　Gr. 4-10
　　Ch. 9 is on Frederick Banting; Chapter 10 is on Alexander Fleming.

**Edwin Hubble: Discoverer of Galaxies*, by Claire Datnow　　Gr. 5-9

**Rocket Man: The Story of Robert Goddard*, by Thomas Streissguth　　Gr. 5-10

Bright Design, by Katherine Shippen, Ch. 13　　Gr. 5-12
　　Chapter bios, such as Ch. 13 on J.J. Thomson.

Alexander Fleming: Pioneer with Antibiotics, by Beverley Birch (Giants of Sci.)   Gr. 5-12

Robert Goddard: Space Pioneer, by Anne Dewey   Gr. 5-12

Albert Einstein, by Fiona Macdonald (Giants of Science)   Gr. 5-12

Albert Einstein and Relativity, by Steve Parker (Science Discoveries)   Gr. 5-12

John Logie Baird, by Struan Reid (Groundbreakers)   Gr. 5-12

Alexander Fleming, by Steve Parker (Groundbreakers)   Gr. 5-12

22g🎵 American jazz & national music

Jazz grew from the music of the former slaves. The whole world now enjoys it! Duke Ellington, Louis Armstrong, and "Jelly Roll" Morton were some famous performers, but soon white men, such as George Gershwin and Paul Whiteman, fell in love with jazz and began to add to it. Songwriters such as Irving Berlin, Cole Porter, and George M. Cohan staged popular musicals on Broadway which were often made into movies. Mahalia Jackson was a talented and popular Negro singer.

Charlie Parker Played Be Bop, by Chris Raschka   Gr. 1-3

The Sound that Jazz Makes, by Carole Weatherford   Gr. 1-4

Satchmo's Blues, by Alan Schroeder   Gr. 1-4
  Picture book about young Louis Armstrong working hard to buy a used horn.

Duke Ellington: The Piano Prince and His Orchestra, by Andrea Pinkney   Gr. 1-4

Duke Ellington, by Mike Venezia (Getting to Know...)   Gr. 1-4

George Gershwin, by Mike Venezia (Getting to Know...)   Gr. 1-4

In the *Childhood of Famous Americans* series: Gr. 1-6
  Louis Armstrong, by Dharathula Millender; *Duke Ellington*, by Martha Schaaf; *George Gershwin*, by Bernice Bryant; *George M. Cohan*, by Gertrude Winders; *Mahalia Jackson*, by Montrew Dunham

If I Only Had a Horn: Young Louis Armstrong, by Roxanne Orgill   Gr. 2-6

Say it with Music: A Story about Irving Berlin, by T. Streissguth (Creative Minds) Gr. 2-6

America, I Hear You: A Story about George Gershwin (Creative Minds)   Gr. 2-8
  by Barbara Mitchell

Louis Armstrong: Ambassador Satchmo, by Jean Cornell (Garr. Am. All)   Gr. 2-8

Duke Ellington: King of Jazz, by Elizabeth Montgomery (Garr. Am. All)   Gr. 2-8

Louis Armstrong: Jazz Musician, by P. McKissack (Great African Americans)   Gr. 3-6
    I'm not actually sure of the age recommendation for this book; I've not seen it.

Trumpeter's Tale: Louis Armstrong, by Jeanette Eaton   Gr. 5-12

Mahalia Jackson, by Evelyn Witter (Sower series)   Gr. 5-12

☞ If you'd like to understand jazz, you'll love the video tapes done by Wynton Marsalis, called *Marsalis on Music*. There's a book/CD combo version too. Excellent!

Fiction/Historical Fiction:

The Jazz Fly, by Matthew Gollub   Gr. 1-4
    This book shares the rhythms and energy of jazz in a unique way, from what I hear.

22h❧ Sports

Knute Rockne: Young Athlete, by Guernsey Van Riper, Jr. (Childhood)   Gr. 1-6

Knute Rockne: Notre Dame's Football Great, by George Sullivan (Garr. Am. All)   Gr. 2-8

Fiction/Historical Fiction:

Paperboy, by Mary Kay Kroeger   Gr. 2-4
    A really nice picture book that shows an immigrant boy hard persevering to earn extra money by selling extra newspapers after one of Jack Dempsey's big fights.

Your kids may enjoy reading the heroic, true story of Balto and the other dog sled teams who tried to get serum to Nome, Alaska during a diptheria epidemic.

The Bravest Dog Ever, by Natalie Standiford (Step Into Reading 2)   Gr. K-3
Race Against Death, by Seymour Reit   Gr. 3-12
☞ There is also a Disney film on the topic, *Balto*, if you approve.

---

23 Hard Times–The Great Depression

Well, you've had a taste of the 1920s, and you've seen that many folks were really decent people. But, remember, there was still some bad thinking on the loose. These wrong *Big 2 Beliefs* that we've been seeing, these ones about 'human progress,' were still growing slowly and quietly in the hearts of many Americans. And bad believing makes bad thinking, and bad thinking makes bad doing, and bad doing makes bad problems...not always at first, but eventually. Only God's ways are perfectly right; He made this world and He made us and He knows the truth that holds it all together. He *is* the truth that holds it all together! Anything less than God's right means things are going wrong.

And that's just what happened on a day called Black Tuesday in October of 1929. On that one day, the cheery promises of 'human progress' crumbled...for a time. On that day, a key part of the American money system–the stock market–crashed. It was the beginning of many years of hard times that are called the Great Depression. This time started on Black Tuesday but it lasted through all the 1930s. Many businesses and banks failed, and this meant that many people lost their jobs and their savings. The Great Depression happened for several reasons, most of which you can study when you're older, but just realize now that people were getting a little careless in their optimism about 'human progress.' They started buying things on credit–in a huge way–and the government was encouraging them to borrow (parents: this was done through the Federal Reserve) so the factories could keep humming.[17]

Too, American banks were loaning lots of money to Germany. Do you remember that after the Germans lost World War I the Allies who beat them (including America) required Germany to make huge payments to the various Allied countries? Well, the Germans had no money, so they could only borrow money from American banks to make their payments to the American government. Of course, the Germans also found it impossible to pay back those loans to American banks. This got the banks into a big mess, but they could have guessed there would be problems.

To make matters worse, during the 1930s, there was a terrible, windy drought in the Great Plains states. Things got so dry that the crops died and the barren soil just baked to powder in the sun. Then the fierce wind lifted it up and whipped it around. It sifted into people's homes and made a mess. This sad event was called the *Dust Bowl*. Many farmers lost their lands and homes because they couldn't raise any crops to sell; they couldn't even feed their families. Many headed to California and Oregon to work on farms that were flourishing there.

People *do* need to care for each other during hard times. Mr. Herbert Hoover, who was president during the beginning of the Depression (though the crash had been building since long before Hoover ever became president) wanted to see individuals help each other during

---

[17] Carson 4:262.

the Depression, instead of the government.[18] This was something Hoover knew a lot about, because he had helped feed and care for the starving millions in Europe after World War I! He thought it was so wonderful for everyone's character when people helped people. We'll talk more about that whole issue in the next section.

Well, we don't need to think–at your young age–any more about how it all happened. We can just meet some of the folks who lived through it, and we can see how they managed. There were some shining moments during this hard, hard time.

23a✎ The Great Depression

Rocks in His Head, by Carol Hurst   Gr. 1-4
> This is not about the Depression in general, but about one man's real life during the Depression in particular. It is excellent! Don't miss this one!

> Parents, if you're reading along:
> *Basic History of the United States–Vol. 5*, by Clarence Carson, Ch. 1-4

When Grandpa Wore Knickers, by Fern Brown   Gr. 1-6
> This book is rare. Life for children during the early 1930s.

The Story of the Great Depression, by R. Conrad Stein (Cornerstones)   Gr. 2-8

Fiction/Historical Fiction:

Leah's Pony, by E. Friedrich   Gr. 1-3
> Don't miss this one! A beautiful tale of one girl's sacrifice.

> Margaret Bourke-White became famous for her photographs of the Depression, and later World War II.
> *Margaret Bourke-White* (Childhood)   Gr. 1-6
>   by Montrew Dunham
> *Margaret Bourke-White* (Own My Own) Gr. 2-6
>   by Catherine Welch

The Gardener, by Sarah Stewart   Gr. 1-4
> Optimistic girl cheers her family during the Depression.

The Song of the Trees, by Mildred Taylor   Gr. 2-6
> Story of black girl in the Depression south and ruthless lumbermen.

---

[18] Hoover, quoted in: Clarence Carson, *A Basic History of the United States—Volume 5* (Wadley, AL: American Textbook Committee, 1986) 17: "This is not an issue as to whether people shall go hungry or cold in the United States. It is solely a question of the best method by which hunger and cold shall be prevented.... My own conviction is strongly that if we break down this sense of responsibility of individual generosity to individual and mutual self-help in the country in times of national difficulty, and if we start appropriations of this character [government handouts/taxpayer monies] we have not only impaired something infinitely valuable in the life of the American people but have struck at the roots of self-government. Once this has happened it is not the cost of a few score million but we are faced with the abyss of reliance in future upon Government charity in some form or another.

Black Tuesday, **and**, *The Great Depression*, by Joann Grote (Amer. Adventure)   Gr. 3-8

Christmas After All, by Kathryn Lasky (Dear America)   Gr. 3-8

Ida Early Comes over the Mountain, **and**, *Christmas with Ida Early*, by R. Burch   Gr. 3-9

Overland Escape, by Lee Roddy (and all in "An American Adventure" series) Gr. 3-9
   Christian fiction series set during the Depression
   and the 'Okie' migration to California.

> The beloved film, *It's a Wonderful Life*, seems to be set during the Depression. Enjoy!

Her Majesty, Grace Jones, by Jane Langton   Gr. 3-9
   Loving family during the Depression.

Roll of Thunder, Hear My Cry, **and**, *Let the Circle Be Unbroken*, by Mild. Taylor Gr. 4-12
   Story of loving black family in Depression-ridden Mississippi.

> I've heard *Henner's Lydia*, by Marguerite de Angeli, is set during the 1930s. This warm story of an Amish family is a lovely book for any time! You may also enjoy her *Up the Hill* about a Polish mining family in Pennsylvania.

Queenie Peavy, by Robert Burch   Gr. 5-10
   Tenacious 13-year-old during the Depression.

Where the Red Fern Grows, by Wilson Rawls   Gr. 5-12
   Beloved tale, and rightly so, of Depression-era boy's love for dogs. Film version also.

23b꘡ Dust Bowl

Dust for Dinner, by Ann Turner (Hist. I Can Read)   Gr. K-3

Children of the Dust Bowl, by Jerry Stanley   Gr. 5-12

The Dust Bowl, by John Farris (World Disasters)   Gr. 5-12

Driven from the Land, by Milton Meltzer (Great Journeys)   Unknown

Fiction/Historical Fiction:

What You Know First, by Patricia MacLachlan   Gr. 1-6
   This doesn't say it's set during the Dust Bowl, but it so captures the losses suffered then.
   Really, it's a beauty. Don't miss it!

Journal of C.J. Jackson, a Dust Bowl Migrant, by W. Durbin (My Name is Am.)   Gr. 3-8

Survival in the Storm, by Katelan Janke (Dear America)   Gr. 3-8

Blue Willow, by Doris Gates   Gr. 5-12
   A beloved story of girl and her family migrating to California.

23c🏵 Herbert Hoover (first president born west of the Mississippi River)

Herbert Hoover, by Mildred Comfort (Childhood)   Gr. 1-6

Herbert Hoover, by David Holford (United States Presidents)   Gr. 5-8

Herbert Hoover, by Susan Clinton (Encyclopedia of Presidents)   Gr. 5-12
   It sounds like this book really tries to show what a good person and good president
   Hoover was, even though he's been criticized by liberals since.

The World of Young Herbert Hoover, by Suzanne Hilton   Gr. 5-12

24🏵 Stop and Think...

Well, you'd think after the hard times of the Great Depression that folks would sit up and take notice of God's truths for running countries, banks, businesses, and more, but that's not exactly what happened. You see, some of the most influential people in America–the writers, the artists, the college professors, and many in government–were still convinced that America could soon break into the 'heaven of human progress.' The problem, they thought, was that it was taking too long for Americans to switch *from* their earlier belief that truth is a 'forever, never-changing thing' (even if they weren't personally Christians) *to* the new idea that what was true for people was evolving as people themselves evolved.

Let me try to say this real simply because it's one of the most important ideas in this whole guide: it's the privilege of God to say what is true for this world because He made this world. (Hey, if you make up a new game, you get to make the rules for it too, right?!) But people want to be God (just like Satan did, just like Adam and Eve did). That means they want to say what is true...for themselves and for others. Big problem, but it's the same mistake I made when I stomped out of my house that day. I thought *I* should be able to decide what was good and right for me.

To say this, people had to pretend *they* had made this world, not God. That's a pretty brazen thing to say! Think about it! But people couldn't just, out of the blue, claim to have created the world, so they did it gradually. Very clever! First, they made God sound like some faraway old grandfather who couldn't possibly be an active, strong Creator. Then, they said 'Nature' had the power to *make itself* through evolution. Then, they said people were the most highly evolved creature in nature. Finally, they said people had become *so* high that they could now direct the process of evolution themselves; they could take over from 'Nature.' That meant people were in fact making the world. Wow! Can you believe how they worked out that crazy idea?!

Did you know that they then started teaching this idea in more and more schools?! "Aha," they thought! "We don't have to worry that the older Americans aren't quickly switching their beliefs. We'll teach the new ideas to the kids!" Of course, the early leaders of public schooling, such as Horace Mann and John Dewey,[19] thought they were doing a good thing. They thought they were making America free from fuddy-duddy thinking. They would have known better if they would have checked God's Word! (Parents, you may be interested to know that John Dewey was excited about all that Stalin–the terribly cruel communist ruler–was doing in Russia, before news of his atrocities became widespread–though they should have been anticipated considering his beliefs. Dewey made a visit there because he liked how Stalin was remaking Russia on the basis of human progress, as socialism teaches.[20] Stalin's communism was a type of socialism; Clarence Carson calls it *revolutionary socialism*, while the type we have here in America is *evolutionary socialism*.[21])

So, do you see it?! Do you see this huge-i-mundo change fighting for control of America?! Do you see what a difference it would make if people got to decide what was true about everything instead of accepting and working with the power of what *God* says is true?!

Well, that people-get-to-decide-for-themselves-what-is-true thing, is just what was happening more and more in America. Want two examples? Here goes!

25&♣ Franklin Delano Roosevelt: Was His 'New Deal' the 'Right Deal?'

One of the biggest people-get-to-decide-for-themselves-what-is-true changes happened in government. Remember, people in the early 1900s had already begun looking to the government, rather than to the Lord and their own efforts, as their main source of help because they were being taught that government contains the most human power since it represents so many people. We've already talked about that. Well, when times got tough during the Depression, most folks looked even more to the government to provide for them. (Parents: you'd be interested in the thoughts of a former president, Grover Cleveland, who was astonished

---

[19] Parents! If you'd like some excellent insights on John Dewey, and thus on American education, see: *Seven Men Who Rule the World from the Grave*, by Dave Breese, Ch. 9. In fact, you should read the entire book! Wow! It will really open your eyes to the issues of this era...and today!

[20] Carson 4:243.

[21] Carson 4:63-71.

by this thinking since, he said, governments do not *produce* wealth, they only *consume* it.[22] How could the government make provision for anyone?) Well, folks ignored Cleveland's wisdom, and that meant that someone could get voted in as president who promised that the government would fully take care of people, from cradle to grave, as the saying goes, though it meant the government would have to take control of many more parts of American life. That's just what happened: Franklin Delano Roosevelt, who made such promises, was elected president four times!

Remember, now, that government is not bad; God talks about government in the Bible. It's just that government should be limited; it should not have too much control. It should see itself *only* as a servant of God, *only* doing the things God says should be done, and *only* in the way God says they should be done. It should have the same respect for people as God does; it should give people the same freedom and responsibility as God does.

But that's what was changing in America! Too many people in government didn't see themselves as servants of God; instead they wanted to wield *human power*. Since evolution taught people to reject the idea of *unchanging* truth, these government people thought they had to figure out what was true and best for America *each day*. They did not obey God's commands to do *only* what He said should be done. And too many Americans were either not paying attention or were actually happy that the government was going to be like a big daddy. But that means people were sadly letting go of the good things the Lord had planned for us: the beauty of individuality, the self-respect of personal responsibility, the fire of aspiration, and the strong spine of self-government!

So, back to Mr. Franklin Delano Roosevelt. He said it was the government's job to look after people. Indeed, FDR (that was his nickname) said government should be the *main force* in the country rather than individual Americans, even if it had to borrow tons and tons of money to start big projects. He left the debt for later children to pay (that's you and me!).[23] He also took a lot more power than any other president before him. He called it all the "New Deal." In fact, the Supreme Court had to strike down many of his plans because they were not allowed in the Constitution, but he also got plenty through.

I'm trying to avoid, since you're so young, the details of all FDR said and believed, but I do want you to know that FDR made *major, galactic, enormous* changes to America while he was

---

[22] Carson 5:1.

[23]Parents! If you'd like some excellent insights on the thinking of Franklin Delano Roosevelt, you can read about the man whose ideas he embraced: John Maynard Keynes in: *Seven Men Who Rule the World from the Grave*, by Dave Breese, Ch. 10. In fact, you should read the entire book! Wow! It will really open your eyes to the issues of this era...and today! About Keynes, Breese says in this book: "Keynesian economics preaches the doctrine that the government is the final resource. It can answer every problem; it can create something out of nothing [emphasis mine], namely, prosperity. What can this mean except that the government is God?" Someone admitted to Keynes that his plan seemed to work in the short-term, but what about the financial and social consequences in the long-term? He reportedly answered, "In the long term, we are all dead."

president during most of the 1930s and the first half of the 1940s. Now, FDR's beliefs were those of socialism, but no one called it that because Americans didn't like that word. So, the socialists (who believe that people are basically good so that we don't have to worry about any person having too much power and thus it is okay for the government to run everything) instead said they were just trying to make America into a better democracy. (America is supposed to be a republic according to our Constitution; the founding fathers knew it was the best kind of government.) There's a code word when you're reading: if you see talk of democracy, it's a pretty safe guess that the author wants America to move away from being a republic and instead become more socialistic. Be smart!

So, we're in a rather sticky spot! There are tons of children's books about FDR, but I don't know which ones to recommend because I don't know of one that includes both the story of his life and the truth about his beliefs (according to the basic biblical worldview). Hopefully, you'll find some gems out there. By the way, Franklin's wife, Eleanor, was also very involved in government issues, but she had the same basic beliefs as Franklin. So, I'll leave this decision, as always, up to your mom and dad (admitting, Mom and Dad, that you haven't been able to hear a full exploration of these issues since you're not in the guide for older students covering the same era–*TruthQuest History: Age of Revolution IV*).

Here, then, I'll list some of the books you're likely to find, but I'm not recommending any of them *per se*.

Franklin Delano Roosevelt, by William Wise (See & Read)	Gr. K-3
*Young Eleanor Roosevelt, by Francene Sabin (Troll Easy Biographies)	Gr. 1-4
Eleanor Roosevelt: First Lady of the World, by Charles Graves (Garr. Discovery)	Gr. 1-5
Franklin Roosevelt, by Ann Weil (Childhood)	Gr. 1-6
*Eleanor Roosevelt, by Ann Weil (Childhood)	Gr. 1-6

26❧ The 1930s

Happily, there was more to the 1930s than just the Depression. Movies became popular, while jazz music grew and spawned swing music. Two black women were famous singers: Ella Fitzgerald and Marian Anderson. Families still enjoyed the radio; they also looked forward to *The Saturday Evening Post* magazine with Norman Rockwell's paintings on the cover. The *Art Deco* style showed that technology was making artists feel more modern and sophisticated. Lou Gehrig amazed the world with his grateful attitude when his baseball career was ended by a dreadful disease. Men started building the Golden Gate bridge, and Howard Hughes flew around the entire world in just four days!

Since there is so much you could learn about, I'll just list key events and persons. You'll have to decide who and what to study!

26a꙳ Scientists

Enrico Fermi (nuclear physicist), Igor Sikorsky (helicopter inventor), and Robert Watson-Watt (radar inventor) made discoveries that would impact the coming war.

☞ Enrico Fermi is a very important scientist, but he will be covered later, in connection with the great development of atomic power and the Manhattan Project.

> *Prairie Boy's Summer* and *Prairie Boy's Winter*, by William Kurelek, show a Canadian prairie family in the 1930s. (Gr. 3-8)
>
> *The Education of Little Tree*, by Forrest Carter, is the story of a real Indian boy growing up in the 1930s. (Gr. 5-12)
>
> *T-Model Tommy*, by Stephen Meader, is a boy who wants work, not welfare. (Gr. 5-12)

☞ Mr. Sikorsky will be mentioned in any books about the history of flight. I know of no biography just on his life.

26b꙳ Authors

We'll mention only those authors who could be known by young children: Pearl S. Buck, Walter Edmonds, Marjorie Kinnan Rawlings, and C.S. Forester.

Pearl S. Buck, by Elisabeth Myers (Childhood)   Gr. 1-5

Between Two Worlds: A Story about Pearl Buck, by B. Mitchell (Creative Minds) Gr. 2-6

26c꙳ Grandma Moses and Norman Rockwell were artists of a very homey style!

Norman Rockwell, by Mike Venezia (Getting to Know the World's...)   Gr. 1-6

The Norman Rockwell Storybook, by Jan Wahl   Gr. 1-6
        An unusual book. Wahl made up stories to match Rockwell's paintings.

Grandma Moses: Favorite Painter, by Charles Graves (Garrard Am. All)   Gr. 2-7

Norman Rockwell: Storyteller with a Brush, by Beverly Gherman   Gr. 4-12

Grandma Moses, by Zibby O'Neal   Gr. 4-12

Barefoot in the Grass, by William H. Armstrong   Gr. 4-12

26d☙ Hoover Dam and the Empire State Building (the largest skyscraper in its day) were great feats of engineering

The Story of the Empire State Building, by Patrick Clinton (Cornerstone)	Gr. 3-10
The Hoover Dam, by Elizabeth Mann (Wonders of the World)	Gr. 3-10

26e☙ Amelia Earhart was lost in her attempt to fly around the world

Note: Please do realize that Ms. Earhart did not always exemplify biblical qualities; books about her may be quite feminist in their outlook.

*A Picture Book of Amelia Earhart, by David Adler	Gr. K-2
*Young Amelia Earhart, by Susan Alcott (Troll First-Start)	Gr. K-3
*Amelia Earhart: Adventure in the Sky, by Francene Sabin (Troll)	Gr. 1-4
*Amelia and Eleanor Go for a Ride, by Pam Muñoz Ryan	Gr. 1-5

Based on a true story, Amelia takes Mrs. Roosevelt up for an impromptu ride. This book does emphasize their very "independent" spirits.

Amelia Earhart: Pioneer in the Sky, by John Parlin (Garrard Discovery)	Gr. 1-5
Clear the Pasture, I'm Coming in for a Landing! by Robert Quackenbush	Gr. 1-5
*Amelia Earhart, by Jane Howe (Childhood)	Gr. 1-6
*Vanished! by Monica Killing (Step into Reading 4)	Gr. 2-4
Amelia's Flying Machine, by Barbara Hazen	Gr. 2-7

A true and crazy adventure from Earhart's childhood.

Amelia Earhart: First Lady of the Air, by Jerry Seibert (Piper)	Gr. 2-7
The Story of Amelia Earhart, by Adele de Leeuw (Signature)	Gr. 3-8
Women of Courage, by Dorothy Nathan (Landmark)	Gr. 5-12

Warning: this Landmark seems to promote feminism.

*Lost Star, by Patricia Lauber	Gr. 5-12

26f♣ Hindenburg Disaster–the German dirigible exploded into flame just before landing (Caution, parents! This topic can be very intense and frightening.)

Horror Overhead, by Richard Boning (Incredible Series)	Gr. 3-6
The Hindenburg Disaster, by R. Conrad Stein (Cornerstones)	Gr. 3-7
Disaster of the Hindenburg, by Shelly Tanaka (TimeQuest)	Gr. 4-12

        This book alternates between reliving the event and later discovery.

Fictional/Historical Fiction:

Fire in the Sky, by Candice Ransom (Carolrhoda)	Gr. 3-7

26g♣Jesse Owens, Joe Louis, and Lou Gehrig were great sports heroes: Mr. Owens embarrassed Hitler's horrible belief that blacks weren't capable; Joe Louis was one of the first black boxers to achieve great fame, especially when he beat a Nazi boxer; and, Lou Gehrig showed great courage when his fabulous baseball career was cut short by a sad disease.

When Jo Louis Won the Title, by Belinda Rochelle	Gr. K-3

        Girl, named Jo, learns how she was named after Joe Louis. Try not to miss this wonderful story of a warm black family and their pride in a black hero! Nicely done!

Jesse Owens: Olympic Hero, by Francene Sabin (Troll Easy Biographies)	Gr. 1-4
Lou Gehrig: Pride of the Yankees, by Keith Brandt (Troll Easy Biographies)	Gr. 1-4
A Picture Book of Jesse Owens, by David Adler	Gr. 1-4
Jesse Owens, by Jane Sutcliffe (On My Own)	Gr. 1-4
Jesse Owens: Olympic Star, by Patricia & Frederick McKissack (Great Af.-Am.)	Gr. 1-5
Jesse Owens, by Mervyn Kaufman (Crowell Biography)	Gr. 1-5
Lou Gehrig: The Luckiest Man, by David Adler	Gr. 1-5
Lou Gehrig, by Guernsey Van Riper, Jr. (Childhood)	Gr. 1-6
Jesse: The Man Who Outran Hitler, also titled, *The Jesse Owens Story*	Gr. 5-12

        by Jesse Owens, with Paul Neimark

☞ *The Jesse Owens Story* is a film about Owens's story, and shows how he floored Hitler.

26h Johnstown Flood
 (Parents: This is another sad event you may not want young children to face.)

 Story of the Great Republic, by H.A. Guerber, Ch. LXIX (cited elsewhere also) Gr. 3-7

 The Story of the Johnstown Flood, by R. Conrad Stein (Cornerstones) Gr. 2-7

 Disaster at Johnstown, by Hildegarde Dolson (Landmark) Gr. 4-12

26i 'Big Band' Music

 Once Upon a Time in Chicago: The Story of Benny Goodman, by Jonah Winter Gr. 1-5

27 War Clouds!

Yes, this guide is about American history, but we Americans have always been closely linked with the people in Europe. Why? To answer that you must remember *again* that history is not first about what people do, it's about what they believe to be true, especially the *Big 2 Beliefs—who is God, and who, then, is mankind*. Well, since most American people originally came from Europe, so did their beliefs about God and people. And these 'human progress' beliefs, these 'evolution' beliefs, we've been talking about (they're linked), had been popular in Europe even before they became popular here in the United States.

What does that mean? That means you'll get to see right away if it's true what I've been telling you...that bad beliefs make for bad trouble. You see, Europe had been living with these wrong beliefs for a longer time, and that means you can already see what happened as a result. Though this is reason enough to look at Europe for a little while, we'd have to anyway because Europe's troubles got so big that America jumped in too. Jumped into what? *World War II!*

You see, two terrible men came to power in Europe—Adolf Hitler of Germany and Joseph (Josef) Stalin of Russia. These two guys were one of the main reasons for World War II. They were both socialists, though of different sorts. This means they rejected God's statements about Himself and people. This also means both Hitler and Stalin were horribly powerful rulers (they believed they could be like God in saying what was right and wrong—*Big Belief #1*—and they didn't believe there was a God bigger than them Who could tell them what to do)[24] and they were both horribly cruel (instead of believing that people are special because God has made

---

 [24] Erwin Lutzer, *Hitler's Cross* (Chicago: Moody Press, 1995) Ch. 3, for this quote and other ideas in this section. Though at first calling himself a Christian, Hitler claimed to be a new messiah who was establishing a new religion, the religion of Man-God. He said, "What Christ began I will complete" and "in driving out the Jews I remind myself of Jesus in the temple." And, "At one of the Nuremberg rallies, a giant photo of Hitler was captioned with the words: 'In the beginning was the Word.' The Lord's prayer was changed by some to read, 'Our Father Adolf who art in Nuremberg, Hallowed be thy name, the Third Reich come...'"

them, they said that only people they liked should live–*Big Belief #2*). They killed millions of people they didn't want. Horrible![25]

But you also need to realize that too many German people actually were excited about Hitler because they believed the same socialistic, evolutionary ideas! And many Germans were dabbling in dark things, as Hitler was.[26] They thought books about witches and spells were just for fun, but it was blinding them to the truth. So, even though Germany was filled with churches, people soon looked to Hitler's government to improve their lives after the mess of World War I.[27] Soon, most churches took the Bible off the front table, and put Hitler's book there. They took the cross off the back wall, and put the Nazi swastika there. They weren't even very upset when Hitler killed people and invaded other countries, because they trusted him.[28] Ack!

I won't say anything more than this, but do know that we go into much greater depth in the *TruthQuest History* guide for older students. All you need to know here is that Hitler's Germany and Stalin's Russia (actually, it was called the U.S.S.R. then) began attacking other European countries. The two rulers had made an agreement about which other countries they would each take (as if they were theirs to take!) and they promised not to attack each other, but you can guess that such wicked men didn't keep their promise. The fact is that one of the reasons Hitler wanted to steal neighboring European countries was so he'd have more land and more people...to better attack Stalin! And Stalin had the same idea about attacking Hitler! It wasn't long at all before Hitler and Stalin were fighting each other! What a mess! In fact, most of World War II was fought on the "Eastern Front" between those two countries. We Americans don't think much about that part of the war because we weren't involved in it, but that was the main hot spot.

Well, as Hitler and Stalin started taking European countries, other European countries stepped in to help. Besides, they could guess that Hitler and Stalin might try to take them next. Soon, almost every country in Europe was in the war. And then America came in to help the Allies–countries like England that were fighting Hitler and his buddies.

---

[25] Dave Breese, *Seven Men Who Rule the World from the Grave* (Chicago: Moody Press, 1990) 156: "The opening salvos of any war are the public announcement that the earlier spiritual, intellectual, and mental battle has been lost."

[26] Lutzer, Chapter 3.

[27] Lutzer 104, quoting Hitler: "Do you really believe the masses will be Christian again? Nonsense! Never again. That tale is finished...The parsons will dig their own graves. They will betray their God to us. They will betray anything for the sake of their miserable jobs and incomes."

[28] Lutzer 101, quoting Pastor Julius Leutherser: "Christ has come to us through Hitler...through his honesty, his faith and his idealism, the Redeemer found us....We know today the Savior has come...we have only one task, be German, not Christian."

Now, Hitler did need to be stopped, but there is one sad fact we Americans need to look at right now...and it shows one of the messes of war. Since Stalin was also fighting Hitler, Stalin was part of the Allies, even though Stalin was an even more awful man than Hitler was (at least he killed way more people than Hitler did)! That means that the United States was on the same side of the war (the Allies) as Stalin! What a huge mess!

(Parents: You may wonder why I even bother to mention this. That's a fair question. I guess I just want our children, as they learn about World War II, to not overly glamorize it. When they get older and learn more of the complexities of the war, I don't want them to have had such a white-hat view, that it's hard for them to embrace the more realistic aspects of certain elements of the war. War is an imminently tough business, and though I'm intensely proud of all the American soldiers who fought so bravely, I don't want our children to have too unrealistic a view of some of the progressive thinking that contributed to certain decisions in the war. Again, I repeat: I honor the individual soldiers and support personnel who gave so much to free millions of people from oppression! Yeah! Double yeah! The rest can be learned by the kids when they are older.)

We're ready to tackle the war itself. And what a doozie it was! We'll try to focus on the areas where America was most involved, but we will also include books and topics that give you a somewhat fuller sense of the war. You'll have to decide how to spend your time and you'll have to *decide very carefully which topics are appropriate for your children.* You might even want to check the "Table of Contents" to see all the sub-sections in this section because I've chronologically laid out the events of each year (listed as briefly as possible), and have then listed special topics. That might help you plan your 'attack!'

> Parents, if you're following along in Clarence Carson's book: *Basic History of the United States–Vol. 5*, Ch. 5-6.

27a✎ General Resources

☞ For activities, games, recipes: *World War II Days*, by David King	Various
The First Book of World War II, by Louis Snyder (First Books)	Gr. 3-8
The Military History of World War II series, by Trevor Dupuy (16 volumes)	Gr. 4-12
World War II, by Tom McGowen	Gr. 4-12
The Story of World War II, by Stewart Graff	Gr. 5-12
The Story of World War II, by Robert Leckie (Landmark Giant)	Gr. 5-12

27b≈* Events of 1938–Hitler invades Czechoslovakia, Munich Conference

(No specific books for young children.)

27c≈* Events of 1939–Stalin and Hitler make 'non-aggression pact' (they both agree to take land in eastern Europe and promise not to attack each other); as a result both Hitler and Stalin invade Poland, while Hitler takes smaller areas such as Bohemia and Moravia, and Stalin invades Finland, Latvia, Lithuania, Estonia, etc.; Britain and France both declare war on Germany, and British troops are sent to France; Italy invades Albania; England agrees to help Poland; Battle of the Atlantic begins.

The Invasion of Poland, by G.C. Skipper (World at War)	Gr. 3-7
Battle for the Atlantic, by G.C. Skipper (World at War)	Gr. 3-7
The Battle for the Atlantic, by Jay Williams (Landmark)	Gr. 3-10

Fiction/Historical Fiction:

Bolek, by Antoni Gronowicz Story of Polish children on the verge of the invasion.	Gr. 4-9

27d≈* Events of 1940–Germany invades France, Norway, Denmark, Holland, Belgium, and Luxembourg; British troops must be evacuated from Dunkirk as France falls to Germany; Germany bombs England in what is called 'The Battle of Britain;' London is especially blitzed; Britain begins bombing Germany; Japan joins the Axis (the German side); Italy invades Greece and Egypt; Britain re-opens the Burma Road and attacks the Italians on their North African holdings.

The Battle of Britain, by G.C. Skipper (World at War)	Gr. 3-7
The Battle of Britain, by Quentin Reynolds (Landmark)	Gr. 3-10

Fiction/Historical Fiction:

*The Little Ships, by Louise Borden Partially fact-based, girl helps her father rescue soldiers at Dunkirk. Pretty book!	Gr. 2-6
*Snow Goose, by Paul Gallico Artist helps at Dunkirk.	Gr. 2-8

We Were There at the Battle of Britain, by Clayton Knight (We Were There)   Gr. 3-8
    Fictional kids see real historical events.

Silence Over Dunkerque, by John Tunis   Gr. 4-12
    I *loved* this book as a girl! I think most libraries still have this.

When the Sirens Wailed, by Noel Streatfeild   Gr. 5-12
    Story of children during the bombing of London from good author.

27e꩜ Events of 1941–US begins financial support of Allies with the 'Lend-Lease' program; Battle of Tobruk in North Africa; German battleship *Bismarck* is sunk; Germany invades Greece, Yugoslavia, and the Soviet Union, capturing Kiev and nearing Leningrad (beginning the siege there) and Moscow; Soviet counter-offensive begins; Japan bombs Pearl Harbor, attacks Wake Island, the Philippines, Burma, and captures Hong Kong; the United States enters the war with the Allies.

*Pearl Harbor, by Stephen Krensky (Ready-to-Read 3)   Gr. 1-4

The Story of the U.S.S. Arizona, by R. Conrad Stein (Cornerstones)   Gr. 2-7
    Story of Pearl Harbor and the sinking of a large ship there.

Pearl Harbor, by G.C. Skipper (World at War)   Gr. 3-7

The Invasion of Russia, by R. Conrad Stein (World at War)   Gr. 3-7

The Siege of Leningrad, by R. Conrad Stein (World at War)   Gr. 3-7

*Air Raid–Pearl Harbor! by Theodore Taylor   Gr. 4-12

The Sinking of the Bismarck, by William Shirer (Landmark)   Gr. 4-12

*Exploring the Bismarck, by Robert Ballard (TimeQuest)   Gr. 4-12
    Interesting book shuttles between the events and the later finding of the sunken ship.

Fiction/Historical Fiction:

We Were There at Pearl Harbor, by Felix Sutton (We Were There)   Gr. 3-8
    Fictional kids experience real historical events.

Boris, by Jaap Ter Haar   Gr. 3-10
    Russian boy tries to survive the Siege of Leningrad.

Films:

Sink the Bismarck, starring Kenneth More   Parental decision

Tora! Tora! Tora! starring Martin Balsam, Joseph Cotten, E.G. Marshall   Parental decision

27£▲ **Events of 1942–Japan invades the Dutch East Indies, where there is much oil, then takes Singapore, Java, Rangoon, and Bataan, forcing the American and Filipino prisoners (after Allied surrender) on the 'Bataan Death March;' US government puts Japanese citizens in internment camps; Japan attacks Alaska's Aleutian Islands; Doolittle bombing raids on Tokyo; America beats Japan in the Battle of the Coral Sea, the Battle of Midway, and enters Guadalcanal; German saboteurs working in America, just as German submarines had been patrolling American coast; Battle of El Alamein in North Africa; American soldiers join fighting in North Africa; Germany attacks the Soviet Union near Kharkov and Sebastopol, and begins long ordeal at Stalingrad; British and Indian troops move into Burma; Hitler begins killing Jews in gas chambers (books about the holocaust listed in later section).**

> **General resources on the European/African campaigns:**
>
> *The Road to Rome* (World at War)   Gr. 3-7
>   by R. Conrad Stein
> *From Casablanca to Berlin* (Landmark)   Gr. 5-12
>   by Bruce Bliven, Jr.

The Fall of Singapore, by R. Conrad Stein (World at War)   Gr. 3-7

The Battle of Guadalcanal, by R. Conrad Stein (World at War)   Gr. 3-7

Midway, by Philip Sauvain (Great Battles and Sieges)   Gr. 4-12

Thirty Seconds Over Tokyo, by Ted Lawson (Landmark)   Gr. 4-12
     The story of the Doolittle bombing raids of Tokyo.

Guadalcanal Diary, Richard Tregaskis (Landmark)   Gr. 4-12

Midway: Battle for the Pacific, by Edmund Castillo (Landmark)   Gr. 5-12

*Lost Ships of Guadalcanal, by Robert Ballard   Gr. 5-12
     The well-known Ballard tells of the battles and sunken ships.

Fiction/Historical Fiction:

Baseball Saved Us, by Ken Mochizuki   Gr. 2-5
    Boys play baseball to ease anger in Japanese internment camp in Idaho.

We Were There at the Battle for Bataan, by Benjamin Appel (We Were There)   Gr. 3-8
    Fictional kids experience real events.

The Children's War, by Theodore Taylor   Gr. 5-12
    Alaskan boy is drawn into the war.

Films:
    Thirty Seconds Over Tokyo Parent decision
        starring Spencer Tracy & Van
        Johnson

    Bataan   Parent decision
        starring Robert Taylor

> **General resources on the war in the Pacific:**
>
> *Submarines in the Pacific* (World at War)   Gr. 3-7
>   by G.C. Skipper
> *From Pearl Harbor to Okinawa* (Landmark) Gr. 4-12
>   by Bruce Bliven, Jr.

27g❧ Events of 1943–Roosevelt and Churchill decide at Casablanca to demand 'unconditional surrender' of Germany, which makes it more difficult for Germany–who is already in deep trouble after miseries of Soviet campaign and the defeat at Stalingrad–to cease fighting, and makes it harder for German Resistance to gain support in their attempt to overthrow Hitler; Polish Jews persecuted in the Warsaw Ghetto uprising (books on this topic are listed separately further below); Germany and Italy losing in North Africa; US regains the Aleutian Islands; Allies land in Italy, which had been seized by Germany after the Italian people imprisoned Mussolini and switched to the Allied side; Germany receives destructive bombing; Americans bomb Romanian oilfields–Germany's main source of oil after attacking its former supplier, the Soviet Union; Stalin, Churchill, and Roosevelt meet at Teheran where they basically give Stalin a free hand in eastern Europe, which the Soviet Union will dominate until its collapse; Japan loses many seized islands to the US (such as Tarawa) and begins losing territory in China.

The Fall of the Fox: Rommel, by G.C. Skipper (World at War)   Gr. 3-7

27h❧ Events of 1944–Allies land at Anzio in Italy and then recapture Rome; Allies launch D-Day attack at Normandy and are soon able to liberate parts of France–including Paris–and Brussels; Battle of the Bulge (Ardennes) begins; London experiences another round of air raids, including V-1 and V-2 rockets; Berlin is bombed; Warsaw revolts against Hitler, and is systematically decimated by him; German officers try to assassinate Hitler; Russian forces push further westward, occupying Yugoslavia and Hungary; the US attacks Saipan, bombs southern Japan, begins the battle for Guam, regains the Solomon and Marshall Islands, and wins the Battle of Leyte Gulf in an attempt to regain the Philippines.

The Story of D-Day, by R. Conrad Stein (Cornerstones)	Gr. 2-8
D-Day, by G.C. Skipper (World at War)	Gr. 3-7
MacArthur and the Philippines, by G.C. Skipper (World at War)	Gr. 3-7
Story of the Battle of the Bulge, by R. Conrad Stein (Cornerstones)	Gr. 3-8
The Story of D-Day, by Bruce Bliven, Jr. (Landmark)	Gr. 4-10
The Battle of the Bulge, by John Toland (Landmark)	Gr. 4-12

Fiction/Historical Fiction:

We Were There at the Normandy Invasion, by Clayton Knight (We Were There)	Gr. 3-8
We Were There at the Battle of the Bulge, by David Shepherd (We Were There)	Gr. 3-8

Films:

The Longest Day, starring Richard Burton, Henry Fonda, John Wayne Based on the book, this is an involved portrayal of D-Day.	Parental decision

27i🔊 Events of 1945–Russian forces move further into eastern Europe as Germany is beaten back; Russia takes Poland and finally makes it to Berlin, Germany's capital; Allied troops move in from the west, freeing concentration camps, and also arriving in Berlin; Raoul Wallenberg–a Swedish diplomat who rescued many Jews–disappears in Budapest and has never been seen since; Mussolini is killed by the Italians and Hitler ends his life as Germany falls to the Allies, ending the European phase of World War II; Stalin, Roosevelt, and Churchill meet at the Yalta Conference to discuss end to European war; Franklin Roosevelt dies and Harry Truman becomes president of the US; talks finalize the United Nations, which will supercede the League of Nations; the US regains Luzon in the Philippines, the Burma Road, Iwo Jima, Okinawa, etc.; Japan is on its last leg and then surrenders after atomic bombs are dropped on two Japanese cities–Hiroshima and Nagasaki.

The Story of the Battle for Iwo Jima, by R. Conrad Stein (Cornerstones)	Gr. 2-8
Raoul Wallenberg: Missing Diplomat, by Anita Larsen (History's Mysteries)	Gr. 2-8
The Death of Hitler, by G.C. Skipper (World at War)	Gr. 3-7
The Death of Mussolini, by G.C. Skipper (World at War)	Gr. 3-7

The Battle of Okinawa, by R. Conrad Stein (World at War)   Gr. 3-7

The Battle for Iwo Jima, by Robert Leckie (Landmark)   Gr. 5-12

Films:

**The Sands of Iwo Jima*, starring John Wayne   Parental decision

27j✶ Manhattan Project/Atomic Power/Atomic Bomb
(Parents: Please give special care to studying this topic; some children naturally can't handle learning about the atomic bombs at this young age. Do note that this section also covers the new learning in the field of atomic power.)

You may already have learned that scientists were discovering many things about the power inside atoms. We'll meet some of those scientists in a minute, such as Enrico Fermi who escaped from Mussolini in Italy.

But there's something else we must look at because Albert Einstein, the great German scientist who had fled to America so Hitler couldn't use his science knowledge to help Germany, believed that Hitler was trying to build an atomic bomb that would be used on America or the other Allies. So, the American government decided the only way America could keep Germany from dropping atomic bombs on the world was to have an atomic bomb of our own, so we could hold Germany in check. In other words, Germany would know they would *get* an atomic bomb attack, if they dropped one on other nations. The American government hoped this would stop them. It was later discovered that Germany was *not* working on an atomic bomb, but other countries would soon have them.

So, American scientists, with the help of Canadian and British scientists, set to work. Their efforts were called the Manhattan Project. They did indeed make atomic bombs, and the scientists were shocked at how much more powerful the bombs were than they had even imagined. But please know that not all atomic scientists were working toward bombs; many strongly opposed them.

Near the end of the war, when America wanted Japan to surrender quickly, President Truman (who became president after FDR died) made the decision to drop two atomic bombs on Japan. I don't want to say too much about it here because the bombs created great destruction and there are many issues surrounding Truman's decision we can't discuss with young children. Japan immediately surrendered, and World War II came to an end. (Parents, you must carefully decide if you want your children to tackle this subject; some resources are listed below, but do realize that most books on this issue are highly politicized and graphic...before a child is old enough to understand the issues.)

Enrico Fermi: Father of Atomic Power, by Sam & Beryl Epstein (Garr. Am. All)   Gr. 2-7

The Manhattan Project, by R. Conrad Stein (Cornerstones)   Gr. 3-8

Enrico Fermi: Atomic Pioneer, by Doris Faber   Gr. 3-8

Hiroshima, by R. Conrad Stein (World at War)   Gr. 4-7

Hiroshima and Nagasaki, by Barbara Silberdick (Cornerstone)   Gr. 4-8

Sadako and the Thousand Paper Cranes, by Eleanor Coerr   Gr. 4-8
    Japanese girl, dying from the bomb's radiation, fights for her life.

The Story of Atomic Energy, by Laura Fermi (Landmark)   Gr. 4-12

How Did We Find Out about Nuclear Power? by Isaac Asimov   Gr. 5-12

Fiction/Historical Fiction:

We Were There at the Opening of the Atomic Era, by James Munves (We Were...) Gr. 3-8
    Fictional kids participate in real events.

27k☙ Holocaust/Jewish suffering

(Parents! Again I caution you to carefully consider your children's ability to handle this topic. I've listed some resources, but you must decide what is appropriate for your child. Be aware that some books try to be very gentle or highlight the heroism of those who risked so much to save the Jews, so not all books on the topic are gruesome. Anyway, the age recommendations here refer only to independent reading level, not age-appropriateness.)

Yellow Star, by Carmen Deedy   Gr. 1-4
    The wonderful, true story of King Christian X of Denmark and the people of Denmark who did so much to save the Jews of their country from Nazi capture.

Rose Blanche, by Roberto Innocenti   Gr. 1-4
    I'm nervous about recommending a book I haven't seen for such young children, but it may be worth checking. It's the story of a young girl who sees thin, hungry children behind a fence (they're in a concentration camp, which she doesn't understand), and she innocently decides to bring them food.

112

Passage to Freedom: The Sugihara Story, by Ken Mochizuki   Gr. 2-5
    The true story of a Japanese diplomat to Lithuania who helped 10,000 Jews escape!

Anne Frank, by Vanora Leigh (Great Lives)   Gr. 2-8

Warsaw Ghetto, by R. Conrad Stein (World at War)   Gr. 3-7

The United States Holocaust Memorial Museum, by P. Brooks (Cornerstones)   Gr. 3-7

A Place to Hide, by Jayne Pettit   Gr. 3-10
    True stories of holocaust rescue.

So Young to Die: Hannah Senesh, by Candice Ransom   Gr. 3-12
    Story of young Jewish woman who had a chance to free herself, but went back to help.

Corrie ten Boom, by Janet & Geoff Benge (Christian Heroes)   Gr. 4-10

Daniel's Story, by C. Matas   Gr. 4-12

Anne Frank, by J. Hurwitz   Gr. 4-12

> There are books on both Corrie ten Boom and Dietrich Bonhoeffer in several Christian series: Young Reader's Christian Library (Gr. 1-5), Hero Tales (Gr. 3-7), Christian Heroes, Then and Now (Gr. 3-12), and Heroes of the Faith (Gr. 5-12). The individual titles are simply the name of the person being studied.

Fiction/Historical Fiction:

Butterfly, by Patricia Polacco   Gr. 1-4
    A French girl discovers a Jewish girl hiding in her home; partially fact-based.

Twenty and Ten, by Claire Bishop   Gr. 2-9
    Moving story of French nun and children who harbor Jewish children. Really good!

Star of Danger, by Jane Levin   Gr. 4-12
    The Danish Resistance help Jews escape.

From Anna, by Jean Little   Gr. 5-12
    A Jewish girl, fleeing Germany, faces a new life and vision problems in Canada.

Films:

Miracle at Moreaux, starring Loretta Swit   All ages
    Based on the abovementioned story, *Twenty and Ten*. Wonderful!

27l꙰ Winston Churchill
(This is a corollary topic; cover only if you want to learn about the leader of England during World War II.)

The Story of Winston Churchill, by Alida Malkus (Signature)   Gr. 3-8

Winston Churchill, by Quentin Reynolds (Landmark)   Gr. 5-12

27m꙰ True stories of individuals

Hanna's Cold Winter, by Trish Marx   Gr. 2-6
  True story of family trying to keep hippo in Budapest zoo from starving during the war.

*High Flight, by Linda Granfield   Gr. 2-8
  This is the true story of a young American–John Magee–who decided to fly for the Royal Canadian Air Force in World War II. He lived just a short time, but before death wrote one of the most famous poems about flying, even though it is very brief. "Oh! I have slipped the surly bonds of earth..." This book brings to life not only Magee and the poem, but also life as a World War II pilot.

*War Boy, by Michael Foreman   Gr. 3-8
  An English author/illustrator tells of his childhood during the war.

Radar Commandos, by Bernard Glemser (Winston Adventure)   Gr. 3-8
  True story of teens who help underground spy effort.

*Snow Treasure, by Marie McSwigan   Gr. 3-9
  Don't miss this gem! This is the book men most often tell me they vividly recall from their childhoods. In fact, Dad will probably want to read this one aloud, just to enjoy it again! It's the *true* story of Norwegian children who try to smuggle Norway's gold supply out before the Nazis can seize it.

Medal of Honor Heroes, by Colonel Red Reeder (Landmark)   Gr. 3-9

North of Danger, by Dale Fife   Gr. 3-12
  The true story of a Norwegian boy who tried to ski 200 miles to warn of the Nazis.

Great Escapes of World War II, by George Sullivan   Gr. 3-12

Long Escape, by Irving Werstein   Gr. 4-12
  Belgian woman tries to rescue children who will be exterminated if caught.

Combat Nurses of World War II, by Wyatt Blassingame (Landmark)   Gr. 4-12

A Penny for a Hundred, by Ethel Pochocki   Gr. 4-12
    True story; family spends Christmas with German soldiers.

Operation Escape, by Daniel Madden   Gr. 5-12
    True story of Vatican priest, Hugh O'Flaherty, who helps rescue Nazi targets in Rome.

The Endless Steppe, by Esther Hautzig   Gr. 5-12
    Siberian Jewish girl tries to survive the war.

The Story of the Trapp Family Singers, by Maria Trapp   Gr. 5-12
    This is the true story that was the basis for the film, *The Sound of Music*. Mrs. von Trapp
    expanded and continued the story in, *Maria*.

Sole Survivor, by Ruthanne McCunn   Gr. 5-12
    Boy survives German U-boat torpedo, then is then adrift on a raft.

Medical Corps Heroes of World War II, by Wyatt Blassingame (Landmark)   Gr. 5-12

Films & audios:

The Sound of Music, starring Julie Andrews (film)   All ages
    True story of von Trapp family's attempt to escape.

The Diary of Anne Frank, starring Millie Perkins   Parental decision

The Scarlet and the Black, starring Gregory Peck   Parental decision
    Wow! This is an important film...and it's good! It shows the true story of a Vatican
    priest (Hugh O'Flaherty) who risked his life to help others. His final showdown with
    a Nazi leader is a great lesson in 'higher law.' Excellent! If your kids are old enough to
    handle the tension and punishments suffered, this film is a good teacher.

27n♣ Military leaders

Dwight David Eisenhower, by Red Reeder (Garrard Discovery)   Gr. 1-5

Douglas MacArthur, by Laura Long (Childhood)   Gr. 1-6

Dwight D. Eisenhower, by Wilma Hudson (Childhood)   Gr. 1-6

Omar Nelson Bradley, by Red Reeder   Gr. 2-8

Goering and the Luftwaffe, by G.C. Skipper (World at War)   Gr. 3-7

The Story of Dwight D. Eisenhower, by Arthur Beckhard (Signature)   Gr. 3-8

Great American Fighter Pilots of World War II, by Robert Loomis (Landmark)   Gr. 4-12

Dwight D. Eisenhower, by Malcolm Moos (Landmark)   Gr. 5-12

John F. Kennedy and PT-109, by Richard Tregaskis (Landmark)   Gr. 5-12

Commandoes of World War II, by Hodding Carter (Landmark)   Gr. 5-12

27o੪ Special topics

The Nisei Regiment, by R. Conrad Stein (World at War)   Gr. 3-7
   The story of Japanese-Americans who fought in World War II.

Prisoners of War, by R. Conrad Stein (World at War)   Gr. 3-7

The Home Front, by R. Conrad Stein (World at War)   Gr. 3-7

Resistance Movements, by R. Conrad Stein (World at War)   Gr. 3-7

U.S. Frogmen of World War II, by Wyatt Blassingame (Landmark)   Gr. 4-12

**World War II Submarine*, by Richard Humble (Inside Story)   Gr. 4-12
   Interesting cut-away views. If you're near Chicago, go to the Museum of Science and
   Industry and walk through the *real* World War II submarine there!

The Story of the Paratroops, by George Weller (Landmark)   Gr. 4-12

That Denmark Might Live, by Irving Werstein   Gr. 5-12
   Tells of the amazing Danish Resistance who did so much to save Danish Jews.

The Flying Tigers, by John Toland (Landmark)   Gr. 5-12
   Tells of the American pilots who worked in China.

The Seabees of World War II, by Edmund Castillo (Landmark)   Gr. 5-12
   Tells of the WW2 construction battalions (cb's...seabees).

V is for Victory, by Sylvia Whitman   Gr. 5-12
   Life on the American homefront.

When the Saboteurs Came, by William Wise   Gr. 5-12
    Tells of German sabotage in the United States.

27p² Miscellaneous Fiction/Historical Fiction

All Those Secrets of the World, by Jane Yolen   Gr. 1-3
    Poignant picture book; girl sees her father leave to fight in the war.

*Bicycle Man, by Allen Say   Gr. 1-3
    A Japanese boy (just after the war) remembers a visit by an American soldier.

*Don't You Know There's a War On? by James Stevenson   Gr. 1-3
    See the war through the eyes of a young boy at home in the States.

*The Bracelet, by Yoshiko Uchida   Gr. 1-4
    Based on the author's girlhood, a story in a Japanese-American internment camp.

*New Coat for Anna, by Harriet Ziefert   Gr. 1-4
    This story is actually set just after Germany's collapse, when a mother must barter to obtain a coat for her daughter. I've seen an audio format also.

*Night Crossing, by Karen Ackerman   Gr. 1-5
    Nice story for young children of loving, Austrian-Jewish family trying to escape.

Corporal Keeperupper, by Katherine Milhous   Gr. 1-6
    Old story of toy soldier who wants to help fight in the war.

Augustus Helps the Army, **and,** *Augustus Helps the Navy*, by LeGrand   Gr. 2-6
    Wonderfully warm and funny stories of boy who gets to help out here in the States!

Young Man of the House, by Mabel Leigh Hunt   Gr. 2-6
    Boy tries to help in his father's absence.

*Meet Molly and the rest of the series, by Valerie Tripp (American Girls)   Gr. 2-7

*Flight of the Fugitives, by Dave & Neta Jackson (Trailblazer)   Gr. 3-7
    Fictional kids with Gladys Aylward as she rescues Chinese children during the war.

The Level Land, by Dola DeJong   Gr. 3-8
    Dutch family faces World War II. *Return to the Level Land*, is the sequel.

*Number the Stars, by Lois Lowry   Gr. 3-10
    Newbery Award-winning novel of the Danish Resistance.

The House of Sixty Fathers, by Meindert de Jong   Gr. 3-10
     Another *don't-miss* story of a Chinese boy trying to find his parents. Wonderful!

The Small War of Sergeant Donkey, by Maureen Daly   Gr. 3-10
     Italian boy helps soldier train mules.

Journey to America, **and**, *Silver Days*, by Sonia Levitin   Gr. 3-12
     Beloved stories of German-Jewish family who is separated by the war.

When Hitler Stole the Pink Rabbit, by Judith Kerr   Gr. 4-10
     I'm not familiar with the contents of this.

Escape from Warsaw, by Ian Serraillier (previously titled *Silver Sword*)   Gr. 4-12
     Children must escape Nazis and search for father. Highly recommended!

Heroes in Plenty, by Theodora DuBois   Gr. 4-12
     A fact-based story of the German resistance to Hitler. I've heard it's quite good!

Little Riders, by Margaretha Shemin   Gr. 4-12
     American girl in Holland must try to escape the Nazis.

The Avion My Uncle Flew, by Cyrus Fisher   Gr. 4-12
     Unusual book which gradually inserts French words in place of English.

The Winged Watchman, by Hilda van Stockum   Gr. 5-12
     Long-beloved tale of Dutch family protecting a shot-down British pilot. *Don't miss it!*

Up Periscope; *The Frogmen*; *Flight Deck*; **and**, *The Survivor*, all by Robb White   Gr. 5-12
     Boys love this author! Exciting stories of subs, codes, downed pilots, etc.

Sea Snake; *The Long Trains Roll*, **and**, *Shadow in the Pines*, by Stephen Meader   Gr. 5-12
     Exciting author tells stories of danger at home to Nazi subs, fifth columnists, etc.

When the Typhoon Blows, by Elizabeth Lewis   Gr. 5-12
     Chinese families struggle against Japanese invaders.

Patriot of the Underground, by Robin McKown   Gr. 5-12
     Teen boys help the French Resistance.

No Time for Glory: Stories of World War II, by Phyllis Fenner   Gr. 5-12

The Sword is Drawn, by André Norton   Gr. 5-12
     Can a Dutch jeweler's son keep the Nazis from getting the jewels?

The Little Fishes, by Erik Haugaard   Gr. 5-12
    12-year-old boy must live on the streets during World War II.

Haven for the Brave, by Elizabeth Yates   Gr. 5-12

The Devil's Arithmetic, by Jane Yolen   Gr. 5-12

The Mitchells (also titled *Five for Victory*), *Canadian Summer*, **and**, *Friendly Gables* Gr. 5-12
    All *three* books tell of English children living in Canada due to war dangers in England.
    Beloved author and series.

27q⁀ Miscellaneous Films

Journey for Margaret, starring Robert Young   All ages
    Couple helps orphaned English children.

Inn of the Sixth Happiness, starring Ingrid Bergman   All ages
    The true story of missionary Gladys Aylward who must rescue Chinese children during
    World War II. This episode and her fuller missionary work are related in the *fabulous*
    book about her life, *The Small Woman*, by Alan Burgess (Gr. 7-12) (which also gives a
    vivid feel for China in the early 1900s), as do books in the common Christian series
    about Miss Aylward.

Miracle of the White Stallions, starring Robert Taylor   All ages
    True story of attempt to keep Lipizzan stallions from the Nazis.

Command Decision, starring Clark Gable   Parental decison
    Shows the tense debate about whether to bomb Germany at night when it was safer for
    the Allied fliers but did more damage to German civilians.

Guns of Navarone, starring Gregory Peck   Parental decision
    Gripping film of attempt to take Nazi guns out of Greek stronghold; based on the novel
    by the same name, written by Alistair MacLean.

Twelve O'Clock High, starring Gregory Peck   Parental decision
    Shows the tension felt by Allied bombers.

Miss Rose White, starring Kyra Sedgwick and Maximilian Schell   Parental decision
    This film shows the stress in a Jewish family just after the war. Very moving.

Bridge on the River Kwai, starring Alec Guinness and William Holden   Parental decision
    This is a real favorite for many. Wow! It shows the incredible fortitude of British
    soldiers captured by the Japanese somewhere in the Asian jungles, maybe Burma?

Mortal Storm, starring Jimmy Stewart   Parental decision
         Can Stewart and his fiancé, who grasp the horrors of Nazism, escape in time?

28⚘ Nuremberg Trials

Did you know that after World War II the top Nazis were put on trial?! These sessions were called the *Nuremburg Trials* because the court was held in Nuremburg, Germany. It's not necessary to learn details about the trials, but there is one *very* important point you *should* notice...and here it is: the Nazis told the judge that the horrendous things they did to people were alright because they were simply obeying the laws of Germany![29] *But the laws of Germany had just been made up by Hitler...based on what he wanted! They were not based on God's laws! And that's why they hurt people! Only God's laws are actually good for us!*

Well, now! Doesn't that just scream out the point we've been trying to make!!!!!!! It makes me want to stand on top of the Sears Tower and scream:

> *"Hey, world! Don't you get it?! When people make themselves gods by deciding what is truth, when they decide what is right and wrong, when they make their own laws, when they ignore the true God and His higher law, when they deny the King of all other kings...you end up with utter tragedy! World, that's not safe and that's not right! Can't you see that surrendering to God actually brings freedom, because God's laws are good for everyone?!"*

Of course, this was the same awful thing I did when I ran away from home. I had made my own 'law' and my own 'life-rules' in my own heart; I had decided what was right for me. I ignored God's command to obey my parents because I didn't think it was best for me. Well, what did I know?! And what did the Nazis know?! Did the world they tried to make turn out well? No! It was horrendous! And the same with Stalin! And the same with America, if we don't obey God's perfect rules of life.

> **Parents:** You will be intrigued by the film: *Judgment at Nuremberg*, starring Spencer Tracy
>   I was *very* impressed! I thought it powerfully made the point about *higher law!*

29⚘ The 1940s

Of course, there was more to the 1940s than just war. People wore 'zoot suits,' danced the jitterbug, and watched Joe DiMaggio break an important baseball record. But Jackie Robinson broke an even more important baseball 'record:' he was the first black man to play in the major

---

[29] Lutzer 119.

120

leagues and he had to face great difficulties. Chuck Yeager flew faster than the speed of sound, while Rodgers & Hammerstein created beloved musicals, as did Leonard Bernstein. Mondrian and Henry Moore created more modern art. There was quite a polio scare too. In 1947, the Dead Sea Scrolls were found, proving how accurate the main Bible translations are. Dr. Spock tried to tell Americans to parent their children in a 'modern' way, repeating the humanistic idea that children are born perfect so parents should not discipline them, but should instead focus only on giving their creativity and individuality free rein; you can see what problems that has caused in America. The transistor was invented that same year, and was a tremendous boost to technology. I'll quickly list a few books on some of these topics:

> Mt. Rushmore was 'completed' in 1941, since work stopped when Gutzon Borglum, the sculptor, passed away.
>
> *Story of Mount Rushmore* (Cornerstone) Gr. 2-6
> *Rushmore*, by Lynn Curlee Gr. 4-9

> Parents, you'll be fascinated by:
> *History through Eyes of Faith*, by Ronald Wells, Ch. 15

Leonard Bernstein, by Molly Cone (Crowell Biography)	Gr. 1-3
Teammates, by Peter Golenbock About the relationship between Jackie Robinson and PeeWee Reese.	Gr. 1-4
Jackie Robinson: A Life of Courage, by Keith Brandt (Troll Easy Biographies)	Gr. 1-5
Leonard Bernstein, by Marlene Toby (Rookie)	Gr. 1-5
Jackie Robinson, by Herb Dunn (Childhood)	Gr. 1-6
Joe DiMaggio, by Herb Dunn (Childhood)	Gr. 1-6
Jackie Robinson, by Kenneth Rudeen	Gr. 1-6
Jackie Robinson and the Story of All-Black Baseball, by J. O'Connor (Step...4)	Gr. 2-4
Baseball's Best, by Andrew Gutelle, Ch. 2-3 (Step into Reading 4)	Gr. 2-6
Scientists Who Changed the World, by P. Wilkinson & M. Pollard, pp. 72-74 Describes Alan Turing's work to develop the computer.	Gr. 2-6
Jackie Robinson Breaks the Color Line, by A. Santella (Cornerstones)	Gr. 2-7
Jackie Robinson, by Margaret Davidson (Dell Yearling)	Gr. 3-7
Chuck Yeager Breaks the Sound Barrier, by R. Conrad Stein (Cornerstones)	Gr. 3-7

After the War was Over, by Michael Foreman   Gr. 3-8
    Englishman tells of his real boyhood just after World War II.

*Dead Sea Scrolls, by Ilene Cooper   Gr. 4-8

Cave of Riches: The Story of the Dead Sea Scrolls, by Alan Honour   Gr. 4-9

Quest for the Dead Sea Scrolls, by Geoffrey Palmer   Gr. 5-12

Fiction/Historical Fiction:

Farm Summer 1942, by Donald Hall   Gr. 1-4

When I Was Nine, by James Stevenson   Gr. 1-4
Higher on the Door, by James Stevenson   Gr. 1-4
    These two wonderful books reveal an American boy's life during the 1940s.

*Golden Age, by Martha Wickham (Odyssey)   Gr. 2-6
    Girl imagines herself living during the 1940s and enjoying the radio.

Cotton in My Sack, To Be a Logger, Bayou Suzette, Judy's Journey, by Lois Lenski   Gr. 3-9
    Various stories of life around America: Arkansas and Alabama sharecroppers, etc.

*In the Year of the Boar and Jackie Robinson, by Bette Bao Lord   Gr. 3-10
    Chinese-American immigrant girl is encouraged by Robinson's accomplishment. Unknown content.

You can tell we're hurrying here, as we must. I will simply mention two authors of the 1940s who wrote for children! You know these guys–C.S. Lewis (British) and James Thurber!

☞ There are biographies of Lewis in common Christian series, such as *Hero Tales*, by Dave & Neta Jackson, and the *Heroes of the Faith* series.

30☙ From 'Hot War' to 'Cold War' to 'Hot War' Again!

When World War II ended, the shooting was over, but the conflict was not. You see, Stalin had made his communist Russia (the U.S.S.R.) even bigger and more powerful because he kept all the lands he overran during World War II...as he had planned. In fact, it was Stalin's dream that every country in the world would become communist! He wanted to rule them all! He quickly looked for any countries that were struggling, and he sent his people there to make a communist revolution. At one point, one-third of the world was under the evil power of communism!

Well, you can imagine that Americans were getting mighty concerned! They didn't like the idea of all the communist countries working together and maybe trying to take over America. That's why there was a lot of struggle between America and the communist countries during the 1950s and 1960s. This struggle was called the *Cold War* because soldiers weren't usually in 'hot' battle, but there was still plenty of tension!

Some Americans built shelters in their backyard because they were afraid the Russians would bomb them (especially after Russia also started making atomic bombs). And when a communist man, Fidel Castro, got control of Cuba (an island close to Florida), there were even stronger threats against America. By this time, John F. Kennedy was president of America, and there was almost a war then during the *Cuban Missile Crisis.*

Actually, there were times when the Cold War did become 'hot.' In the 1950s, America (as part of the United Nations) was fighting the communist Koreans who were trying to take over that land. And in the 1960s, Americans (again as part of the United Nations) were fighting the communist Vietnamese who were trying to take over that land. Those wars were very frustrating for the brave Americans who were fighting them because the American government was being very fickle. It was *not* resisting communism as hard as it should have been because communism is a form of socialism and many of America's highest leaders–such as Harry Truman–were rather socialistic (progressive) themselves, so they often managed things in a way that took America two steps forward in fighting the communists, but then one step back, as the saying goes.[30] And there was lots of arguing here in America about the wars. It turned out to be a bitter time in American history, even though young men and women were heroically sacrificing themselves to resist communism and help people who didn't want their countries to fall under that evil power.

If you're old enough, you may want to learn a bit about these wars and struggles, but be aware that it wasn't just the fear of communism that got America involved in other conflicts around the world. You see, America was getting pretty hoity-toity with her 'human progress' ideas; she seemed to think she should 'fix' other countries with her 'human wisdom' (humanism) instead of godly wisdom. A lot of this was done through an organization called the United Nations, but we'll talk about that in the guide for older students. You're too young now. But I can tell you that we ended up dabbling in some messy situations where we really didn't know very much

---

[30] Carson 5:146-182.

123

and we ended up supporting some very nasty leaders because they promised they wouldn't be friends with Russia...even though they often double-crossed us and *did* support Russia.[31] Again you see that any time people decide for themselves how things ought to be, instead of obeying what God already has said is good for people and nations, things get very sticky! God knows how each nation should treat others!

30a▲ The Cold War

The Story of the Cold War, by Leila Foster (Cornerstones)   Gr. 2-7

The Rosenbergs, by Anita Larsen (History's Mysteries)   Gr. 3-9
    Story of American couple convicted of spying for Russia & passing atomic information.

30b▲ The Korean War

War in Korea (Landmark)   Gr. 4-12
    by Robert Leckie

*The Korean War, by Tom McGovern Gr. 5-12

> Parents, you'll be surprised by the info about the Korean War in: **Basic History of the United States—Vol. 5*, by Clarence Carson, pp. 162-169.

Fiction/Historical Fiction:

Sabre Pilot, by Stephen Meader   Gr. 5-12

30c▲ The Cuban Missile Crisis

*Story of the Cuban Missile Crisis, by Susan Clinton (Cornerstones)   Gr. 3-9

30d▲ The Vietnam War

Leaving Vietnam, by Sarah Kilborne (Ready to Read 3)   Gr. 1-3

*A Wall of Names, by Judy Donnelly (Step Into Reading 4)   Gr. 1-5
    Tells of the memorial and the war.

The Story of the Saigon Airlift, by Zachary Kent (Cornerstones)   Gr. 2-8

The Vietnam Women's Memorial, by Deborah Kent (Cornerstones)   Gr. 2-8

The Vietnam Veterans Memorial, by David Wright (Cornerstones)   Gr. 2-8

---

[31] Maybury mentioned throughout his books, *World War I* and *World War II*.

The Wall, by Eve Bunting   Gr. 3-7

The Vietnam War, by John Devaney   Gr. 5-12

Fiction/Historical Fiction:

The Lotus Seed, by Sherry Garland   Gr. 1-6
    Wonderful, beautiful picture book; Vietnamese woman remembers her homeland.

The Land I Lost **and** *Water Buffalo Days*, by Huynh Quang Nhuong   Gr. 3-7
    Tender stories of Vietnamese boy. Really warm.

31🕊 The Cold War "Takes Off" (Space Exploration)

The Cold War didn't just take place on earth though, it also went into outer space! "What are you talking about?" you ask! The space race! Americans were afraid of Russia's space program, and I can understand why. When Russia first sent a man in orbit around the earth, people worried that Russia could attack America from space! President Kennedy made it America's goal to put the first man on the moon. Well, you'll see what happened!

What is a Space Shuttle? by Chris Arvetis *et al* (Just Ask)   Gr. K-2

One Giant Leap: The Story of Neil Armstrong, by Don Brown   Gr. 1-4

Apollo 13: Space Race, by Gail Herman (All Aboard Reading)   Gr. 1-4
    Story of ill-fated mission.

This is Cape Canaveral, by Miroslav Sasek   Gr. 1-4

Skylab, by Dennis Fradin (New True Book)   Gr. 1-4

Space Shuttles, by Margaret Friskey (New True Books)   Gr. 1-5

Moonwalk: First Trip to the Moon, by Judy Donnelly (Step Into Reading 4)   Gr. 1-5

One Giant Leap, by Mary Ann Fraser   Gr. 1-6
    A very handsome book!

Virgil I. Grissom, by Carl Chappell (Childhood)   Gr. 1-6

Neil Armstrong, by Montrew Dunham (Childhood)   Gr. 1-6

John Glenn: Young Astronaut, by Michael Burgan (Childhood)   Gr. 1-6

Let's Go to the Moon, by Janis Wheat (National Geographic)   Gr. 1-6

Scientists Who Changed the World, by P. Wilkinson & M. Pollard, pp. 82-90   Gr. 2-5

Launch Day, by Peter Campbell   Gr. 2-6
    Nice illustrations show the work necessary to prepare the space shuttle for launch.

Space Exploration, by Michael George   Gr. 2-12
    Beautiful images, in a book that also includes Russian accomplishments.

The Story of Apollo 11: First Man on the Moon, by R. Conrad Stein (Cornerstone) Gr. 3-8

One Giant Leap: The First Moon Landing, by Dana Rau (Smithsonian Odyssey) Gr. 3-8

Sally Ride, Astronaut, by June Behrens   Gr. 3-8
    Biography of first woman astronaut to orbit earth.

*Flight of the Falcon: The Thrilling Adventures of Colonel Jim Irwin   Gr. 3-10
    by Paul Thomsen (Creation Adventure)
    This is the interesting biography of a strongly Christian astronaut.

The Story of the Challenger Disaster, by Zachary Kent (Cornerstones)   Gr. 4-9

First on the Moon, by Barbara Hehner   Gr. 4-9
    Story is told from point of view of Buzz Aldrin's daughter.

Rocket! How a Toy Launched the Space Age, by Richard Maurer   Gr. 5-12
    A narrative history of the development of the rocket.

21 Scientists Who Believed the Bible, by Ann Lamont, pp. 240-251   Gr. 5-12
    A brief introduction to Wernher von Braun, rocket scientist.

Space Exploration, by Carole Stott (Eyewitness)   Gr. 5-12

Christa McAuliffe: Pioneer Space Teacher, by Charlene Billings   Gr. 5-12
    True story of teacher who was aboard the space shuttle *Challenger* when it exploded.

Just for fun for the little tykes:

I Want to Be an Astronaut, by Byron Barton   Gr. PK-K

32❧ The 1950s & 1960s

Let's look now at life for the average American during the 1950s and 1960s. It was a peppy time because, after World War II, soldiers, sailors, and nurses came home ready to enjoy peace and freedom in America! Many married, started families (these years were called the *Baby Boom*), and built houses in new suburbs. The television set and its impact became common in many homes. Alaska and Hawaii became states in the late 50s. Two doctors made a polio vaccine which was appreciated by many who had feared the disease. The *Nautilus* became a nuclear submarine in 1954. The laser was invented in 1960, and the SST took its first test flight in 1969.

> Writers of the 50s and 60s who produced some books children could enjoy:
>
> Catherine Marshall, Dr. Seuss, Isaac Bashevis Singer, Carl Sandburg, Robert Frost, and J.R.R. Tolkien (British).

But all was not 'sweetness and light.' You see, after World War II, people had very deep questions about the promises of 'human progress.' Why? Because the terrible deeds of Hitler and Stalin (for example) had caused many Americans to lose husbands and brothers and sons during the war! And hadn't those men done horrible things to Jews and others?! Yes, they had!

So, why did the big preachers and big presidents and big college professors and big authors keep telling folks that people had 'evolved' beyond being sinful (and thus beyond needing God's laws to control them and help guide them) in spite of all that happened during World War II? I can give you what I think is *part* of the answer...that to face the truth about humankind would have meant they needed God, they needed to surrender to Him, they needed His salvation through Jesus Christ, *and* that people weren't controlling the evolution of the world, but were in fact creatures who had been made by God. And all of human history boils down to the decision of each person's heart: will he believe what God says about Himself and about people, or will he try to make up his own way. That's what we've been talking about this whole time!

And I think another *part* of the answer is that too many folks who really *did* know the truth about the Lord weren't living that truth each and every day in a way that made a difference their neighbors could see, they weren't so filled with God's light that folks could see they had a hold of real life and truth. But guess what! I face the very same challenge in my own life! Is *my* heart so turned to the Lord that I glow with His light? Have a planted *my*self beside His streams of living water (Psalm 1) so that I make good 'fruit' for those around me? Well, I need to...or I will be part of America's problems, not part of the solution!

But, though Americans were asking questions about 'human progress,' I'm sad to report that few turned to the truth for answers. Instead of being honest about how much people need the Lord (as the life of Hitler and Stalin shows us), the experts just said those two guys were *madmen*. But, the truth is that those two guys were acting just as evolution and socialism had taught them! They believed they could make their own rules for life since there was no higher God who had the wisdom and power to control the universe.

In a not-so-different way, American presidents continued with the American style of socialism, the kind that says we can all pool our 'human power' together and work through human government to fix all the problems of life...not just the ones God wants government to fix, but even the ones only He can fix! Yes, the presidents of the 1950s and 1960s–Eisenhower, Kennedy, Johnson–were still putting many 'human progress' plans into place, rather than looking directly to God's Word for wisdom on solving the problems of the human heart and for instructing human actions. (Eisenhower said he would resist such plans, but he did little more than move at a slower pace than did Kennedy and Johnson–who were both very committed to 'human progress' ideas.)

But I'm not saying it very well; it was much more personal. You see, too many American grownups *talked* about God, they even *believed* in God, but they hadn't *surrendered* to Him and thus they hadn't agreed that the only way to have a close, personal, life-changing relationship with God was through Jesus Christ. Yes, too many tried to make their own Christianity based on 'human progress' and 'human goodness;' in fact, all they were really after was making money and having peaceful lives, while ignoring the needs of others.[32] Well, the teens saw their parents' style of Christianity, and they knew it wasn't real. They were right![33] But they thought the problem was the Christianity...when it fact it was the *falseness* of their parents' Christianity. So, the teens of the 50s and 60s moved further from God instead of closer to Him...and the problems only got worse.

Yes, the young people thought they had to find their own 'answers' for life, and in the 1960s they thought they *had* found them: they joined the artists and musicians who realized that their parents' beliefs about human progress didn't add up. But the young kids kept the idea that people could run their own lives without God, and then added a new twist. They said that truth wasn't in the 'big blue sky of human wonderfulness,' but was to be found in the heart and mind and experiences of each person. (Big people have a fancy name for this idea–*existentialism*–but you don't need to worry about that.)

But do think about this! Because they believed truth was in themselves, their focus was on themselves. People now thought they had the right to do things that were selfish, naughty, and even destructive if it would help them 'find themselves' or 'express themselves.' But it wasn't just selfish, it was also sad. People were still running away from God and insisting they could take care of themselves, just like I did when I ran away from home...and they were just as lost as I would have been if I hadn't gone back to Mom!

And these young people didn't just reject God, they also rejected their parents...and almost everything their parents thought was good. It was called the *generation gap*.[34] Since their parents liked to be clean-cut, the teens were sloppy. They were called hippies and had long hair

---

[32] Throughout his book, Schaeffer calls this the quest for "personal peace and affluence."

[33] Schaeffer 208: "The young people wanted more to life than personal peace and affluence. They were right in their analysis of the problem, but they were mistaken in their solutions."

[34] Schaeffer 182.

and baggy clothes. They said they were going to care about others, but too often they were just selfish drifters who quit jobs and schools so they could drive around in VW vans trying to "do their own thing." They had their own music–rock and roll–which wasn't even trying to sound beautiful or flowing; instead, groups like the Beatles were trying to express the frustration of teens, the disconnectedness they felt from their parents' world, and the pounding 'power' of their new self-focused beliefs.[35] In fact, one writer of the time called these youths the *Beat Generation*, from the throbbing beat of their music; they were nicknamed *beatniks*. They started riots on their college campuses. They defied parents, government, and the police (who were now called nasty names). They had "love-ins," which were really sinful parties, and they started wearing very immodest miniskirts. Mr. Schaeffer says:

> *Why should anybody have been surprised? ...Was it not natural that one generation would begin to live on the basis of what they had been taught?*[36]

Remember, these teens and twenty-somethings had been told as young children that there was no real, active God Who had lovingly and intelligently created a meaningful world. They had been taught in school and in too many churches that they had just evolved out of muck under their own power and had to find answers themselves. What emptiness they must have felt, for if there was no real Creator-God, if life was only chemical reactions in billion-year-old ooze, there was nothing to give meaning to life. There would then be no God Who could lovingly teach them how life ought to be lived.

So what came of all the promises of evolution and human progress? They left people totally alone and adrift...hoping they might have some lucky experience that would help them understand life...thiuking they were nothing more than evolved ooze. How sad. How very sad.

But what an opportunity for those who *did* know the Lord of Truth! They could share the good news, but it was going to be a tough job because these wrong ideas we've been talking about where *everywhere* in America... in music, movies, books, schools, churches, and on the nightly newscasts![37] As Mr. Lutzer wisely said, "the ideas of a nation can change

Parents, if you're following along, you'll be fascinated...and moved...by:

Seven Men Who Rule the World from the Grave, by Dave Breese, Ch. 11

How Should We Then Live? by Francis Schaeffer, Ch. 9 & 10 (Or Video Episode #7 & #8)

History Through the Eyes of Faith, by Ronald Wells, Ch. 16-17.

---

[35] Wells 216: The new rock-n-roll movement "gave popular voice to the essential incoherence of life, and, often times, the desire for personal gratification because that is all there is."

[36] Schaeffer 206.

[37] Schaeffer 197, 201.

if enough people say the same thing often enough."[38] That's just what had happened! Ack! But the same is true the other way! What happens when a lot of us tell the truth?! Yeah!

32a☙ General events and ideas of the 1950s and 1960s

Benny's Flag, by P. Krasilovsky Gr. 1-5
> I love this story of the real boy who designed Alaska's flag as it joined the union.

*Wilma Unlimited, by Kathleen Krull   Gr. 1-6
> True tale of polio-stricken girl–Wilma Rudolph–who became great Olympic champion.

Scientists Who Changed the World, by P. Wilkinson & M. Pollard, pp. 79-81   Gr. 2-6
> Describes the work of Francis & Crick, and others.

<table>
<tr><td>You could learn about the Eskimos of Alaska now too, if desired, since Alaska became a state in 1958-1959. There are so many books on your library shelf, that a list here is unnecessary. We looked at Hawaii earlier in this guide.</td><td>Story of Jonas Salk...Discovery of the Polio Vaccine Gr. 3-7
by Zachary Kent (Cornerstone)

The Story of Television Gr. 3-7
by Zachary Kent (Cornerstones)

The Story of the Great Society Gr. 3-7
by Leila Foster (Cornerstones)
President Johnson's progressivist/socialist plan.</td></tr>
</table>

*Kent State, by Arlene Erlbach (Cornerstones)   Gr. 4-8
> Caution! This covers one of the most violent student riots.

Fiction/Historical Fiction:

We Were There on the Nautilus, by Robert Webb (We Were There)   Gr. 3-8
> Fictional kids have adventures on first atomic submarine.

32b☙ Presidents Eisenhower, Kennedy, Johnson, and families

Note: Eisenhower was cited in the World War II section (biographies of him cover both his war service and his presidency); those biographies won't be listed here again. I know of no particular books on Johnson, other than the ones in the same in-print series cited below, so you can extrapolate from this list to find them, if desired. Thus, only biographies of Kennedy and his family will be listed here. Please be careful, though! Kennedy has been made a great hero by the folks who espouse humanistic progressivism, since he carried the torch for their cause.

---

[38] Lutzer 120.

A Picture Book of John F. Kennedy, by David Adler   Gr. 1-4

Meet John F. Kennedy, by Nancy White (Step Up)   Gr. 1-4

John F. Kennedy: New Frontiersman, by Charles Graves (Garrard Discovery)   Gr. 1-5

Robert F. Kennedy: Man Who Dared..., by Charles Graves (Garr. Am. All)   Gr. 1-5

John F. Kennedy, by Lucy Frisbee (Childhood)   Gr. 1-6

Who Shot the President? by Judy Donnelly (Step into Reading 4)   Gr. 2-5

The Story of the Assassination of John F. Kennedy, by R. Conrad Stein (Corner...) Gr. 3-7

The Assassination of Robert F. Kennedy, by Andrew Santella (Cornerstones)   Gr. 3-7

John F. Kennedy, by Hal Marcovitz (Childhood of the Presidents)   Gr. 3-7

John F. Kennedy, by Paul Joseph (United States Presidents)   Gr. 3-7

> Books on the other presidents in this era can be found in the some of the in-print series listed here. There's no need for me to mention the specific titles on each.

When John & Caroline Lived in the White House, by Laurie Coulter   Gr. 4-8

John F. Kennedy: Thirty-fifth President of the United States (Enc. of Presidents)   Gr. 4-9
    by Zachary Kent

The Story of President Kennedy, by Iris Vinton (Signature)   Gr. 5-12

The Story of Jacqueline Kennedy, by Alida Malkus (Signature)   Gr. 5-12

I'm reminded of a great quote that you parents will appreciate!

The republic that sinks to sleep, trusting to constitutions and machinery, to politicians and to statesmen, for the safety of its liberties, never will have any. The people are to be waked to a new effort, just as the Church as to be regenerated in each age....Never, to our latest posterity, can we afford to do without prophets...to stir up the monotony of wealth, and reawake the people to the great ideas that are constantly fading out of their minds...

(Wendell Phillips, quoted by Douglas Miller in *Then was the Future* (New York: Knopf, 1973) 103-104.)

33⚬ The Civil Rights Movement

Guess what! That was *another* huge thing that happened during the 1950s and 60! There was a great struggle for the black folks in this country to have the full rights they deserved. This was called the *civil rights movement.* Maybe you did not know that earlier in this country, black people (some now like to be called African-Americans, since their earliest ancestors came from Africa) were treated very unfairly. They were told they must keep separate from white people. For example, they were required to use different drinking fountains, restaurants, theaters, schools, colleges, and to ride in the worst train cars and in the back seats of the bus. They were given only the very worst jobs and they weren't welcome in white neighborhoods.

By the 1950s and 60s, though, some black people (and some white) were fighting for this unfairness to end. One day, a black lady, Mrs. Rosa Parks, refused to sit in the back of the bus! The civil rights movement was on! Soon marches were organized, and "sit-ins" were held at segregated diners. ('Segregation' was the separating of people by color.) This really upset many of the white folks, and things sometimes got really rough, especially when the local police wanted segregation and didn't treat the marchers fairly. Often, the federal government had to send troops in to keep the peace when the freedoms of blacks had to be protected, such as when the first black students entered a college or school.

One of the leaders of the civil rights movement was a man named Martin Luther King, Jr. You may have heard of him because there is a national holiday in his honor now. He gave a famous speech at a big gathering in Washington, D.C. It was called, "I Have a Dream!"

But before you explore this topic, please know that though there were some very admirable people fighting for civil rights, not everyone who was involved had the right beliefs or the right attitudes. Yes, God did absolutely want black people to be treated fairly, as He wants *all* people to be treated with respect because He created and loves them all! The Lord must have been *very* disappointed that so many Christians did so little for so long while the blacks were suffering.[39] That means that even more of the folks who *were* working to make things fair weren't doing it according to God's ways (which would deal with the sin of unfairness and unlovingness and would teach people the correct reason for the value of human life, the source of civil rights, and the job of government in these issues). So...too many of the civil rights workers, though not all, wanted to cure the problems in a 'human progress' or 'socialist' way: through governmental power, by ignoring the spiritual part of the problem, and by rejecting God's family design, for example. Some even went to hurtful, revengeful extremes, while also encouraging black people to put away Christianity and become Muslims instead. All this means their 'cures' have made even bigger problems!

And this is a very sensitive issue, naturally. It is also a very political issue, and you'll find that most books on the topic come from some very strong political points of view. You're going to have to discern very carefully when borrowing books from your library. But what I think is

---

[39] On the other hand, some of the earliest folks to fight against the former slavery of blacks *were* strong Christians! They often risked a great deal to protect black slaves, such as on the Underground Railroad.

important to remember is that the Lord wants His people, His church (the general body of believers) to be the most caring, helpful, sacrificial, truth-oriented people on earth. To me, that means that Christians should be among the first to speak up about unfair treatment of others. And we also should be the first to offer God-honoring solutions, not 'human progress' solutions.

As with all heated situations, it's best for us not to assume we understand it all, because it is hard for those who haven't experienced unfairness to know what it's really like. Instead, let's ask the Lord for *His* view of the situation. Only He holds the key to real human worth, justice, and freedom.

Let's now meet some of the leaders of the civil rights movement, and you can see those who really sought the Lord's values and those who didn't. You can also see how the church responded.

☞ *Warning! Some of these books are relevant, but not recommended, as is the case in other sections of this guide as well. The philosophical and spiritual bases for some are very unbiblical. This does not undermine the legitimate concerns of the civil rights movement or racial equality—which is a given—but only warns that some authors have a stridently militant and anti-Judeo-Christian*

Parents, if you're following along: *Basic History of the United States–Volume 5*, by Clarence Carson, pp. 234-241.

view. Indeed, some will be pro-Muslim since many blacks, especially black separatists, have found a religious home there. Others see government as the issuer of rights and the righter of wrongs, rather than focusing on the need to change sinful attitudes in individuals. Still others feel an all-too-common, modern 'tribalism,' which emphasizes differences; these folks have rejected the goal of unity in Christlikeness—which transcends race and gender. Don't forget! Wrongs have been grievously suffered by slaves, so repentance and forgiveness are key. Parents, you must preview.

Picture Book of Martin Luther King, Jr., by David Adler	Gr. K-3
Picture Book of Rosa Parks, by David Adler	Gr. K-3
Meet Martin Luther King, Jr., by James DeKay (StepUp Books)	Gr. K-3
Martin Luther King [Jr., one citation includes] and the March on Washington by Frances Ruffin (All Aboard Reading 2)	Gr. 1-3
Young Martin Luther King, Jr.: I Have a Dream, by J. Mattern (Troll First-Start)	Gr. 1-3
Young Rosa Parks: Civil Rights Heroine, by Anne Benjamin (Troll First-Start)	Gr. 1-3
Cracking the Wall: Struggles of the Little Rock Nine (On My Own), by E. Lucas Tells of the nine black students who first attended an all-white high school.	Gr. 1-4
Happy Birthday, Martin Luther King, by Jean Marzollo	Gr. 1-4

I am Rosa Parks, by Rosa Parks & Jim Haskins (Puffin Easy to Read)   Gr. 1-4

If a Bus Could Talk: The Story of Rosa Parks, by Faith Ringgold   Gr. 1-4

My Dream of Martin Luther King, by Faith Ringgold   Gr. 1-4
    Girl has dream about life of King.

Story of Ruby Bridges, by Robert Coles   Gr. 1-4
    Story of six-year-old black girl who is the first to enter a formerly segregated school.

Rosa Parks, by Eloise Greenfield (Crowell Biography)   Gr. 1-5

Martin's Big Words: The Life of Dr. Martin Luther King, Jr., by D. Rappaport   Gr. 1-5

Martin Luther King, Jr., by Dharathula Millender (Childhood)   Gr. 1-6

Rosa Parks: Young Rebel, by Kathleen Kudlinski (Childhood)   Gr. 1-6
    This is a new addition to the series.

Rosa Parks, by Keith Brandt (Troll Easy Biographies)   Gr. 2-5

North Star Shining, by Hildegarde Swift   Gr. 2-12
    Poetic history of blacks in America for all ages, really.

Rosa Parks, by Eloise Greenfield (Trophy Chapter Books)   Gr. 3-7
    I've not seen this, and am not sure of the age recommendation.

If You Lived at the Time of Martin Luther King, by Ellen Levine   Gr. 3-7

Hero Tales—Vol. II, by Dave & Neta Jackson, pp. 128-139   Gr. 3-7
    Tells of John Perkins, a black Christian working in the South during the 1960s.

The Story of the Montgomery Bus Boycott, by R. Conrad Stein (Cornerstones)   Gr. 3-8

The Assassination of Martin Luther King, Jr., by R. Conrad Stein (Cornerstones)   Gr. 3-8

Civil Rights Marches, by Linda & Charles George (Cornerstones)   Gr. 3-8

The Freedom Riders, by Deborah Kent (Cornerstones)   Gr. 3-8

Malcolm X, Jack Slater (Cornerstones)   Gr. 3-8

Martin Luther King, Jr.: Man of Peace, by L. Patterson (Garr. Americans All)   Gr. 3-8

Coretta Scott King, by Lillie Patterson (Garrard Americans All)   Gr. 3-8

Whitney Young, Jr.: Crusader for Equality, by Peggy Mann (Garr. Am. All)   Gr. 3-8

Malcolm X: Black and Proud, by Florence White (Garr. Americans All)   Gr. 3-8

Don't Ride the Bus on Monday, by Louise Meriwether   Gr. 3-8
     Biography of Rosa Parks.

Black Rage: Malcolm X, by David R. Collins (People in Focus)   Gr. 3-12
     I *think* this is the same Collins who wrote some of the Sower series, so this might be a good choice if you're going to study Malcolm X, who became a strident, Muslim, black separatist.

Time of Trial, Time of Hope, by Milton Meltzer   Gr. 5-12
     Shows life of black Americans between the world wars.

*Rosa Parks: My Story, by Rosa Parks   Gr. 5-12

Video/Film:

*Ruby Bridges, starring Penelope Ann Miller

Fiction/Historical Fiction:

New Boy in School, by May Justus   Gr. 2-6

Bright April, by Marguerite de Angeli   Gr. 2-8
     Delightful story of brave, wonderful black family in Philadelphia.

The Empty Schoolhouse, by Natalie Savage Carlson   Gr. 3-8
     Two girlfriends, one black and one white, face school desegregation.

Roosevelt Grady, by Louis Shotwell   Gr. 4-7

Mary Jane, by Dorothy Sterling   Gr. 4-12

34🐾 People...and Nature

Guess what! There was *another* movement that began during the 1960s. A book helped start it: *Silent Spring*, written by Rachel Carson in 1962. It warned people that nature was being harmed by chemicals. And this brings up another sticky situation!

You see, the Lord *did* tell people to take care of nature (though they haven't always done a good job). Why did He give the job to people? Because mankind is God's special creation and He has given us a lot of authority over the earth He has lovingly made.

But you can maybe guess that anyone who believes in evolution disagrees totally with what I just said. And that makes us look again at the 'slippery slope' of evolution, for though evolution *says* mankind is the greatest creature, it actually takes away mankind's specialness and authority because it says that mankind evolved just like birds and salamanders did, so people are 'equal' with birds and salamanders and moths and owls and toads.

Do you get the point here? Instead of being careful of the environment *because* mankind is the God-appointed caretaker of it, evolution has taught too many people to think that mankind is hogging it...when he's no more important than the other animals. In fact, evolution says that 'nature' is the force that is evolving us, so it is like their god. That means that some folks who believe in evolution aren't just taking care of nature, they're worshiping it as their Maker!

Now, I don't know what Mrs. Carson's view was, but I know that nature is really God's creation. I like to think of it as the 'clothes' He wears. Because He is spirit, we can't see Him with our eyes; but in nature, He shows us some of His beauty, intelligence, creativity, strength, and awesomeness!

Rachel Carson: Friend of the Earth, by Francene Sabin (Troll Easy Bio)　　　Gr. 1-4

Rachel Carson: Who Loved the Sea, by Jean Lee Latham (Garrard Discovery)　　　Gr. 1-5

Listening to Crickets: A Story about Rachel Carson, by C. Ransom (Creat. Minds) Gr. 2-7

Rachel Carson and the Environmental Movement, by Leila Foster (Cornerstones)　Gr. 3-8

Rachel Carson, by Kathleen Kudlinski (Women of Our Time)　　　Gr. 3-9

35ঌ From the 1970s...to Today!

Well, we must close this guide fairly quickly, so I'll just list some key people and events of the last thirty years. You might want to take special note of Mr. Ronald Reagan who did some things that really helped America. There was also the Gulf War, as well as other

Parents, if you're following along: *Basic History of the United States–Vol. 5*, by Clarence Carson, pp. 289-end, and, *Basic History of the United States–Vol. 6*, by Clarence Carson (whole book).

presidents, the fall of communism, the September 11, 2001 attacks, and many heroes of faith, business, and science. Your parents will help you know how to spend your time exploring this era. We'll talk about one final issue of this era, a deep one, in the next section.

Frankie Wonders...What Happened Today, by Yvonne Conte　　　Gr. K-2
　　　Like many of the other books listed in this section, I've not seen this simple explanation of the September 11, 2001 terrorist attacks.

Richard Nixon, by Helen Olds (See & Read)   Gr. 1-3

Gerald Ford, by Charles Mercer (See & Read)   Gr. 1-3

Jimmy Carter, by Charles Mercer (See & Read)   Gr. 1-3

*Fireboat, by Maira Kalman   Gr. 1-3
    Relates the events of the September 11th tragedies (as well as a little New York City
    history) and the true role of a rescue fireboat.

*September 11, 2001, by Nancy Poffenberger   Gr. 1-4

Sandra Day O'Connor, by Carol Greene   Gr. 1-5
    Life of first female U.S. Supreme Court justice.

*Several in the *Young Reader's Christian Library* series   Gr. 1-5
    Billy Graham; Luis Palau

*Ronald Reagan, by Montrew Dunham (Childhood)   Gr. 1-6

The Story of the Persian Gulf War, by Leila Foster (Cornerstones)   Gr. 2-7

*The Fall of the Soviet Union, by Miles Harvey (Cornerstones)   Gr. 3-7

The Story of Watergate, by Jim Hargrove (Cornerstones)   Gr. 3-7

The Iran Hostage Crisis, by R. Conrad Stein (Cornerstones)   Gr. 3-7

*Meet great Christians in the *Hero Tales* series by Dave & Neta Jackson   Gr. 3-7
    For example: Jim Elliot, Brother Andrew, Billy Graham, Betty Greene, Clarence Jones,
    Luis Palau, Gordon McLean, Ricky & Sherialyn Byrdsong, Ben Carson, Joy Ridderhof,
    Tom White.

*Operation Rawhide, by Paul Thomsen (Creation Adventure Series)   Gr. 3-8
    A Christian book about Reagan's attempted assassination ordeal.

*Ronald Reagan, by T. Orr (Childhoods of the Presidents)   Gr. 3-8

*Ronald W. Reagan: Our Fortieth President, by Cynthia Klingel (Our Presidents) Gr. 3-9

*James Earl Carter: Our 39th President, by Lori Hobkirk (Our Presidents) Gr. 3-9

> I've given samples of the various series on the presidents. There's no need to list each title for each president. Just see what's at your library, but beware the political view!

Ronald Reagan, by Paul Joseph (United States Presidents)	Gr. 3-9
Jimmy Carter, by Paul Joseph (United States Presidents)	Gr. 3-9
Ronald Reagan: Fortieth President, by Zachary Kent (Encyclopedia of Pres.)	Gr. 3-9
Saddam Hussein, by Paul Deegan	Gr. 4-8
*Saddam Hussein, by Charles Shields (Major World Leaders)	Gr. 4-10
The Gulf Crisis, by Michael Evans Tells of the Iraq-Iran War, and related conflicts.	Gr. 4-10
*Several in the Christian Heroes, Then and Now series Such as Nate Saint, etc.	Gr. 4-10

*Several in the Heroes of the Faith series:
    Billy Graham, Francis and Edith Schaeffer, Jim Elliot, Luis Palau, Peter and Catherine
    Marshall, etc. (Various authors.)
	Gr. 5-12

Fiction/Historical Fiction:

*Books in the Trailblazers series, by Dave & Neta Jackson Race for the Record (about Joy Ridderhof), The Fate of the Yellow Woodbee (about Nate Saint)	Gr. 3-9

☞ Dover publishes paper doll sets covering Ronald Reagan, George W. Bush, the Kennedys, and other presidents. They are titled: *Ronald Reagan and His Family Paper Dolls*, etc. They are all by Tom Tierney.

☞ There is a zany, wordless book, though with humor for older students, called *Good Dog, Millie*, by Andy Mayer. In it, Vice President Dan Quayle and President George Bush's dog, Millie, have fun while Bush is away!

36☙ Another Wrong Turn (Postmodernism)

Well, you know that during the 1950s and 1960s, there was a new 'toying' with truth. It was popular to believe that people could find truth in their own heads, their own hearts, and their

own experiences. Well, the next generation–the kids that came of age in the 1970s, 80s, and 90s–couldn't help but notice that if their parents' 'truth' was that fickle, then it wasn't really truth at all!

But instead of realizing that truth comes from God and is therefore true for all times and for all people, this next generation went even further the wrong way...just as their parents and grandparents had! You see, this new generation said there was no truth at all!

Well, you may think we're talking about a bunch of gobbledy-gook here, but this is huge-i-mundo, pal! Why? Because the sweet goodness

> *ThinkWrite 3: "The truth about loving the lovely truth!"*
>
> The Lord tells us (in II Timothy 2:10b-12) that we need to have a *love for the truth*. What do you think that means, and why would that be important?

of God–which is all wrapped up like a fantastic gift in His truths and in His laws–is the *only* thing that can make life be good, happy, decent, safe, and free. *Without that truth, we don't have anything!* (Do *ThinkWrite 3* as you complete this final section.)

How utterly aimless and hopeless it must be to live without truth. Well, actually, it sounds fun for a few minutes; hey, you could run your own show...just like I did when I ran away from home. You could decide to do whatever pleased you! You could say that everything you did was right for you. That way, if anything went wrong, you could blame it on someone else. Sounds rather fun...for a while.

But the thrill of being your own god wouldn't last for very long because you're *not* a god. You *don't know* what's best. Only what is *truly* right is going to be best. And only what is right and best is going to make you happy, believe it or not. Yes, God made us very special, but we're not God! We didn't make ourselves, we didn't make this world, and we don't know, by ourselves, how it all should work. We have to humble ourselves and learn from the Master Creator! Like me, you have to admit that you don't know it all...and that's the smartest thing you'll ever say! Happily, He loves to teach us!

Don't believe me?! Well think about it this way. If everyone gets to 'do their own thing,' what happens when that 'thing' hurts others? What then? You already know what it's like to play with people who are selfish, or who make up the rules of the game as they go along. It's awful! How would you like to live in a whole country like that?! You can ask the people of Germany and Russia; they've already lived through that with Hitler and Stalin. But sadly, America is heading toward this same way of thinking–that God doesn't have the right to guide everyone's thinking

Parents, there are some great things for you to read, if you're following along:

How Should We Then Live? by Francis Schaeffer
Ch. 11 to end of book
(Or Video Episodes IX & X)

Postmodern Times, by Gene Edward Veith, Jr.

History Through the Eyes of Faith
by Ronald Wells, Ch. 17

and behavior with His truth—even though that truth is the very thing (and the *only* thing) that brought such freedom and blessing to America! That's why you've learned American history, so you can know this awesome truth...and so you can share it with others!

This 'whatever-I-want' and 'whatever-I-feel' belief has a fancy name: *postmodernism*, but you don't need to remember that. You already know in your own heart how easy it is to think like that too, but you also know the truth! And you know which is better...in the long run! Yeah! And our country needs to learn that truth all over again! So how about speaking up?!

Really, many people are hungry for truth! You know they are finding disappointment in their *God*less beliefs. You know they can't find real solutions for real problems when they are not dealing with the spiritual heart of issues. They must have realized that in spite of all the people-can-do-anything-through-the-power-of-government programs and the we-can-fix-problems-ourselves movements, there are still deep problems in our country—broken families, need, and sadness.

But be encouraged! Think of what the Bible and history show us: *it's the work of God to change the hearts and thinking of mankind...to heal them of their wrongness and sin whenever they will turn to Him!* That is the flow of God in history, and when you're participating in God's work, you're in the strongest flow in the entire universe! I know that sounds big, but it *is* big!

> The epilogue of *History Through the Eyes of Faith* cites examples of individuals who made a difference!

This is the exciting adventure you're in when you're a child of God, when you take the time and trouble to learn the truth, when you live the truth by being generous, forgiving, hard-working, and honest, and when you care enough to bless people by sharing it with them! Wonderful!

When we're like a tree planted by rivers of water, when we put our roots down deep into His truth, when we turn our leaf-faces to His light...then we produce 'fruit' that helps our nation! Remember, we are not carrying the burden for this nation; only God can do that. But we do need to love and honor Him and love the truth, and then He works through us to make a difference! How thrilling!

Remember the oft-quoted verse:

> *If...My people who are called by My name will humble themselves and pray and turn from their wicked ways, then I will hear from heaven, and will forgive their sin, and will heal their land. (II Chron. 7:14)*

On we go in Him and through Him and by Him! Hooray!

APPENDIX 1: *ThinkWrite* Responses

Parents, you may want to prevent your students from seeing these pages until after they have completed their own responses, for I have here mentioned some of the key thoughts you will want to see your children discovering. If your children are too young to come to such conclusions on their own, these responses will help you understand the key points you're trying to communicate to them during your warm discussion times.

ThinkWrite 1: "What's the big deal?"

Though it may be hard, try your best to explain why it's so important that we know God created us and the whole world.

It is *impossible* to overstate the importance of understanding that God is the Creator of mankind and the entire world. My father likes to point out that God Himself emphasized His Creatorhood quite often throughout Scripture. That tells us a lot, so maybe you'd like to have your children find and memorize a few of the scads of verses that assert this truth! God knew that it undergirded all of our other thinking. Indeed! The One who has made us alive has the authority to tell us how best to live. That authority traces directly back to His Creatorhood. That's why evolution is so impactful. It not only says that people came from monkeys or primordial ooze, it says God did not create us, thus we can rule ourselves. How wrong, yet widely believed, that is!

But God wants us to understand that He created us for another reason, and what a loving reason it is (which is typical of our dear Lord!) He knows that our very value as human beings rests on the knowledge that He especially created us. We were not accidents, chemical reactions, or lucky mutations. We are the apple of His eye, made expressly in His very image! Without that basis for human worth, mankind can be seen as merely a blob of tissue, a highly-evolved animal, an impersonal biochemical machine, a tool of the state, a pariah, or whatever those in leadership decide. Human life is at the whim of the powerful when it is not solidly based on God's creation of it.

So the irony is that people thought they'd be more magnificent if they jettisoned God. In fact, they have utterly debased themselves, for God is the source of their life and worth.

ThinkWrite 2: "What do you make of it?!"

Why don't you pick one inventor and talk about something he/she made or discovered. But can you also dig a little deeper and find out what the person believed to be true about God and people? Then you can understand this person's life and work even better!

Because each child may select a different inventor or scientist, no 'Sample Response' can be given here. But do help your child realize that knowing what a person *did* is only a small part of understanding them, or their role in history. It's their *Big 2 Beliefs*–what they thought to be true about God and people–that really shaped their life, their achievements, and thus their impact on history. If there is any difficulty in locating this 'belief' information on your selected topic, don't despair. At least you've taken your child through the process of thinking about these deeper questions and seeking answers to them.

ThinkWrite 3: "The truth about loving the lovely truth!"

The Lord tells us (in II Timothy 2:10b-12) that we need to have a *love for the truth*. What do you think that means, and why would that be important?

Let's get one thing clear right off the bat! God doesn't just tell us the truth; He *IS* truth! (John 14:6) When we love truth, we're actually loving God Himself! And if we love truth it means that we love God's ways...and we admit that they are higher than our ways:

> *For {as} the heavens are higher than the earth, So are My ways higher than your ways And My thoughts than your thoughts. (Isaiah 55:9, NAS)*

Furthermore, if we love truth, we will seek it, and He promises we will find it:

> *Ask, and it will be given to you; seek, and you will find; knock, and it will be opened to you. (Matthew 7:7, NAS)*

Then, all the good things that flow out of truth will be in our lives! And that's good for us and all those around us!

I like how my friend, Gina Snyder, puts it. She says it's easy to agree that some idea is true. But we *love* it when we're willing to obey, whether or not that truth seems easy or fun.

The modern world tells us to 'find ourselves.' That's because they believe truth is *inside* us. But we know that God IS truth, so what we need to do in all of our studies, including history, is to find God! Then we find the truth! And that truth is true for all people and for all times because God loves everyone equally and He is the same yesterday, today, and forever. God is never changing, so truth is never changing! (Hebrews 13:8) Fantastic! We can trust it fully!

Appendix 2: List of Resources Cited in this Guide

✦ <u>Not all of these sources are 'recommended.' Some are listed as only 'relevant.' Cautionary notes are in the main text of this guide.</u> Many I've never even seen, but because folks requested inclusion of a greater number of current books, I've listed more in-print books, even though I'm *not* familiar with them all. Parents, as always, monitor what your children are reading.

✦ The books marked with an asterisk (*) are those deemed to be in-print at this time. They do *not* denote preferred books.

✦ The size of this list proves that TruthQuest History does not require the use of any particular books, but only offers many suggestions (though a handful are highly recommended in the main text of this guide!)

Books:

19th Century Frontier Fort, by Scott Steedman (Inside Story)*	Gr. 4-8
19th Century Railway Station, by Fiona Macdonald (Inside Story)*	Gr. 4-12
A. P. Giannini, by Marie Hammontree (Childhood)	Gr. 1-6
Aaron Copland, by Mike Venezia (Getting to Know...)*	Gr. 1-5
Across America on an Emigrant Train, by Jim Murphy*	Gr. 4-12
Adam Bradford, Cowboy, by Don Russell (Garrard Americans All)	Gr. 1-4
Addie Across the Prairie, by Laurie Lawlor*	Gr. 3-8
Admiral Byrd of Antarctica, by Michael Gladych (Messner)	Gr. 5-12
Adventure in Courage, by Frances Cavanah	Gr. 3-8
Adventurous Spirit, by Ethlie Vare (Creative Minds)*	Gr. 2-6
After the War was Over, by Michael Foreman	Gr. 3-8
Ahoy! Ahoy! Are You There? by Robert Quackenbush	Gr. 2-6
Air Raid–Pearl Harbor! by Theodore Taylor*	Gr. 4-12
Alaska Gold Rush, by May McNeer (Landmark)	Gr. 3-10
Albert Einstein, by Marie Hammontree (Childhood)*	Gr. 1-6
Albert Einstein, by Fiona Macdonald (Giants of Science)*	Gr. 5-12
Albert Einstein, by Saviour Pirotta (Scientists Who Made History)*	Gr. 2-6
Albert Einstein and Relativity, by Steve Parker (Science Discoveries)*	Gr. 5-12
Alcott Family Christmas, by Alexandra Wallner*	Gr. 1-5
Aleck Bell, by Mabel Widdemer (Childhood)	Gr. 1-5
Alexander Fleming, by Steve Parker (Groundbreakers)*	Gr. 5-12
Alexander Fleming: Pioneer with Antibiotics, by Beverley Birch (Giants of Sci.)*	Gr. 5-12
Alexander Graham Bell, by Leonard Everett Fisher*	Gr. 5-10
Alexander Graham Bell, by Victoria Sherrow (On My Own)*	Gr. 1-4
Alexander Graham Bell and the Telephone, by Steve Parker (Science Discoveries)*	Gr. 4-8
Alexander Graham Bell: Man of Sound, by E. Montgomery (Garr. Discovery)	Gr. 1-4

Alice Ramsey's Grand Adventure, by Don Brown*	Gr. 1-4
All the Places to Love, by Patricia MacLachlan*	All ages
All Those Secrets of the World, by Jane Yolen	Gr. 1-3
All-of-a-Kind Family series, by Sydney Taylor*	Gr. 3-9
Along Came the Model T! by Robert Quackenbush	Gr. 2-6
Alvin C. York, by Ethel Weddle (Childhood)	Gr. 1-6
Amazing Voyage of the New Orleans, by Judith St. George	Gr. 3-8
Amelia and Eleanor Go for a Ride, by Pam Muñoz Ryan*	Gr. 1-5
Amelia Earhart, by Jane Howe (Childhood)*	Gr. 1-6
Amelia Earhart: Adventure in the Sky, by Francene Sabin (Troll)*	Gr. 1-4
Amelia Earhart: First Lady of the Air, by Jerry Seibert (Piper)	Gr. 2-7
Amelia Earhart: Pioneer in the Sky, by John Parlin (Garrard Discovery)	Gr. 1-5
Amelia's Flying Machine, by Barbara Hazen	Gr. 2-7
America, I Hear You: A Story about George Gershwin (Creative Minds)*	Gr. 2-8
America's First World War, by Henry Castor (Landmark)	Gr. 4-9
America's Own Mark Twain, by Jeanette Eaton	Gr. 5-12
American Adventure series, by Lee Roddy (there are three series by this name)	Gr. 3-9
American Indian, by Sydney Fletcher	Gr. 4-12
American Indian, by Oliver LaFarge	Gr. 5-12
American Indian Foods, by Jay Miller (True Books)*	Gr. 2-6
American Indian Games, by Jay Miller (True Books)*	Gr. 2-6
American Indian Story, by May McNeer	Gr. 4-12
Among the Plains Indians, by Lorenz Engel	Gr. 3-12
Amy Carmichael, by Janet & Geoff Benge (Christian Heroes)*	Gr. 4-10
Amy Carmichael, by Sam Wellman (Heroes of the Faith)	Gr. 5-12
Anasazi, by Leonard Everett Fisher*	Gr. 3-9
Ancient Skyscrapers, by Sherry Paul	Gr. 2-8
Andrew Carnegie, by Joanne Henry (Childhood)	Gr. 1-6
Andrew Carnegie, by Clara Ingram Judson	Gr. 3-10
Andrew Carnegie and the Age of Steel, by Katherine Shippen (Landmark)	Gr. 3-9
Andrew Carnegie: Giant of Industry, by Mary Malone (Garrard Americans All)	Gr. 1-5
Angel on the Square, by Gloria Whelan*	Gr. 4-10
Anna, Grandpa, and the Big Storm, by Carla Stevens	Gr. 2-6
Anne Frank, by J. Hurwitz*	Gr. 4-12
Anne Frank, by Vanora Leigh (Great Lives)	Gr. 2-8
Anne Morrow Lindbergh: Pilot and Poet, by Roxanne Chadwick (Carolrhoda)*	Gr. 3-6
Annie Oakley, by Ellen Wilson (Childhood)*	Gr. 1-5
Annie Oakley: The Shooting Star, by Charles Graves (Garrard Discovery)	Gr. 1-4
Annie Sullivan, by Mary Malone (See & Read)	Gr. K-3
Annushka's Voyage, by Bruce Degen*	Gr. 1-4
Apache, by Andrew Santella (True Books)*	Gr. 2-6
Apache Indians, by Sonia Bleeker	Gr. 3-12
Apache Indians, by Nicole Claro (Junior Library of American Indians)*	Gr. 4-12

Apollo 13: Space Race, by Gail Herman (All Aboard Reading)*	Gr. 1-4
Apprentice to Liberty, by Mary Fox	Gr. 4-12
Arapaho Indians, by V. Haluska (Junior Library of American Indians)*	Gr. 4-12
Arctic Explorer, by Jeri Ferris (Carolrhoda)*	Gr. 3-6
Around the World with Nellie Bly, by Emily Hahn (North Star)	Gr. 5-12
Art of American in the Early Twentieth Century, by Shirley Glubok	Gr. 5-12
Art of the Gilded Age, by Shirley Glubok	Gr. 5-12
Art of the Old West, by Shirley Glubok	Gr. 5-12
Art of the Plains Indians, by Shirley Glubok	Gr. 4-12
Art of the Southwest Indians, by Shirley Glubok	Gr. 4-12
Artist in Overalls: The Life of Grant Wood, by John Duggleby*	Gr. 5-10
Assassination of Martin Luther King, Jr., by R. Conrad Stein (Cornerstones)*	Gr. 3-8
Assassination of Robert F. Kennedy, by Andrew Santella (Cornerstones)*	Gr. 3-7
Augustus Helps the Army, by LeGrand	Gr. 2-6
Augustus Helps the Navy, by LeGrand	Gr. 2-6
Automobiles Past and Present, by Walter Buehr	Gr. 4-9
Avion My Uncle Flew, by Cyrus Fisher	Gr. 4-12
Babe Ruth, by Guernsey Van Riper, Jr. (Childhood)*	Gr. 1-6
Babe Ruth Ballet School, by Tim Shortt	Gr. 3-8
Babe Ruth: Home Run Hero, by Keith Brandt (Troll Easy Biographies)*	Gr. 1-5
Back of Beyond, by George Cory Franklin (American Heritage)	Gr. 4-10
Bandannas, Chaps, and Ten-Gallon Hats, by Bobbie Kalman*	Gr. 3-9
Barefoot in the Grass, by William H. Armstrong	Gr. 4-12
Baseball Saved Us, by Ken Mochizuki*	Gr. 2-5
Baseball's Best: Five True Stories, by A. Gutelle (Step Into Reading 4)*	Gr. 2-5
Basic History of the United States, Vol. 3-6, by Clarence Carson	Parents
Bat Masterson, by Dale White	Gr. 5-12
Battle for Iwo Jima, by Robert Leckie (Landmark)	Gr. 5-12
Battle for the Atlantic, by G.C. Skipper (World at War)	Gr. 3-7
Battle for the Atlantic, by Jay Williams (Landmark)	Gr. 3-10
Battle of Britain, by Quentin Reynolds (Landmark)	Gr. 3-10
Battle of Britain, by G.C. Skipper (World at War)	Gr. 3-7
Battle of Guadalcanal, by R. Conrad Stein (World at War)	Gr. 3-7
Battle of Okinawa, by R. Conrad Stein (World at War)	Gr. 3-7
Battle of the Bulge, by John Toland (Landmark)	Gr. 4-12
Bayou Suzette, by Lois Lenski	Gr. 3-9
Be Ever Hopeful, Hannalee, by Patricia Beatty*	Gr. 3-10
Beautiful Land, by Nancy Antle (Once Upon America)*	Gr. 3-7
Beckoning Hills, by Gage (Land of the Free)	Gr. 4-12
Benny's Flag, by P. Krasilovsky	Gr. 1-5
Berta Benz and the Motorwagen: The Story of the First Automobile Journey	Unknown
Best Friends, by Loretta Krupinski*	Gr. 1-5
Betsy-Tacy series, by Maud Lovelace*	Gr. 3-7

Better Mousetraps, by Nathan Aaseng*   Gr. 5-12

Between Two Worlds: A Story about Pearl Buck, by B. Mitchell (Creative Minds)* Gr. 2-6

Bicycle Man, by Allen Say*   Gr. 1-3

Big Balloon Race, by Eleanor Coerr (I Can Read)*   Gr. K-3

Big Book of Cowboys, by Sydney Fletcher   Gr. 1-4

Big Book of the Wild West, by Sydney Fletcher   Gr. 1-4

Big Bridge to Brooklyn, by Frances Browin (Aladdin's American Heritage)   Gr. 3-8

Big Fire in Baltimore, by Rosa Eichelberger   Gr. 3-9

Bigfoot Wallace and the Hickory Nut, by Helen Rushmore (Am. Folk Tales)   Gr. 1-4

Bijou, Bonbon & Beau: The Kittens Who Danced for Degas, by Joan Sweeney*   Gr. 1-4

Bill Pickett: Rodeoridin' Cowboy, by Andrea Pinkney*   Gr. 1-4

Billy Sunday, by Robert Allen (Sower series)*   Gr. 5-12

Billy Sunday, by Rachael Phillips (Heroes of the Faith)   Gr. 5-12

Black Cowboy, Wild Horses: A True Story, by Julius Lester*   Gr. 1-5

Black Rage: Malcolm X, by David R. Collins (People in Focus)   Gr. 3-12

Black Robe Peacemaker: Pierre de Smet, by J.G.E. Hopkins (Am. Background) Gr. 4-12

Black Tuesday, by Joann Grote (Amer. Adventure)*   Gr. 3-8

Black Whiteness: Admiral Byrd Alone in the Antarctic, by Robert Burleigh* Gr. 4-9

Blackfeet Indians, by Annemarie Hendrickson (Junior Library of...)   Gr. 4-12

Blizzard of 1896, by E.J. Bird*   Gr. 1-6

Blondin: Hero of Niagara, by Richard Boning (Incredible Series)   Gr. 1-6

Blowing Wand, by Ziegler (Land of the Free)   Gr. 4-12

Blue Willow, by Doris Gates*   Gr. 5-12

Bolek, by Antoni Gronowicz   Gr. 4-9

Bomba series, by Roy Rockwood   Gr. 4-10

Book of Cowboys, by Holling Clancy Holling   Gr. 3-9

Book of Indians, by Holling Clancy Holling   Gr. 4-12

Book of the West, by Charles Chilton   Gr. 4-10

Booker T. Washington, by Thomas Amper (On My Own)*   Gr. 1-3

Booker T. Washington, by Lillie Patterson (Garrard Discovery)*   Gr. 1-5

Booker T. Washington, by Augusta Stevenson (Childhood)   Gr. 1-6

Booker T. Washington, by William Wise (See & Read)   Gr. 1-3

Boom Town Boy, by Lois Lenski   Gr. 3-8

Boris, by Jaap Ter Haar   Gr. 3-10

Bracelet, by Yoshiko Uchida*   Gr. 1-4

Brave Balloonists: America's First Airmen, by Esther Douty (How They Lived) Gr. 3-8

Brave Cowboy, by Joan Walsh Anglund*   Gr. K-2

Brave the Wild Trail, by Milly Howard*   Gr. 3-8

Bravest Dog Ever, by Natalie Standiford (Step Into Reading 2)*   Gr. K-3

Bright April, by Marguerite de Angeli   Gr. 2-8

Bright Design, by Katherine Shippen   Gr. 5-12

Brighty of the Grand Canyon, by Marguerite Henry*   Gr. 4-10

Brilliant Streak, by K. Lasky*   Gr. 4-8

Brooklyn Bridge, by Lynn Curlee*	Gr. 3-7
Brooklyn Bridge, by Elizabeth Mann (Wonders of the World)*	Gr. 3-10
Broomtail: Brother of Lightning, by Miriam Mason	Gr. 1-5
Bruce Carries the Flag: They Came from Scotland, by Clara Ingram Judson	Gr. 4-10
Buckboard Stranger, by Stephen Meader	Gr. 5-12
Buckey O'Neill of Arizona, by Jeanette Eaton	Gr. 4-12
Buffalo Bill, by Frank Beals (American Adventure, older series)	Gr. 2-7
Buffalo Bill, by Ingri & Edgar Parin d'Aulaire*	Gr. 1-4
Buffalo Bill, by Mary Davidson (Garrard Discovery)	Gr. 1-4
Buffalo Bill, by Shannon Garst (Messner)	Gr. 4-12
Buffalo Bill, by Carl Green	Gr. 4-12
Buffalo Bill, by August Stevenson (Childhood)	Gr. 1-5
Buffalo Bill and the Pony Express, by Eleanor Coerr (History I Can Read)*	Gr. K-2
Buffalo Bill's Great Wild West Show, by Walter Havighurst (Landmark)	Gr. 3-9
Buffalo Boy, by Edna Walker Chandler	Gr. 2-6
Buffalo Harvest, by Glen Rounds	Gr. 3-8
Buffalo Hunt, by Russell Freedman*	Gr. 5-12
Build Your Own Wells Fargo Stagecoach, by Richard Mansir	Various
Building of the First Transcontinental Railroad, by Adele Nathan (Landmark)	Gr. 3-8
Bull's-Eye: A Photobiography of Annie Oakley, by Sue Macy*	Gr. 3-8
Butch Cassidy, by Carl Green	Gr. 4-12
Butterfly, by Patricia Polacco*	Gr. 1-4
Caddie Woodlawn, by Carol Ryrie Brink*	Gr. 3-9
Calamity Jane, by Doris Faber	Gr. 4-12
Caleb's Story, by Patricia MacLachlan*	Gr. 1-6
Call It Courage, by Armstrong Sperry*	Gr. 2-6
Call Me Ahnighito, by Pam Conrad*	Gr. 1-5
Calvin Coolidge, by Zachary Kent (Encyclopedia of Presidents)*	Gr. 5-12
Camel Express, by Olive Burt (Winston Adventure)	Gr. 3-9
Camels are Meaner than Mules, by Mary Calhoun	Gr. 2-6
Canadian Summer, by Hilda van Stockum	Gr. 5-12
Carl Sandburg (Poetry for Young People)	Gr. 3-12
Carl Sandburg, by Grace Melin (Childhood)	Gr. 1-6
Carl Sandburg: Voice of the People, by Ruth Franchere	Gr. 3-8
Carvers' George, by Florence Means	Gr. 3-7
Casey Over There, by Staton Rabin*	Gr. 1-3
Cave of Riches: The Story of the Dead Sea Scrolls, by Alan Honour	Gr. 4-9
Chariot in the Sky, by Bontemps (Land of the Free)	Gr. 4-12
Charles Babbage, by Neil Champion (Groundbreakers)*	Unknown
Charles Lindbergh: Hero Pilot, by David Collins (Garrard Discovery)*	Gr. 1-5
Charles Sheldon, by Ellen Caughey (Heroes of the Faith)	Gr. 5-12
Charlie Drives the Stage, by Eric Kimmel*	Gr. 1-6
Charlie Parker Played Be Bop, by Chris Raschka	Gr. 1-3
Cherokee Strip: The Race for Land, by Aileen Fisher (Aladdin's Am. Heritage)	Gr. 3-8

Cheyenne, by Andrew Santella (True Books)*   Gr. 2-6

Chief Joseph, by Olive Burt (Childhood)   Gr. 1-5

Chief Joseph, by M. Taylor (North American Indians of Achievement)*   Gr. 4-10

Chief Joseph: Guardian of His People, by Elizabeth Montgomery (Garr. Am. Ind.) Gr. 1-5

Chief Joseph of the Nez Percés, by Shannon Garst (Messner)   Gr. 4-12

Chief Red Horse Tells about Custer, edited by Jessie McGraw   Various

Chief Seattle: Great Statesman, by Elizabeth Montgomery (Garr. Am. Ind.)   Gr. 1-5

Child's History of Art, by V.M. Hillyer & E.G. Huey (OR, *Young People's....*)   Gr. 2-8

Children of the Dust Bowl, by Jerry Stanley*   Gr. 5-12

Children Who Stayed Alone, by Bonnie Worline (aka: *Sod House Adventure*)   Gr. 3-10

Children's War, by Theodore Taylor   Gr. 5-12

Christa McAuliffe: Pioneer Space Teacher, by Charlene Billings   Gr. 5-12

Christmas After All, by Kathryn Lasky (Dear America)*   Gr. 3-8

Christmas Tree in the White House, by Gary Hines*   Gr. 1-4

Christmas with Ida Early, by Robert Burch   Gr. 3-9

Christy, by Catherine Marshall*   Gr. 5-12

Chuck Yeager Breaks the Sound Barrier, by R. Conrad Stein (Cornerstones)*   Gr. 3-7

Chumash Indians, by Bill Lund (Native Peoples)*   Gr. 2-5

Chumash Indians, by Martin Schwabacher* (Junior Library of...)   Gr. 4-12

Circus Days Under the Big Top, by R. Glendinning (How They Lived)   Gr. 3-8

Cities: Through the Eyes of Artists, by Wendy & Jack Richards*   Various

Civil Rights Marches, by Linda & Charles George (Cornerstones)*   Gr. 3-8

Clara and the Bookwagon, by Nancy Levinson (I Can Read)*   Gr. K-2

Clear the Pasture, I'm Coming in for a Landing! by Robert Quackenbush   Gr. 1-5

Click! A Story about George Eastman, by Barbara Mitchell (Carolrhoda)*   Gr. 1-5

Cliff Dwellers of Walnut Canyon, by Carroll Fenton & Alice Epstein   Gr. 2-8

Climb a Lofty Ladder, by the Havighursts (Land of the Free)   Gr. 4-12

Clouds of Terror, by Catherine Welch (On My Own)*   Gr. 1-4

Clyde Tombaugh and the Search for Planet X, by M. Wetterer (On My Own)*   Gr. 1-4

Coast to Coast with Alice, by Patricia Hyatt*   Gr. 5-10

Cochise: Apache Chief, by M. Schwartz (North American Indians of Achieve...) Gr. 4-12

Cochise: Apache Warrior and Statesman, by Edgar Wyatt   Gr. 3-8

Cochise of Arizona, by Oliver LaFarge (Aladdin's American Heritage)   Gr. 3-9

Comanche, by David Appel   Gr. 4-12

Comanche and His Captain, by A.M. Anderson (American Adventure)   Gr. 2-8

Comanche Indians, by Martin Mooney (Junior Library of American Ind.)*   Gr. 4-12

Combat Nurses of World War II, by Wyatt Blassingame (Landmark)   Gr. 4-12

Coming to America, by Betsy Maestro*   Gr. 2-5

Commandoes of World War II, by Hodding Carter (Landmark)   Gr. 5-12

Conquest of the North and South Poles, by Russell Owen (Landmark)   Gr. 3-10

Contests at Cowlick, by Richard Kennedy   Gr. 1-4

Coolies, by Yin*   Gr. 2-6

Copper Kings of Montana, by Marian Place (Landmark)   Gr. 4-10

Copper Lady, by Alice Ross (On My Own)*   Gr. 1-4

Copper-Toed Boots, by Marguerite de Angeli*	Gr. 2-6
Coretta Scott King, by Lillie Patterson (Garrard Americans All)	Gr. 3-8
Corporal Keeperupper, by Katherine Milhous	Gr. 1-6
Corrie ten Boom, by Janet & Geoff Benge (Christian Heroes)*	Gr. 4-10
Corrie ten Boom, by Sam Wellman (Heroes of the Faith)*	Gr. 5-12
Cotton in My Sack, by Lois Lenski	Gr. 3-9
Cowboy, by David Murdoch (Eyewitness)*	Gr. 4-12
Cowboy ABC, by Chris Demarest*	Gr. 1-3
Cowboy Artist, by Shannon Garst (Messner)	Gr. 5-12
Cowboy Country, by Ann Scott*	Gr. K-3
Cowboy Jamboree, by Harold Felton	Various
Cowboy Sam series, by Edna Walker Chandler	Gr. 1-5
Cowboy Tommy's Roundup, by Sanford Tousey	Gr. 1-5
Cowboy Trade, by Glen Rounds*	Gr. 3-12
Cowboys, by Doug & Marie Gorsline*	Gr. 1-3
Cowboys, by Glen Rounds	Gr. 1-3
Cowboys and Cattle Drives, by Edith McCall (Frontiers of America)	Gr. 2-8
Cowboys and Cattle Trails, by Shannon Garst (American Adventure, older ser.)	Gr. 3-7
Cowboys, Cowboys, Cowboys, edited by Phyllis Fenner	Gr. 3-12
Cowboy's Handbook, by T. Cody*	Gr. 4-12
Cowboys of the Wild West, by Russell Freedman*	Gr. 5-12
Cowman's Kingdom, by Edmund Collier (Aladdin's American Heritage)	Gr. 4-9
Cracking the Wall: The Struggles of the Little Rock Nine (On My Own)*	Gr. 1-4
Crazy Horse, by Glen Dines (See & Read)	Gr. 1-3
Crazy Horse: Sioux Warrior, by Enid Meadowcroft (Garr. Am. Indian)	Gr. 1-5
Crow, by E. Tarbescu (Watts Library: Indians of the Americas)*	Gr. 4-12
Crow Indians, by Sonia Bleeker	Gr. 3-12
Custer: Fighter of the Plains, by Shannon Garst (Messner)	Gr. 5-12
Custer's Last Stand, by Quentin Reynolds (Landmark)	Gr. 3-10
D.L. Moody, by Bonnie Harvey (Heroes of the Faith)	Gr. 5-12
Dakota Dugout, by Ann Turner*	Gr. K-3
Dancing Cloud, by Mary & Conrad Buff	Gr. 2-8
Dandelions, by Eve Bunting*	Gr. 1-7
Danger at Dry Creek, by Irving Werstein	Gr. 4-10
Danger on the Flying Trapeze, by Dave & Neta Jackson (Trailblazer)*	Gr. 3-9
Dangerous Journey, by László Hámori	Gr. 4-12
Daniel's Duck, by Clyde Robert Bulla (I Can Read History)*	Gr. K-2
Daniel's Story, by Carol Matas*	Gr. 4-12
Day the Circus Came to Lone Tree, by Glen Rounds	Gr. 2-6
D-Day, by G.C. Skipper (World at War)	Gr. 3-7
Dead Sea Scrolls, by Ilene Cooper*	Gr. 4-8
Dear Levi: Letters from the Overland Trail, by Elvira Woodruff*	Gr. 1-7
Death of Hitler, by G.C. Skipper (World at War)	Gr. 3-7

Death of Mussolini, by G.C. Skipper (World at War)	Gr. 3-7
Deep Treasure, by Blackford (Land of the Free)	Gr. 4-12
Defeat of the Ghost Riders, by Dave & Neta Jackson (Trailblazer)*	Gr. 3-9
Desert Harvest, by Oakes (Land of the Free)	Gr. 4-12
Devil's Arithmetic, by Jane Yolen*	Gr. 5-12
Diary of Thomas A. Edison, by Thomas Edison, edited by K. McGuirk	Gr. 4-12
Disaster at Johnstown, by Hildegarde Dolson (Landmark)	Gr. 4-12
Disaster of the Hindenburg, by Shelly Tanaka (TimeQuest)	Gr. 4-12
Discover the Titanic, by Eric Kentley*	Gr. 4-12
Discovering Great Artists, by MaryAnn Kohl*	Various
Doctors Who Conquered Yellow Fever, by Ralph Hill (Landmark)	Gr. 3-9
Don't Ride the Bus on Monday, by Louise Meriwether	Gr. 3-8
Don't You Dare Shoot that Bear! by Robert Quackenbush	Gr. 1-6
Don't You Know There's a War On? by James Stevenson*	Gr. 1-3
Douglas MacArthur, by Laura Long (Childhood)	Gr. 1-6
Down the Colorado with Major Powell, by James Ullman (North Star)	Gr. 4-10
Down the Mississippi, by Clyde Robert Bulla	Gr. 1-6
Dr. Elizabeth, by Patricia Clapp	Gr. 4-12
Dr. Morton: Pioneer in the Use of Anesthesia, by Rachel Baker (Messner)	Gr. 5-12
Drake Drills for Oil, by Louis Wolfe	Gr. 2-6
Drawn by a China Moon, by Dave & Neta Jackson (Trailblazer)*	Gr. 3-9
Dreaming of America, by Eve Bunting*	Gr. 1-4
Driven from the Land, by Milton Meltzer (Great Journeys)*	Unknown
Duke Ellington, by Martha Schaaf (Childhood)	Gr. 1-6
Duke Ellington, by Mike Venezia (Getting to Know...)*	Gr. 1-4
Duke Ellington: King of Jazz, by Elizabeth Montgomery (Garr. Am. All)	Gr. 2-8
Duke Ellington: The Piano Prince and His Orchestra, by Andrea Pinkney*	Gr. 1-4
Dust Bowl, by John Farris (World Disasters)	Gr. 5-12
Dust Bowl, by Patricia Lauber	Gr. 6-12
Dust for Dinner, by Ann Turner (History I Can Read)*	Gr. K-3
Dwight D. Eisenhower, by Wilma Hudson (Childhood)	Gr. 1-6
Dwight D. Eisenhower, by Malcolm Moos (Landmark)	Gr. 5-12
Dwight David Eisenhower, by Red Reeder (Garrard Discovery)	Gr. 1-5
Early Days of Automobiles, by Elizabeth Janeway (Landmark)	Gr. 3-10
Early Loggers and the Sawmill, by Adams	Gr. 4-12
Earthquake! by Kathleen Kudlinski (Once Upon America)*	Gr. 3-8
Easter Fires, by Wilma Pitchford Hays	Gr. 1-5
Eddie Rickenbacker, by Cathrine Cleven (Childhood)	Gr. 1-6
Edith Cavell, by Adele de Leeuw (Spies of the World)	Gr. 3-10
Edith Cavell: Heroic Nurse, by Juliette Elkon (Messner)	Gr. 4-12
Edna St. Vincent Millay (Poetry for Young People)	Gr. 3-12
Education of Little Tree, by Forrest Carter*	Gr. 5-12
Edward Bok: Young Editor, by Elisabeth Myers (Childhood)	Gr. 1-6

Edward Hopper, by Mike Venezia (Getting to Know the World's Greatest...)   Gr. 1-5

Edward MacDowell and His Cabin In the Pines, by Opal Wheeler & S. Deucher   Gr. 1-6

Edwin Hubble: Discoverer of Galaxies, by Claire Datnow*   Gr. 5-9

Eleanor Roosevelt, by Ann Weil (Childhood)*   Gr. 1-6

Eleanor Roosevelt: First Lady of the World, by Charles Graves (Garr. Discovery)   Gr. 1-5

Elizabeth Blackwell, by Matthew Grant   Gr. 1-5

Elizabeth Blackwell, by Joanne Henry (Childhood)*   Gr. 1-5

Elizabeth Blackwell, by Jean Lee Latham (Garrard Discovery)   Gr. 1-4

Elizabeth Blackwell, by Francene Sabin (Troll)*   Gr. 1-3

Elizabeth Blackwell: First Woman Doctor, by Carol Greene (Rookie)   Gr. 1-3

Elsie Dinsmore series, by Martha Finley*   Gr. 4-12

Emily, by Michael Bedard*   Gr. 1-4

Emily Dickinson, edited by Frances Bolin (Poetry for Young People)*   Gr. 2-7

Emily Dickinson, by Carol Greene (Rookie)*   Gr. 1-5

Emily Dickinson's Letters to the World, by Jeanette Winter*   Gr. 2-5

Empty Schoolhouse, by Natalie Savage Carlson   Gr. 3-8

End O' Steel: Men and Railroads, by Glenn Dines   Gr. 4-9

Endless Steppe, by Esther Hautzig*   Gr. 5-12

Enrico Fermi: Atomic Pioneer, by Doris Faber   Gr. 3-8

Enrico Fermi: Father of Atomic Power, by Sam & Beryl Epstein (Garr. Am. All)   Gr. 2-7

Escape from Warsaw, by Ian Serraillier* (aka: *Silver Sword*)   Gr. 4-12

Eureka! It's an Airplane, by Jeanne Bendick*   Gr. 2-7

Eureka! It's an Automobile, by Jeanne Bendick*   Gr. 3-8

Exploring the Bismarck, by Robert Balland (TimeQuest)*   Gr. 4-12

Exploring the Titanic, by Robert Ballard (Time Quest)   Gr. 3-12

F.W. Woolworth, by Elisabeth Myers (Childhood)   Gr. 1-6

Fall of Singapore, by R. Conrad Stein (World at War)   Gr. 3-7

Fall of the Fox: Rommel, by G.C. Skipper (World at War)   Gr. 3-7

Famous American Indians, by S. Carl Hirsch   Gr. 3-12

Famous Authors, by Ramon Coffmann   Gr. 5-12

Famous Indian Tribes, by William Moyers   Gr. 1-6

Famous Mathematicians, by Frances Stonaker   Gr. 3-10

Famous Pioneers, by Franklin Folsom   Gr. 4-12

Fanny Crosby, by Sandy Dengler   Gr. 4-12

Fanny Crosby, by Bernard Ruffin (Heroes of the Faith)   Gr. 5-12

Farm Summer 1942, by Donald Hall   Gr. 1-4

Fate of the Yellow Woodbee, by Dave & Neta Jackson (Trailblazers)*   Gr. 3-9

Fire in the Sky, by Candice Ransom (Carolrhoda)*   Gr. 3-7

Fireboat, by Maira Kalman*   Gr. 1-3

First Book of Cowboys, by Benjamin Brewster (First Bks)   Gr. 3-7

First Book of Pioneers, by Walter Havighurst (First Books)   Gr. 3-8

First Book of the Panama Canal, by Patricia Markun (First Books)   Gr. 3-8

First Book of World War II, by Louis Snyder (First Books)   Gr. 3-8

First Flight, by George Shea (I Can Read)*   Gr. 2-4

First on the Moon, by Barbara Hehner*	Gr. 4-9
First Steamboat Down the Mississippi, by George Richter*	Gr. 3-7
First Steamboat on the Mississippi, by Sterling North (North Star)	Gr. 5-12
First Transatlantic Cable, by Adele Gutman (Landmark)	Gr. 3-9
First Woman Doctor, by Rachel Baker*	Gr. 5-10
First World War, edited by John Clare (Living History)	Gr. 4-9
Fish Fry, by Susan Saunders	Gr. 1-3
Flight, by Robert Burleigh*	Gr. 1-4
Flight Deck, by Robb White	Gr. 5-12
Flight of the Falcon, by Paul Thomsen (Creation Adventures)*	Gr. 3-10
Flight of the Fugitives, by Dave & Neta Jackson (Trailblazer)*	Gr. 3-7
Flight of the Union, by Tekla White (On My Own)*	Gr. 1-4
Fly High! The Story of Bessie Coleman, by Louise Borden*	Gr. 1-5
Flying Aces of World War I, by Gene Gurney (Landmark)	Gr. 4-12
Flying Tigers, by John Toland (Landmark)	Gr. 5-12
Foods the Indian Gave Us, by Wilma Pitchford Hays	Adult needed
Footprints of the Dragon, by Vanya Oakes (Land of the Free)	Gr. 4-12
Forty Acres and Maybe a Mule, by Harriette Robinet*	Gr. 5-10
Forty-Acre Swindle, by Dave & Neta Jackson (Trailblazer)*	Gr. 3-9
Frances Willard, by Miriam Mason (Childhood)	Gr. 1-6
Francis Parkman and the Plains Indians, edited by J. Shuter (Hist. Eyewitness)*	Gr. 5-12
Frankie Wonders...What Happened Today, by Yvonne Conte*	Gr. K-2
Franklin Delano Roosevelt, by William Wise (See & Read)	Gr. K-3
Franklin Roosevelt, by Ann Weil (Childhood)	Gr. 1-6
Frederic Remington, by Clyde Moore (Childhood)	Gr. 1-5
Frederic Remington, by Ernest Raboff (Art for Children)	Gr. 3-9
Frederic Remington: Artist on Horseback, by LaVere Anderson	Gr. 4-12
Freedom Riders, by Deborah Kent (Cornerstones)*	Gr. 3-8
Friday, the Arapaho Indian., by A.M. Anderson (Am. Adventure, older series)	Gr. 1-6
Friendly Gables, by Hilda van Stockum	Gr. 5-12
Frogmen, by Robb White	Gr. 5-12
From Anna, by Jean Little*	Gr. 5-12
From Casablanca to Berlin, by Bruce Bliven, Jr. (Landmark)	Gr. 5-12
From Kite to Kittyhawk, by Richard Bishop	Gr. 5-12
From Pearl Harbor to Okinawa, by Bruce Bliven, Jr. (Landmark)	Gr. 4-12
From Rags to Riches, by Nathan Aaseng*	Gr. 5-12
Frontier Home, by Raymond Bial*	Gr. 3-10
Frontier Leaders and Pioneers, by Dorothy Heiderstadt	Gr. 3-10
Frontier Surgeons, by Emily Crofford (Carolrhoda's Creative Minds)*	Gr. 1-6
Full Steam Ahead, by Rhoda Blumberg*	Gr. 5-12
Gallaudet: Friend of the Deaf, by Etta De Gering	Gr. 4-12
Gardener, by Sarah Stewart*	Gr. 1-4
Gasoline Buggy of the Duryea Brothers, by Robert Jackson	Gr. 3-12
Gay-Neck, by Dhan Mukerji*	Gr. 5-12

Gene Rhodes, Cowboy, by B. F. Day (Messner) — Gr. 4-12
General Crook: Indian Fighter, by Fairfax Downey — Gr. 5-12
George Carver, by Augusta Stevenson (Childhood) — Gr. 1-6
George Custer, by Augusta Stevenson (Childhood) — Gr. 1-6
George Dewey, by Laura Long (Childhood) — Gr. 1-6
George Dewey: Admiral of the Navy, by Fredrika Smith — Gr. 5-12
George Eastman, by Joanne Henry (Childhood) — Gr. 1-6
George Eastman, by Lynda Pflueger* — Unknown
George Gershwin, by Bernice Bryant (Childhood) — Gr. 1-6
George Gershwin, by Mike Venezia (Getting to Know...)* — Gr. 1-4
George M. Cohan, by Gertrude Winders (Childhood) — Gr. 1-6
George Pullman: Young Sleeping Car Builder, by Elisabeth Myers (Childhood) — Gr. 1-6
George W. Goethals: Panama Canal Engineer by Jean Latham (Garr. Discovery) — Gr. 1-5
George Washington Carver, by Janet & Geoff Benge (Christian Heroes)* — Gr. 4-10
George Washington Carver, by Andy Carter (On My Own)* — Gr. 1-3
George Washington Carver, by David Collins (Sower)* — Gr. 5-12
George Washington Carver, by S. & B. Epstein (Garr. Discovery) — Gr. 1-4
George Washington Carver, by Carol Greene (Rookie) — Gr. 1-5
George Washington Carver, by Peter Towne (Crowell Bio) — Gr. 1-3
George Washington Carver, by Sam Wellman (Heroes of the Faith)* — Gr. 5-12
George Washington Carver, by Ann White (Landmark) — Gr. 3-10
George Washington Carver, What do You See? by J. Benge (Another...)* — Gr. 3-4
George Westinghouse, by Montrew Dunham (Childhood) — Gr. 1-6
George Westinghouse: A Genius for Invention, by B. Ravage (Innovative Minds)* — Unknown
Georgia O'Keeffe, by Linda Lowery (On My Own)* — Gr. 1-5
Georgia O'Keeffe, by Mike Venezia (Getting to Know the World's Greatest...)* — Gr. 1-5
Georgia O'Keeffe: The 'Wideness and Wonder' of Her World, by B. Gherman* — Gr. 4-12
Gerald Ford, by Charles Mercer (See & Read) — Gr. 1-3
Geronimo, by M. Schwarz (North American Indians of Achievement)* — Gr. 4-12
Geronimo: Fighting Apache, by Ronald Syme — Gr. 2-8
Geronimo: The Last Apache War Chief, by Edgar Wyatt — Gr. 3-8
Geronimo: Wolf of the Warpath, by Ralph Moody (Landmark) — Gr. 4-10
Geronimo: Young Warrior, by George Stanley (NEW *Childhood of...* series)* — Gr. 2-6
Ghosts of the 20ᵗʰ Century, by Cheryl Harness* — Gr. 3-10
Gift of Magic Sleep, by Irwin Shapiro — Gr. 4-8
Gil Morgan, Oilman, by Ariane Dewey — Gr. 1-4
Girl Who Struck Out Babe Ruth, by Jean Patrick (On My Own)* — Gr. 2-5
Glenn Martin: Boy Conqueror of the Air, by R.W. Harley (Childhood) — Gr. 1-6
Glorious Flight, by Alice & Martin Provensen* — Gr. 1-4
Goering and the Luftwaffe, by G.C. Skipper (World at War) — Gr. 3-7
Going West, by Jean Van Leeuwen — Gr. 1-3
Gold Miners' Rescue, by Dave & Neta Jackson (Trailblazer)* — Gr. 3-9
Golden Age, by Martha Wickham (Odyssey)* — Gr. 2-6
Golden Age of Railroads, by Stewart Holbrook (Landmark) — Gr. 3-12

Good Dog, Millie, by Andy Mayer	All ages
Good Morning, Mr. President: A Story about Carl Sandburg (Carolrhoda)*	Gr. 2-6
Good-bye, Charles Lindbergh, by Louise Borden*	Gr. 1-5
Grandma Essie's Covered Wagon, by David Williams	Gr. 1-4
Grandma Moses, by Zibby O'Neal	Gr. 4-12
Grandma Moses: Favorite Painter, by Charles Graves (Garrard Am. All)	Gr. 2-7
Grandmother and the Runaway Shadow, by Liz Rosenberg*	Gr. 1-4
Grant Marsh, Steamboat Captain, by A.M. Anderson (American Adventures)	Gr. 2-6
Grant Wood, by Mike Venezia (Getting to Know the World's Greatest...)*	Gr. 1-5
Grasshopper Summer, by Ann Turner*	Gr. 2-8
Great American Fighter Pilots of World War II, by Robert Loomis (Landmark)	Gr. 4-12
Great Chicago Fire, by Mary Kay Phelan	Gr. 5-12
Great Depression, by Joann Grote (Amer. Adventure)*	Gr. 3-8
Great Escapes of World War II, by George Sullivan	Gr. 3-12
Great Horse-less Carriage Race, by Michael Dooling*	Gr. 2-6?
Great Men of Medicine, by Ruth Hume (Landmark)	Gr. 4-9
Great Migration, by Walter Dean Myers*	Gr. 1-6
Greatest Adventure, by F. Lane (Aladdin's American Heritage)	Gr. 4-8
Green Ginger Jar, by Clara Ingram Judson	Gr. 4-10
Green Grows the Prairie: Arkansas in the 1890s, by Charlie May Simon	Gr. 4-10
Guadalcanal Diary, Richard Tregaskis (Landmark)	Gr. 4-12
Guglielmo Marconi and Radio, by Steve Parker (Science Discoveries)*	Gr. 3-9
Guglielmo Marconi: Radio Pioneer, by Beverley Birch (Giants of Science)*	Gr. 5-12
Gulf Crisis, by Michael Evans	Gr. 4-10
Hah-Nee of the Cliff Dwellers, by Mary & Conrad Buff	Gr. 3-8
Hanna's Cold Winter, by Trish Marx	Gr. 2-6
Hannah, by Gloria Whelan*	Gr. 2-8
Hannah's Brave Year, by Rhoda Wooldridge	Gr. 3-12
Happy Birthday, Martin Luther King, by Jean Marzollo*	Gr. 1-4
Harvey S. Firestone, by Adrian Paradis (Childhood)	Gr. 1-6
Hats Off to John Stetson, by Mary Christian*	Gr. 3-10
Haven for the Brave, by Elizabeth Yates	Gr. 5-12
Hawaii: Gem of the Pacific, by Oscar Lewis (Landmark)	Gr. 3-9
He Heard America Sing, by C. Purdy (Messner)	Gr. 4-12
Heartland, by Diane Siebert*	All ages
Helen Keller, by Janet Benge (Another Great Achiever)*	Gr. 3-7
Helen Keller, by Margaret Davidson (Scholastic Biography)*	Gr. 1-6
Helen Keller, by Jane Sucliffe (Carolrhoda's On My Own)*	Gr. 1-3
Helen Keller, by Katharine Wilkie (Childhood)*	Gr. 1-5
Helen Keller and the Big Storm, by Pat Lakin (Ready to Read 2)*	Gr. 1-2
Helen Keller: Courage in the Dark, by J. Hurwitz (Step Into Reading 3)*	Gr. 1-4
Helen Keller: Toward the Light, by Stewart & Polly Graff (Garr. Disc.)*	Gr. 1-4
Helen Keller's Teacher, by Margaret Davidson*	Gr. 3-10

Henner's Lydia, by Marguerite de Angeli*	Gr. 3-9
Henry Ford, by Hazel Aird (Childhood)*	Gr. 1-6
Henry Ford, by Adrian Paradis (See & Read)	Gr. 1-4
Henry Ford: Maker of the Model T, by Miriam Gilbert (Piper)	Gr. 2-8
Her Majesty, Grace Jones, by Jane Langton	Gr. 3-9
Herbert Hoover, by Susan Clinton (Encyclopedia of Presidents)*	Gr. 5-12
Herbert Hoover, by Mildred Comfort (Childhood)	Gr. 1-6
Herbert Hoover, by David Holford (United States Presidents)*	Gr. 5-8
Here a Plant, There a Plant, by Robert Quackenbush	Gr. 2-6
Hero Over Here, by Kathleen Kudlinski (Once Upon America)*	Gr. 3-8
Hero Tales–Volumes I-IV, by Dave & Neta Jackson*	Gr. 3-7
Heroes in Plenty, by Theodora DuBois	Gr. 4-12
Heroes of the Faith series:*	Gr. 5-12
Billy Graham, Francis and Edith Schaeffer, Jim Elliot, Luis Palau, Mother Teresa, Peter and Catherine Marshall, etc. (Various authors)	
Heroic Pigeons, by Arch Whitehouse	Gr. 5-12
Heroine of the Titanic, by Joan Blos*	Gr. 2-8
Heroines of the Early West, by Nancy Wilson Ross (Landmark)	Gr. 4-12
Hidden Jewel, by Dave & Neta Jackson (Trailblazer)*	Gr. 3-9
High Flight, by Linda Granfield*	Gr. 2-8
High Wind for Kansas, by Mary Calhoun	Gr. 1-4
Higher on the Door, by James Stevenson	Gr. 1-4
Hindenburg Disaster, by R. Conrad Stein (Cornerstones)	Gr. 3-7
Hiroshima, by R. Conrad Stein (World at War)	Gr. 4-7
Hiroshima and Nagasaki, by Barbara Silberdick (Cornerstone)	Gr. 4-8
History Makers of the Scientific Revolution, by Nina Morgan (History Makers)*	Gr. 4-9
History Through the Eyes of Faith, by Ronald Wells	Parents
Holt and the Teddy Bear, by Jim McCafferty	Gr. 2-6
Home Front, by R. Conrad Stein (World at War)	Gr. 3-7
Home Run: The Story of Babe Ruth, by Robert Burleigh*	Gr. 2-6
Homestead of the Free: The Kansas Story, by Aileen Fisher (American Heritage)	Gr. 4-10
Homeward the Arrow's Flight, by Marion Marsh Brown	Gr. 5-12
Hoover Dam, by Elizabeth Mann (Wonders of the World)	Gr. 3-10
Hope and Have, by Oliver Optic*	Gr. 5-12
Horror Overhead, by Richard Boning (Incredible Series)	Gr. 3-6
Horsemen of the Western Plateaus, by Sonia Bleeker	Gr. 3-10
House of Sixty Fathers, by Meindert de Jong*	Gr. 3-10
How Did We Find Out about Nuclear Power? by Isaac Asimov	Gr. 5-12
How Should We Then Live? by Francis Schaeffer* (for parents)	Parents
Hundred Dresses, by Eleanor Estes*	Gr. 2-6
I am Rosa Parks, by Rosa Parks & Jim Haskins (Puffin Easy to Read)*	Gr. 1-4
I Gave Thomas Edison My Sandwich, by Floyd Moore	Gr. 5-8
I Have Heard of a Land, by Joyce Thomas*	Gr. 1-4
I Want to Be an Astronaut, by Byron Barton	Gr. PreK-K

Ida Early Comes over the Mountain. By Robert Burch*	Gr. 3-9
If a Bus Could Talk: The Story of Rosa Parks, by Faith Ringgold*	Gr. 1-4
If I Only Had a Horn: Young Louis Armstrong, by Roxanne Orgill*	Gr. 2-6
If You Lived 100 Years Ago, by Ann McGovern*	Gr. 3-8
If You Lived at the Time of Martin Luther King, by Ellen Levine*	Gr. 3-7
If You Lived at the Time of the Great San Francisco Earthquake, by Ellen Levine*	Gr. 1-6
If You Lived in the Alaska Territory, by Nancy Levinson*	Gr. 4-8
If You Lived with the Indians of the Northwest Coast, by Anne Kamma*	Gr. 2-7
If You Lived with the Sioux Indians, by Ann McGovern*	Gr. 1-4
If Your Name was Changed at Ellis Island, by Ellen Levine*	Gr. 3-8
If You're Not from the Prairie, by Dave Bouchard*	All ages
Ike & Mama and the Once-in-a-Lifetime Movie, by Carol Snyder	Gr. 2-6
Immigrant Kids, by Russell Freedman*	Gr. 4-12
In Grandma's Attic series, by Arleta Richardson*	Gr. 3-9
In My Mother's House, by Ann Nolan Clark	Gr. K-3
In Search of the Grand Canyon, by Mary Ann Fraser*	Gr. 5-8
In the Year of the Boar and Jackie Robinson, by Bette Bao Lord*	Gr. 3-10
Indian Annie: Kiowa Captive, by Alice Marriott	Gr. 4-12
Indian Boyhood, by Ohiyesa (about Charles Eastman)	Gr. 5-12
Indian Chiefs, by Russell Freedman*	Gr. 5-12
Indian Chiefs of the West, by Felix Sutton (Messner)	Gr. 4-12
Indian Crafts, by Keith Brandt*	Gr. 1-6
Indian Fighter: Nelson A. Miles, by Ralph Bailey	Gr. 5-12
Indian Fishing and Camping, Indian Hunting, Indians at Home, Indian Games and Crafts, Indian Sign Language, The Indian and the Buffalo etc., by Robert Hofsinde	Gr. 3-12
Indian Harvests, by William Grimm (Inappropriate drawing on cover.)	Gr. 4-12
Indian Hill, by Clyde Robert Bulla	Gr. 1-6
Indian Paint, by Glen Balch	Gr. 4-12
Indian Tribes of America, by Marion Gridley	Gr. 3-9
Indian Two Feet series, by Margaret Friskey	Gr. K-2
Indian Uprising, by George Cory Franklin	Gr. 4-9
Indian Wars and Warriors–West, by Paul Wellman (North Star)	Gr. 6-12
Indian Winter, by Russell Freedman	Gr. 5-12
Indians and Cowboys, by Sanford Tousey	Gr. 2-6
Indians, Indians, Indians, by Phyllis Fenner	Gr. 3-12
Indians Knew, by Tillie Pine	Various
Indians on Horseback, by Alice Marriott	Gr. 5-12
Indians: The First Americans, by Patricia Miles Martin	Gr. 1-5
Indians Who Lived in Texas, by Betty Warren	Gr. 3-8
Inside the Titanic, by Ken Marschall*	Gr. 4-10
Into the Air, by Robert Burleigh* (See note.)	Gr. 5-8
Into the Ice, by Lynn Curlee*	Gr. 2-6
Invasion of Poland, by G.C. Skipper (World at War)	Gr. 3-7
Invasion of Russia, by R. Conrad Stein (World at War)	Gr. 3-7

Invention, by Lionel Bender (Eyewitness)*	Gr. 5-12
Invincible Louisa, by Cornelia Meigs*	Gr. 4-12
Iran Hostage Crisis, by R. Conrad Stein (Cornerstones)	Gr. 3-7
Iron Horses, by Verla Kay*	Gr. 1-4
Ishi: The Last of His People, by David Petersen	Gr. 2-6
Island of the Blue Dolphins, by Scott O'Dell*	Gr. 4-12
J.C. Penney, by Wilma Hudson (Childhood)	Gr. 1-6
Jackie Robinson, by Margaret Davidson (Dell Yearling)*	Gr. 3-7
Jackie Robinson, by Herb Dunn (Childhood)	Gr. 1-6
Jackie Robinson, by Kenneth Rudeen (Trophy Chapter)*	Gr. 1-6
Jackie Robinson: A Life of Courage, by Keith Brandt (Troll Easy Biographies)*	Gr. 1-5
Jackie Robinson and the Story of All-Black Baseball, by J. O'Connor (Step...4)*	Gr. 2-4
Jackie Robinson Breaks the Color Line, by A. Santella (Cornerstones)*	Gr. 2-7
Jackson Pollock, by Mike Venezia (Getting to Know....)*	Gr. 1-6
Jacqueline Cochran, by Marquita Fisher (Garrard Americans All)	Gr. 1-8
Jacqueline of the Carrier Pigeons, by Augusta Seaman	Gr. 4-12
James Earl Carter: Our 39th President, by Lori Hobkirk (Our Presidents)*	Gr. 3-9
James J. Hill: Young Empire Builder, by Mildred Comfort (Childhood)	Gr. 1-6
Jazz Fly, by Matthew Gollub*	Gr. 1-4
Jesse: Man Who Outran..., by J. Owens & P. Neimark (aka: *Jesse Owens Story*)*	Gr. 5-12
Jesse Owens, by Mervyn Kaufman (Crowell Biography)	Gr. 1-5
Jesse Owens, by Jane Sutcliffe (On My Own)*	Gr. 1-4
Jesse Owens: Olympic Hero, by Francene Sabin (Troll Easy Biographies)*	Gr. 1-4
Jesse Owens: Olympic Star, by Patricia & Frederick McKissack (Great Af.-Am.)*	Gr. 1-5
Jim Thorpe, by Guernsey Van Riper, Jr. (Childhood)*	Gr. 1-6
Jim Thorpe: All-Around Athlete, by George Sullivan (Americans All)	Gr. 2-7
Jim Thorpe: Young Athlete, by Laurence Santrey (Troll)	Gr. 2-5
Jimmy Carter, by Paul Joseph (United States Presidents)*	Gr. 3-9
Jimmy Carter, by Charles Mercer (See & Read)	Gr. 1-3
Joe DiMaggio, by Herb Dunn (Childhood)	Gr. 1-6
John D. Rockefeller, by Elisabeth Myers (Childhood)	Gr. 1-6
John F. Kennedy, by Lucy Frisbee (Childhood)*	Gr. 1-6
John F. Kennedy, by Paul Joseph (United States Presidents)*	Gr. 3-7
John F. Kennedy, by Hal Marcovitz (Childhood of the Presidents)*	Gr. 3-7
John F. Kennedy and His Family Paper Dolls, by Tom Tierney	Various
John F. Kennedy and PT-109, by Richard Tregaskis (Landmark)	Gr. 5-12
John F. Kennedy: New Frontiersman, by Charles Graves (Garrard Discovery)	Gr. 1-5
John F. Kennedy: Thirty-fifth President..., by Z. Kent (Enc. of Presidents)*	Gr. 4-9
John Fitch: Steamboat Boy, by Augusta Stevenson (Childhood)	Gr. 1-6
John Glenn: Young Astronaut, by Michael Burgan (Childhood)*	Gr. 1-6
John Henry: An American Hero, by Ezra Jack Keats*	Gr. 1-5
John Henry and His Hammer, by Harold Felton	Gr. 3-10
John Henry: Steel-Drivin' Man, by Adele deLeeuw	Gr. 2-6

John J. Pershing, by Arch Whitehouse	Gr. 5-12
John Logie Baird, by Struan Reid (Groundbreakers)*	Gr. 5-12
John Muir, by Glen Dines (See & Read)	Gr. 1-3
John Muir, by Montrew Dunham (Childhood)	Gr. 1-5
John Muir, by Charles Graves (Crowell Biography)	Gr. 1-4
John Muir: Friend of Nature, by Margaret Goff Clark (Garrard Discovery)	Gr. 1-4
John Philip Sousa, by Ann Weil (Childhood)	Gr. 1-6
John Singer Sargent: The Life of an Artist, by Eshel Kreiter*	Unknown
John Wanamaker, by Olive Burt (Childhood)	Gr. 1-6
John Wesley Powell: Canyon's Conqueror, by Marian Place (Piper)	Gr. 3-8
Johnny Texas, by Carol Hoff	Gr. 2-9
Johnny Texas on the San Antonio Road, by Carol Hoff	Gr. 2-9
Journal of C.J. Jackson, a Dust Bowl Migrant, by W. Durbin (My Name is Am.)*	Gr. 3-9
Journal of Josh Loper, a Black Cowboy, by W. Myers (My Name is America)*	Gr. 3-9
Journal of Sean Sullivan, by William Durbin (My Name is America)*	Gr. 3-9
Journey to America, by Sonia Levitin*	Gr. 3-12
Journey to Ellis Island, by Carol Bierman *et al**	Gr. 3-8
Juanito Makes a Drum, by Edna Walker Chandler	Gr. 1-3
Judge Roy Bean, by Carl Green	Gr. 4-12
Judy's Journey, by Lois Lenski	Gr. 3-9
Jules Verne: His Life, by Catherine Owens Peare	Gr. 4-10
Julia Ward Howe, by Jean Wagoner (Childhood)	Gr. 1-6
Kaiulani, by Ellen White (Royal Diaries)*	Gr. 4-12
Kala's Pet, by Edna Chandler	Gr. 1-3
Karl Benz, by Brian Williams	Gr. 4-12
Kate Douglas Wiggin: Little Schoolteacher, by Miriam Mason (Childhood)	Gr. 1-6
Kate Shelley and the Midnight Express, by Margaret Wetterer (Carolrhoda)*	Gr. 1-5
Kate Shelley: Bound for Glory, by Robert San Souci*	Gr. 1-6
Katie Meets the Impressionists, by James Mayhew*	Gr. 1-4
Keeping Quilt, by Patricia Polacco*	Gr. 1-5
Kent State, by Arlene Erlbach (Cornerstones)* (Caution!)	Gr. 4-8
Kickin' Up Some Cowboy Fun, by Monica Hay Cook*	Various
KIDS Discover magazine: *Immigration* (April, 1998)	Gr. 2-8
King of Prussia and a Peanut Butter Sandwich, by Alice Fleming	Gr. 2-8
Kiowa Indians, by Terrance Dolan (Junior Library of American...)*	Gr. 4-12
Klara's New World, by Jeanette Winter*	Gr. 2-6
Klondike Cat, by Julie Lawson*	Gr. 2-5
Knots on a Counting Rope, by Bill Martin, Jr.	Gr. 1-4
Knute Rockne: Notre Dame's Football Great, by George Sullivan (Garr. Am. All)	Gr. 2-8
Knute Rockne: Young Athlete, by Guernsey Van Riper, Jr. (Childhood)*	Gr. 1-6
Korean War, by Tom McGovern*	Gr. 5-12
Kwakiutl Indians, by Scott Prentzas (Junior Library of American Indians)*	Gr. 4-12
Lady with the Lamp, by Lee Wyndham*	Gr. 3-10

Lakota Sioux, by Andrew Santella (True Books)*	Gr. 2-6
Land I Lost, by Huynh Quang Nhuong*	Gr. 3-7
Land of Gray Gold, by August Derleth (Aladdin's American Heritage)	Gr. 3-8
Langston Hughes, by Montrew Dunham (Childhood)*	Gr. 2-6
Language of Doves, by Rosemary Wells* (See note.)	Gr. 1-4
Lantern in Her Hand, by Bess Streeter Aldrich	Gr. 5-12
Last Hawaiian Queen, by Paula Guzzetti*	Gr. 3-6
Last Princess, by Fay Stanley*	Gr. 3-8
Last Queen of Hawaii, by Hazel Wilson	Gr. 5-12
Launch Day, by Peter Campbell*	Gr. 2-6
Laura Ingalls Wilder, by Gwenda Blair	Gr. 1-4
Laura Ingalls Wilder Country, by William Anderson	Gr. 4-12
Laura Ingalls Wilder Country Cookbook, by William Anderson	Gr. 4-12
Laura Ingalls Wilder Songbook, by Eugenia Garson*	Various
Lawless Land, by Mark Boesch (Winston Adventure)	Gr. 3-9
Leah's Pony, by Elizabeth Friedrich*	Gr. 1-3
Leaving Vietnam, by Sarah Kilborne (Ready to Read 3)	Gr. 1-3
Ledgerbook of Thomas Blue Eagle, by Gay Matthaei & Jewel Grutman*	Various
Lee DeForest, by Lavinia Dobler (Childhood)	Gr. 1-6
Legend of Jimmy Spoon, by Kristiana Gregory (Great Episodes)*	Gr. 4-10
Legend of Scarface, by Robert San Souci	Gr. 1-6
Legend of the Bluebonnets, by Tomie de Paola*	Gr. 1-3
Leonard Bernstein, by Molly Cone (Crowell Biography)	Gr. 1-3
Leonard Bernstein, by Marlene Toby (Rookie)	Gr. 1-5
Let the Circle Be Unbroken, by Mildred Taylor*	Gr. 4-12
Let's Be Indians, by Peggy Parish	Various
Let's Go to the Moon, by Janis Wheat (National Geographic)	Gr. 1-6
Level Land, by Dola DeJong	Gr. 3-8
Liberty, by Lynn Curlee*	Gr. 4-9
Life of the California Coast Nations, by Molly Aloian (Native Nations)*	Gr. 4-9
Liliuokalani: Queen of Hawaii, by Mary Malone (Garrard)	Gr. 1-5
Liliuokalani: Young Hawaiian Queen, by S. Newman (Childhood)	Gr. 1-6
Linda Richards: First Trained...., by David Collins (Garrard Discovery)	Gr. 1-4
Lion in the Box, by Marguerite de Angeli	Gr. 2-6
Listening to Crickets: A Story about Rachel Carson, by C. Ransom (Creat. Minds)*	Gr. 2-7
Little Bighorn, by Philip Steele (Great Battles and Sieges)	Gr. 5-10
Little Cedar's Tooth, by Edna Walker Chandler	Gr. 1-4
Little Chief, by Syd Hoff (I Can Read)*	Gr. K-2
Little Colonel, by Annie Fellows Johnston*	Gr. 4-10
Little Fishes, by Erik Haugaard	Gr. 5-12
Little House, by Virginia Burton*	Gr. 1-3
Little House on the Prairie series, by Laura Ingalls Wilder	Gr. 2-8
Little House Cookbook, by Barbara Walker*	Various
Little Indian Basket Maker, by Ann Nolan Clark	Gr. K-4
Little Indian Pottery Maker, by Ann Nolan Clark	Gr. K-2
Little Obie and the Flood, by Martin Waddell*	Gr. 2-6

Little Riders, by Margaretha Shemin   Gr. 4-12

Little Shepherds of Navajo Land, by Marian Schoolland   Gr. 3-12

Little Ships, by Louise Borden*   Gr. 2-6

Little Sioux Girl, by Lois Lenski   Gr. 2-9

Little Sure Shot: Story of Annie Oakley, by S. Spinner (Step Into Reading 3)*   Gr. 1-3

Little Women Book, by Lucille Penner*   Gr. 3-12

Little Yellow Fur, by Wilma Pitchford Hays   Gr. 1-4

Lives of Poor Boys Who Became Famous, by Sarah Bolton   Gr. 5-12

Lives of the Artists, by Kathleen Krull*   Gr. 3-7

Lives of the Writers, by Kathleen Krull*   Gr. 3-7

Locks, Crocs, and Skeeters, by Nancy Winslow Parker*   Gr. 1-5

Lone Hunter and the Cheyennes, by Donald Worcester   Gr. 4-10

Long Escape, by Irving Werstein   Gr. 4-12

Long Knife, by Glen Dines   Gr. 3-7

Long Trains Roll, by Stephen Meader   Gr. 5-12

Long Way to a New Land, by Joan Sandin (I Can Read)*   Gr. K-2

Long Way Westward, by Joan Sandin (I Can Read)*   Gr. K-2

Look Out! Here Comes the Stanley Steamer, by K.C. Tessendorf   Gr. 4-12

Looking at Pictures, by Joy Richardson*   Various

Lost Battalion, by Irving Werstein   Gr. 5-12

Lost Lakes, by Catherine Peare (Winston Adventure)   Gr. 3-9

Lost Ships of Guadalcanal, by Robert Ballard*   Gr. 5-12

Lost Star, by Patricia Lauber*   Gr. 5-12

Lost Violin: They Came from Bohemia, by Clara Ingram Judson   Gr. 4-10

Lotus Seed, by Sherry Garland*   Gr. 1-6

Lou Gehrig, by Guernsey Van Riper, Jr. (Childhood)*   Gr. 1-6

Lou Gehrig: Pride of the Yankees, by Keith Brandt (Troll Easy Biographies)*   Gr. 1-4

Lou Gehrig: The Luckiest Man, by David Adler*   Gr. 1-5

Louis Armstrong, by Dharathula Millender (Childhood)*   Gr. 1-6

Louis Armstrong: Ambassador Satchmo, by Jean Cornell (Garr. Am. All)   Gr. 2-8

Louis Armstrong: Jazz Musician, by P. McKissack (Great African Americans)*   Gr. 3-6

Louis Pasteur, by Beverley Birch & Fiona Macdonald*   Unknown

Louis Pasteur and Germs, by Steve Parker (Science Discoveries)*   Gr. 3-9

Louis Pasteur: Germ Killer, by John Mann   Gr. 2-5

Louis Pasteur: Young Scientist, by Francene Sabin (Troll Easy Biography)*   Gr. 1-3

Louisa Alcott, by Jean Wagoner (Childhood)*   Gr. 1-5

Louisa May Alcott, by Helen Papashvily (North Star)   Gr. 4-10

Louisa May Alcott, by Laurence Santrey (Troll Easy Biography)*   Gr. 1-3

Louisa May Alcott Cookbook, by Gretchen Anderson   Various

Louisa May Alcott: Girlhood Diary, by Alcott, edited by Cary Ryan*   Gr. 2-12

Louisa May Alcott: Her Life, by Catherine Owens Peare   Gr. 4-12

Lucy's Summer, by Donald Hall*   Gr. 1-4

Lumber Camp Library, by Natalie Kinsey-Warnock*   Gr. 2-6

Lumberjack, by William Kurelek   Gr. 4-12

Lumberjack, by Stephen Meader	Gr. 5-12
Lumberjacks of the North Woods, by Lillie Patterson (How They Lived)	Gr. 3-8
Luther Burbank: Boy Wizard, by Olive Burt (Childhood)	Gr. 1-6
Luther Burbank: Nature's Helper, by Lillian Bragdon (Makers of America)	Gr. 2-7
Luther Burbank: Partner of Nature, by Doris Faber (Garrard Discovery)	Gr. 1-5
MacArthur and the Philippines, by G.C. Skipper (World at War)	Gr. 3-7
Magical Melons, by Carol Ryrie Brink*	Gr. 3-9
Mahalia Jackson, by Montrew Dunham (Childhood)	Gr. 1-6
Mahalia Jackson, by Evelyn Witter (Sower series)*	Gr. 5-12
Mailing May, by Michael Tunnell*	Gr. 1-4
Making the Mississippi Shout, by Mary Calhoun	Gr. 4-10
Malcolm X, Jack Slater (Cornerstones)	Gr. 3-8
Malcolm X: Black and Proud, by Florence White (Garr. Americans All)	Gr. 3-8
Mama's Bank Account, by Kathryn Forbes*	Gr. 4-12
Man Who Painted Indians, by N. Plain*	Gr. 3-7
Mandie series, by Lois Gladys Leppard*	Gr. 2-8
Manhattan Project, by R. Conrad Stein (Cornerstones)	Gr. 3-8
Marconi's Battle for Radio, by Beverley Birch*	Gr. 1-5
Margaret Bourke-White, by Montrew Dunham (Childhood)	Gr. 1-6
Margaret Bourke-White, by Catherine Welch (Own My Own)*	Gr. 2-6
Maria Mitchell: Girl Astronomer, by Grace Melin (Childhood)	Gr. 1-6
Maria Mitchell: Stargazer, by Katharine Wilkie (Garrard Discovery)	Gr. 1-4
Maria's Comet, by Deborah Hopkinson*	Gr. 1-4
Marie Curie, by Edwina Conner (Great Lives)	Gr. 3-7
Marie Curie, by Leonard Everett Fisher	Gr. 5-10
Marie Curie, by Robin McKown	Gr. 2-8
Marie Curie and the Discovery of Radium, by Ann Steinke (Solutions)*	Gr. 3-9
Marie Curie and Radium, by Steve Parker (Science Discoveries)*	Gr. 4-8
Marie Curie: Brave Scientist, by Keith Brandt (Troll)*	Gr. 1-3
Marie Curie: Woman of Genius, by Adele de Leeuw	Gr. 3-12
Marie Curie's Search for Radium, by Beverley Birch*	Gr. 1-5
Marigold Garden, by Kate Greenaway*	Gr. 2-8
Mark T-W-A-I-N! by David Collins (Creative Minds)*	Gr. 3-7
Mark Twain, by Carol Greene (Rookie)*	Gr. 1-5
Mark Twain, by Miriam Mason (Childhood)*	Gr. 1-6
Mark Twain and the Queens of the Mississippi, by Cheryl Harness*	Gr. 1-6
Mark Twain and the River, by Sterling North (North Star)	Gr. 5-12
Mark Twain: His Life, by Catherine Owens Peare	Gr. 3-7
Mark Twain? What Kind of Name is That? by Robert Quackenbush	Gr. 2-7
Martin Luther King, by Frances Ruffin (All Aboard Reading 2)*	Gr. 1-3
Martin Luther King, Jr., by Dharathula Millender (Childhood)*	Gr. 1-6
Martin Luther King, Jr.: Man of Peace, by L. Patterson (Garr. Americans All)	Gr. 3-8
Martin's Big Words: The Life of Dr. Martin Luther King, Jr., by D. Rappaport*	Gr. 1-5

Marven of the Great North Woods, by Kathryn Lasky*	Gr. 1-5
Mary Cassatt, by Thomas Streissguth*	Gr. 5-10
Mary Cassatt, by Mike Venezia (Getting to Know the World's Greatest...)*	Gr. 1-5
Mary Jane, by Dorothy Sterling	Gr. 4-12
Mary Mapes Dodge: Jolly Girl, by Miriam Mason (Childhood)	Gr. 1-6
Mary McLeod Bethune, by Olive Burt (Childhood)	Gr. 1-5
Mary McLeod Bethune, by Eloise Greenfield (Crowell Biography)*	Gr. 1-5
Mary McLeod Bethune, by Ruby Radford (See & Read)	Gr. 1-4
Mary McLeod Bethune, by Emma Gelder Sterne	Gr. 5-12
Matthew A. Henson, by Charles Graves (See & Read)	Gr. K-2
Matthew Henson & Robert Peary, by Laurie Rozakis (Partners)	Gr. 2-5
Matthew Henson and the North Pole Expedition, by A. Gaines (Journey to Free...)*	Unknown
Matthew Henson: Arctic Hero, by Sheldon Ripley (Piper)	Gr. 3-8
Mayo Brothers, by Jane Goodsell (Crowell Biography)	Gr. 1-4
McBroom and the Big Wind, by Sid Fleischman	Gr. 1-5
Me and the Man on the Moon-eyed Horse, by Sid Fleischman	Gr. 2-6
Medal of Honor Heroes, by Colonel Red Reeder (Landmark)	Gr. 3-9
Medical Corps Heroes of World War II, by Wyatt Blassingame (Landmark)	Gr. 5-12
Meet John F. Kennedy, by Nancy White (Step Up)*	Gr. 1-4
Meet Kirsten, by Janet Shaw (American Girls)*	Gr. 1-6
Meet Martin Luther King, Jr., by James DeKay (StepUp Books)	Gr. K-3
Meet Molly series, by Valerie Tripp (American Girls)*	Gr. 2-7
Meet Samantha series, by Susan Adler (American Girls)*	Gr. 2-7
Meet the North American Indians, by Elizabeth Payne (Step-Up)	Gr. 1-5
Meet Theodore Roosevelt, by Ormonde de Kay (Step-Up Books)	Gr. 1-4
Men of Flight: The Conquest of the Air, by Charles Verral (Al.'s Am. Heritage)	Gr. 3-8
Men of Science, Men of God, by Henry Morris*	Gr. 5-12
Men on Iron Horses, by Edith McCall (Frontiers of America)	Gr. 2-7
Michael's Victory: They Came from Ireland, by Clara Ingram Judson	Gr. 4-10
Middle Sister, by Miriam Mason	Gr. 1-6
Midway, by Philip Sauvain (Great Battles and Sieges)	Gr. 4-12
Midway: Battle for the Pacific, by Edmund Castillo (Landmark)	Gr. 5-12
Mike Fink, by Steven Kellogg*	Gr. 1-4
Mike Fink: Best of the Keelboatmen, by Harold Felton	Gr. 5-12
Military History of the Korean War, by S.L.A. Marshall	Gr. 6-12
Military History of World War II series, by Trevor Dupuy (16 volumes)	Gr. 4-12
Miranda's Last Stand, by Gloria Whelan	Gr. 4-9
Mirette & Bellini Cross Niagara Falls, by Emily McCully*	Gr. 1-4
Missions Indians, by Sonia Bleeker	Gr. 4-12
Mississippi Steamboat Days, by James McCague (How They Lived)	Gr. 3-8
Mitchells, by Hilda van Stockum (aka: *Five for Victory*)	Gr. 5-12
Model T: How Henry Ford Built a Legend, by David Weitzman*	Gr. 3-8
Molly's Pilgrim, by Barbara Cohen*	Gr. 1-5

Moonwalk: First Trip to the Moon, by Judy Donnelly (Step Into Reading 4)*	Gr. 1-5
More than Anything Else, by Marie Bradby*	Gr. 1-4
Mosquitoes in the Big Ditch, by R. Burlingame (Winston Adventure)	Gr. 3-8
Mouse of Amherst, by Elizabeth Spires*	Gr. 3-6
Mr. Bell Invents the Telephone, by Katherine Shippen (Landmark)	Gr. 3-9
Mr. Penney, by Harry Albus	Gr. 4-10
Mr. Yowder and the Steamboat and others in the series, by Glen Rounds	Gr. 1-6
Mrs. Katz and Tush, by Patricia Polacco*	Gr. 1-4
Muir of the Mountains, by William Douglas (North Star)	Gr. 4-12
Mustang: Wild Spirit of the West, by Marguerite Henry*	Gr. 4-12
My Cowboy Book, by Bruce Grant	Gr. K-2
My Dream of Martin Luther King, by Faith Ringgold*	Gr. 1-4
My First Little House series, by Laura Ingalls Wilder (adapted versions)*	Gr. K-2
Sample titles: *Sugar Snow, Prairie Day, A Deer in the Wood, Going to Town, Farmer Boy Birthday, Winter on the Farm*, etc.	
My Name is Georgia, by Jeanette Winter*	Gr. 2-6
Mysterious Rays of Dr. Röntgen, by Beverly Gherman*	Gr. 3-8
Nat Love, Negro Cowboy, by Harold Felton	Gr. 3-7
Nations of the Northwest Coast, by Kathryn Smithyman (Native Nations)*	Gr. 4-9
Native American Doctor, by Jeri Ferris (Carolrhoda)*	Gr. 2-6
Navaho Land, by Solveig Russell	Gr. 2-6
Navajo, by Andrew Santella (True Books)*	Gr. 2-6
Navajo, by Nancy Bonvillain*	Gr. 5-12
Navajo: Herders, Weavers, and Silversmiths, by Sonia Bleeker	Gr. 3-10
Neil Armstrong, by Montrew Dunham (Childhood)*	Gr. 1-6
Nellie Bly: Reporter for the World, by C. Graves (Garr. Americans All)	Gr. 1-4
Nellie Bly's Monkey, by Joan Blos*	Gr. 2-5
New Boy in School, by May Justus	Gr. 2-6
New Coat for Anna, by Harriet Ziefert*	Gr. 1-4
New Hope, by Henri Sorensen*	Gr. 1-4
Nez Percé, by Alice Osinski (New True Book)*	Gr. 1-6
Nez Percé Indians, by Mark Rifkin (Junior Library of American Indians)*	Gr. 4-12
Nickels and Dimes, by Nina Brown Baker (biography of Woolworth)	Gr. 3-12
Night Crossing, by Karen Ackerman*	Gr. 1-5
Nils, by Ingri & Edgar Parin d'Aulaire	Gr. 1-4
Nisei Regiment, by R. Conrad Stein (World at War)	Gr. 3-7
No Hero for the Kaiser, by Rudolf Frank	Gr. 5-12
No Time for Glory: Stories of World War II, by Phyllis Fenner	Gr. 5-12
Norman Rockwell, by Mike Venezia (Getting to Know the World's...)*	Gr. 1-6
Norman Rockwell Storybook, by Jan Wahl	Gr. 1-6
Norman Rockwell: Storyteller with a Brush, by Beverly Gherman*	Gr. 4-12
North American Indian, by Doug Murdoch (DK)*	Gr. 4-12
North American Indians, by Marie Gorsline*	Gr. K-2
North American Indians, by Susan Purdy	Various

North of Danger, by Dale Fife	Gr. 3-12
North Star Shining, by Hildegarde Swift	Gr. 2-12
Number the Stars, by Lois Lowry*	Gr. 3-10
Oak's Long Shadow, by Burt (Land of the Free)	Gr. 4-12
Ol' Paul, the Mighty Logger, by Glen Rounds	Gr. 1-8
Old Bones the Wonder Horse, by Mildred Pace	Gr. 3-10
Old Chisholm Trail, by Rosalyn Schanzer*	Gr. 1-4
Old Yeller, by Fred Gipson*	Gr. 4-12
Omaha Indians, by M. Anderson (Watts Library: Indians of the Americas)*	Gr. 4-12
Omar Nelson Bradley, by Red Reeder	Gr. 2-8
On Board the Titanic, by S. Tanaka*	Gr. 4-9
Once Upon a Time in Chicago: The Story of Benny Goodman, by Jonah Winter*	Gr. 1-5
Once Upon the Little Big Horn, by Evelyn Lampman	Gr. 5-12
One Bad Thing about Father, by F.N. Monjo (History I Can Read)*	Gr. 1-5
One Bit of Land, by Edith Blackburn (Aladdin's American Heritage)	Gr. 3-8
One Giant Leap, by Mary Ann Fraser*	Gr. 1-6
One Giant Leap: The First Moon Landing, by Dana Rau (Smithsonian Odyssey)*	Gr. 3-8
One Giant Leap: The Story of Neil Armstrong, by Don Brown*	Gr. 1-4
One More River, by Lynne Reid Banks*	Gr. 4-12
Only Opal, by Opal Whiteley*	Gr. 1-3
Operation Rawhide, by Paul Thomsen (Creation Adventure Series)*	Gr. 3-8
Operation Escape, by Daniel Madden (about priest during WW2)	Gr. 5-12
Ordinary Genius: The Story of Albert Einstein, by S. McPherson (Carolrhoda)*	Gr. 3-6
Orphan Train series, by Joan Lowery Nixon*	Gr. 3-9
Orphan Train Rider: One Boy's True..., by Andrea Warren*	Gr. 5-12
Orphans' Journey series, by Arleta Richardson*	Gr. 3-9
Over the Waves, by Marianne Olson*	Gr. 4-12
P.T. Barnum: Circus Boy, by Augusta Stevenson (Childhood)	Gr. 1-6
P.T. Barnum: King of the Circus, by Lynn Groh (Garrard Discovery)	Gr. 1-5
Painter of the Wild West, by Robin McKown (Messner)	Gr. 5-12
Painting the Wind, by Michelle Dionetti*	Gr. 1-4
Panama Canal, by Bob Considine (Landmark)	Gr. 3-9
Panama Canal, by Elizabeth Mann (Wonders of the World)*	Gr. 3-10
Paperboy, by Mary Kay Kroeger*	Gr. 2-4
Passage to Freedom: The Sugihara Story, by Ken Mochizuki*	Gr. 2-5
Pasteur's Fight Against Microbes, by Beverley Birch*	Gr. 1-5
Pat and the Iron Horse, by Polly Angell (Aladdin's American Heritage)	Gr. 3-8
Patriot of the Underground, by Robin McKown	Gr. 5-12
Paul Bunyan, by Steven Kellogg*	Gr. K-4
Pearl Harbor, by Stephen Krensky (Ready-to-Read 3)*	Gr. 1-4
Pearl Harbor, by G.C. Skipper (World at War)	Gr. 3-7
Pearl S. Buck, by Elisabeth Myers (Childhood)	Gr. 1-5
Peary to the Pole, by Walter Lord	Gr. 4-10
Pecos Bill, by Brain Gleeson	Gr. 1-4

Pecos Bill, by Steven Kellogg	Gr. 1-4
Pecos Bill and Lightning, by Leigh Peck	Gr. 3-8
Pecos Bill Finds a Horse, by Kathy Darling	Gr. 1-4
Pecos Bill: Texas Cowpuncher, by Harold Felton	Gr. 4-12
Penny for a Hundred, by Ethel Pochocki*	Gr. 4-12
People on Long Ago Street, by Lillian Budd	Gr. 1-4
Peppe the Lamplighter, by Elisa Bartone*	Gr. 1-4
Peter Spier's Circus, by Peter Spier	Gr. K-4
Picnic in October, by Eve Bunting*	Gr. 1-4
Picture Book of Amelia Earhart, by David Adler*	Gr. K-2
Picture Book of George Washington Carver, by David Adler*	Gr. 1-3
Picture Book of Helen Keller, by David Adler*	Gr. 1-3
Picture Book of Jesse Owens, by David Adler*	Gr. 1-4
Picture Book of John F. Kennedy, by David Adler*	Gr. 1-4
Picture Book of Martin Luther King, Jr., by David Adler*	Gr. K-3
Picture Book of Rosa Parks, by David Adler*	Gr. K-3
Picture Book of Thomas Alva Edison, by David Adler*	Gr. K-3
Picture History of Great Inventors, by Gillian Clement	Gr. 2-7
Picture-Skin Story, by Alex Bealer III	Gr. 1-4
Pieces of Home, by Miska Miles	Gr. 1-5
Pilot Jack Knight, by A.M. Anderson (American Adventure)	Gr. 1-6
Pioneer Bear, by Joan Sandin (Step Into Reading 2)*	Gr. K-2
Pioneer Buckaroo, by Irene Estep	Gr. 2-8
Pioneer Engineer, by Irene Estep	Gr. 1-6
Pioneer Girl, by William Anderson*	Gr. 1-5
Pioneer Show Folk, by Edith McCall (Frontiers of America)	Gr. 3-7
Pioneer Sodbuster, by Irene Estep	Gr. 1-6
Pioneer Stories for Boys, by C. Richard Schaare	Gr. 3-7
Pioneer Tenderfoot, by Irene Estep	Gr. 2-8
Pioneer Traders, by Edith McCall (Frontiers of America)	Gr. 3-7
Pioneering on the Plains, by Edith McCall (Frontiers of America)	Gr. 3-7
Pioneers on Early Waterways, by Edith McCall (Frontiers of America)	Gr. 2-6
Place to Hide, by Jayne Pettit*	Gr. 3-10
Plains Indians, by Henry Pluckrose (Small World)*	Gr. K-3
Pocketful of Goobers, by Barbara Mitchell (Creative Minds)*	Gr. 2-8
Polar the Titanic Bear, by D. Spedden*	Gr. 1-4
Pollyanna, by Eleanor Porter*	Gr. 3-12
Polynesians Knew, by Tillie Pine	Gr. 2-8
Pony of the Sioux, by M.J. Pearson (Signal)	Gr. 3-9
Popcorn at the Palace, by Emily McCully*	Gr. 1-4
Portugee Phillips and the Fighting Sioux, by A.M. Anderson (Am. Adventures)	Gr. 2-8
Postmodern Times, by Gene Edward Veith, Jr.*	Parents
Prairie Boy's Summer, by William Kurelek*	Gr. 3-8

Prairie Boy's Winter, by William Kurelek*	Gr. 3-8
Prairie Primer A to Z, by Caroline Stutsman*	Gr. K-3
Prairie-Town Boy, by Carl Sandburg (Odyssey Classic)*	Gr. 5-12
Prisoners of War, by R. Conrad Stein (World at War)	Gr. 3-7
Pueblo Indians, by Sonia Bleeker	Gr. 3-12
Pueblo Indians, by Liza Burby (Junior Library of American Indians)*	Gr. 4-12
Pueblos, by Alice Flanagan (True Books)*	Gr. 2-6
Pushers, Spads, Jennies, and Jets, by Leonard Everett Fisher	Gr. K-3
Quanah Parker: Indian Warrior for Peace, by LaVere Anderson (Garr. Am. All)	Gr. 3-8
Queenie Peavy, by Robert Burch	Gr. 5-10
Quest for the Dead Sea Scrolls, by Geoffrey Palmer	Gr. 5-12
Quest of Louis Pasteur, by Patricia Lauber	Gr. 3-8
Race Against Death, by Seymour Reit	Gr. 3-12
Race for the Record, by Dave & Neta Jackson (Trailblazers)*	Gr. 3-9
Race to the South Pole, by Rupert Matthews (Great Journeys)	Gr. 3-8
Rachel Carson, by Kathleen Kudlinski (Women of Our Time)*	Gr. 3-9
Rachel Carson and the Environmental Movement, by Leila Foster (Cornerstones)*	Gr. 3-8
Rachel Carson: Friend of the Earth, by Francene Sabin (Troll Easy Bio)*	Gr. 1-4
Rachel Carson: Who Loved the Sea, by Jean Lee Latham (Garrard Discovery)	Gr. 1-5
Radar Commandos, by Bernard Glemser (Winston Adventure)	Gr. 3-8
Radio Boy, by Sharon Denslow*	Gr. 1-4
Raggin': A Story about Scott Joplin, by Barbara Mitchell (Creative Minds)*	Gr. 2-7
Railroad Book, by E. Boyd Smith*	Gr. 3-12
Railroads Yesterday and Today, by Walter Buehr	Gr. 4-9
Raoul Wallenberg: Missing Diplomat, by Anita Larsen (History's Mysteries)	Gr. 2-8
Rascal, by Sterling North*	Gr. 4-12
Real Book about Cowboys, by Michael Gorham (Real Books)	Gr. 3-8
Real Book about Indians, by Michael Gorham (Real Books)	Gr. 4-10
Real Book about the Texas Rangers, by Allyn Allen (Real Books)	Gr. 3-8
Real Book about the Wild West, by Adolph Regli (Real Books)	Gr. 3-8
Real Tom Thumb, by Helen Cross	Gr. 3-12
Rebecca of Sunnybrook Farm, by Kate Douglas Wiggin*	Gr. 4-12
Reconstruction, by Brendan January (Cornerstones)*	Gr. 3-7
Reconstruction, by Judith Peacock (Let Freedom Ring)*	Unknown
Red Cloud, by Shannon Garst	Various
Red Cloud: Sioux War Chief, by Virginia Voight (Garr. Am. Indian)	Gr. 1-5
Red Eagle, by Shannon Garst	Gr. 4-9
Red Horse Hill, by Stephen Meader	Gr. 5-12
Red Man in Art, by Rena Coen	Gr. 4-12
Renegade in the Hills, by Andy Thomson	Gr. 3-9
Resistance Movements, by R. Conrad Stein (World at War)	Gr. 3-7
Return to the Level Land, by Dola DeJong	Gr. 3-8
Richard Byrd, by Guernsey Van Riper, Jr. (Childhood)*	Gr. 1-6

Richard E. Byrd: Adventurer to the Poles, by Adele de Leeuw (Garr. Discovery)   Gr. 1-5
Richard Nixon, by Helen Olds (See & Read)   Gr. 1-3
Richthofen, the Red Baron, by Nicholas Fisk   Gr. 3-8
Ride a Northbound Horse, by Richard Wormser   Gr. 3-9
Ride on the Wind, by Alice Dalgliesh   Gr. 2-6
Rider in the Sky: How an American Cowboy Built England's First..., by Hulls*   Gr. 4-12
Ringling Brothers, by R. & S. Glendinning (Garrard Discovery)   Gr. 1-5
Ringling Brothers: Circus Boys, by Olive Burt (Childhood)   Gr. 1-6
Rise and Fall of Adolf Hitler, by William Shirer (Landmark)   Gr. 4-9
River-Boy: The Story of Mark Twain, by Isabel Proudfit (Messner)   Gr. 5-12
Road to Rome, by R. Conrad Stein (World at War)   Gr. 3-7
Roaring Twenties, by R. Conrad Stein (Cornerstones)*   Gr. 3-7
Robert E. Peary: North Pole Conqueror, by Erick Berry (Garrard Discovery)   Gr. 1-5
Robert F. Kennedy: Man Who Dared..., by Charles Graves (Garr. Am. All)   Gr. 1-5
Robert Frost (Poetry for Young People)   Gr. 3-12
Robert Frost, by Ellen Wilson (Childhood)   Gr. 1-6
Robert Frost: America's Poet, by Doris Faber   Gr. 2-7
Robert Goddard, by Clyde Moore (Childhood)   Gr. 1-6
Robert Goddard, by Lola Schaefer (Famous People in Transportation)*   Gr. 3-6
Robert Goddard: Space Pioneer, by Anne Dewey   Gr. 5-12
Robert Goddard: Space Pioneer, by Milton Lomask (Garrard Discovery)   Gr. 1-5
Robert Goddard: Trail Blazer to the Stars, by Charles Daugherty   Gr. 2-6
Robert Peary, by Electa Clark (Childhood)   Gr. 1-6
Rocket Man: The Story of Robert Goddard, by Thomas Streissguth*   Gr. 5-10
Rocket Pioneer, by Charles Coombs (American Adventure, older series)   Gr. 3-7
Rocket! How a Toy Launched the Space Age, by Richard Maurer   Gr. 5-12
Rocks in His Head, by Carol Hurst*   Gr. 1-4
Rocky Ridge series, by Roger McBride   Gr. 3-8
Roll of Thunder, Hear My Cry, by Mildred Taylor*   Gr. 4-12
Roller Skates, by Ruth Sawyer*   Gr. 3-10
Ronald Reagan, by Montrew Dunham (Childhood)*   Gr. 1-6
Ronald Reagan, by Paul Joseph (United States Presidents)*   Gr. 3-9
Ronald Reagan, by T. Orr (Childhoods of the Presidents)*   Gr. 3-8
Ronald Reagan and His Family Paper Dolls & others in series, by Tom Tierney*   Various
Ronald Reagan: Fortieth President, by Zachary Kent (Encyclopedia of Pres.)*   Gr. 3-9
Ronald W. Reagan: Our Fortieth President, by Cynthia Klingel (Our Presidents)*   Gr. 3-9
Rooftop Astronomer, by Stephanie McPherson (Creative Minds)*   Gr. 1-6
Roosevelt Grady, by Louis Shotwell   Gr. 4-7
Rosa Parks, by Keith Brandt (Troll Easy Biographies)*   Gr. 2-5
Rosa Parks, by Eloise Greenfield (Crowell Biography)   Gr. 1-5
Rosa Parks, by Eloise Greenfield (Trophy Chapter Books)*   Gr. 3-7
Rosa Parks: My Story, by Rosa Parks*   Gr. 5-12
Rosa Parks: Young Rebel, by Kathleen Kudlinski (Childhood)*   Gr. 1-6

Rose Blanche, by Roberto Innocenti*	Gr. 1-4
Rosenbergs, by Anita Larsen (History's Mysteries)	Gr. 3-9
Runaway Cattle, by Verne Davis	Gr. 2-6
Runaways, by Glenn Balch	Gr. 5-10
Rushmore, by Lynn Curlee*	Gr. 4-9
Ruth Law Thrills a Nation, by Don Brown*	Gr. K-3
Sadako and the Thousand Paper Cranes, by Eleanor Coerr*	Gr. 4-8
Saddam Hussein, by Paul Deegan	Gr. 4-8
Saddam Hussein, by Charles Shields (Major World Leaders)*	Gr. 4-10
Sadie Rose series, by Hilda Stahl*	Gr. 4-7
Sally Ride, Astronaut, by June Behrens	Gr. 3-8
Sam Ellis's Island, by Beatrice Siegel	Gr. 5-10
Samuel Clemens, by Charles Daughtery (Crowell Biography)	Gr. 1-4
Samuel Morris, by Terry Whalin (Heroes of the Faith)	Gr. 5-12
Sandra Day O'Connor, by Carol Greene	Gr. 1-5
Santee Sioux, by Terrance Dolan (Junior Library of American Indians)*	Gr. 4-12
Sarah, Plain and Tall, by Patricia MacLachlan*	Gr. 1-6
Satchmo's Blues, by Alan Schroeder	Gr. 1-4
Savage Sam, by Fred Gipson*	Gr. 4-12
Say it with Music: A Story about Irving Berlin, by T. Streissguth (Creative Minds)*	Gr. 2-6
Scientists Who Changed the World, by Philip Wilkinson *et al**	Gr. 3-7
Sea and Cedar: How the Northwest Coast Indians Lived, by Lois McConkey	Unknown
Sea Hunters, by Sonia Bleeker	Gr. 4-12
Sea Snake, by Stephen Meader	Gr. 5-12
Seabees of World War II, by Edmund Castillo (Landmark)	Gr. 5-12
Seasons Sewn, by Ann Paul*	Gr. 2-8
Seek the Dark Gold, by Lundy (Land of the Free)	Gr. 4-12
September 11, 2001, by Nancy Poffenberger*	Gr. 1-4
Sergeant York: Reluctant Hero, by Peter Andrews	Gr. 3-6
Seven Men Who Rule the World from the Grave, by Dave Breese*	Parents
Seward's Folly, by Melissa Whitcraft (Cornerstones "Second" series)*	Gr. 3-8
Shadow in the Pines, by Stephen Meader	Gr. 5-12
Sheriff at Waterstop, by Andy Thomson	Gr. 3-9
Shoes for Everyone, by Barbara Mitchell (Creative Minds)*	Gr. 2-6
Shooting for the Moon: Amazing Life and Times of Annie Oakley, by S. Krensky*	Gr. 1-4
Shoshone Indians, by Nathaniel Moss (Junior Library of American...)*	Gr. 4-12
Siege of Leningrad, by R. Conrad Stein (World at War)	Gr. 3-7
Sign of the Golden Fish, by Robinson (Land of the Free)	Gr. 4-12
Silence Over Dunkerque, by John Tunis	Gr. 4-12
Silver and Lead, by Ralph Moody	Gr. 3-8
Silver Days, by Sonia Levitin*	Gr. 3-12
Silver Sword, by Ian Serraillier (aka: *Escape from Warsaw**)	Gr. 4-12
Sing Down the Moon, by Scott O'Dell*	Gr. 4-12

Sing in the Dark, by Thomas (Land of the Free)	Gr. 4-12
Singing Tree, by Kate Seredy*	Gr. 4-12
Sinking of the Bismarck, by William Shirer (Landmark)	Gr. 4-12
Sioux Indians: Hunters and Warriors, by Sonia Bleeker	Gr. 4-10
Sitting Bull, by B. Bernotas (North American Indians of Achievement)*	Gr. 4-12
Sitting Bull, by Augusta Stevenson (Childhood)*	Gr. 1-6
Sitting Bull: Great Sioux Chief, by LaVere Anderson (Garr. Am. Indian)	Gr. 1-5
Sketchbook of Thomas Blue Eagle, by Gay Matthaei & Jewel Grutman*	Various
Sketches of America Past, by Eric Sloane*	Various
Skylab, by Dennis Fradin (New True Book)	Gr. 1-4
Skylark, by Patricia MacLachlan*	Gr. 1-6
Small War of Sergeant Donkey, by Maureen Daly	Gr. 3-10
Smithsonian Visual Timeline of Inventions, by Richard Platt*	Gr. 5-12
Snow Goose, by Paul Gallico*	Gr. 2-8
Snow Treasure, by Marie McSwigan*	Gr. 3-9
Snow Walker, by Margaret Wetterer (On My Own)*	Gr. 1-4
So Young to Die: Hannah Senesh, by Candice Ransom	Gr. 3-12
Sod-House Winter: They Came from Sweden, by Clara Ingram Judson	Gr. 4-10
Sod Houses on the Great Plains, by Glen Rounds	Gr. 1-6
Soldier Doctor, by Clara Ingram Judson	Gr. 3-12
Sole Survivor, by Ruthanne McCunn*	Gr. 5-12
Song of the Pines, by Walter & Marion Havighurst (Land of the Free)	Gr. 4-12
Song of the Trees, by Mildred Taylor	Gr. 2-6
Sons of the Big Muddy: The Dakota Territory in the 1880s, by W. Granberg	Gr. 4-10
Sound that Jazz Makes, by Carole Weatherford*	Gr. 1-4
Sounder, by William Armstrong*	Gr. 5-12
Space Exploration, by Michael George*	Gr. 2-12
Space Exploration, by Carole Stott (Eyewitness)*	Gr. 5-12
Space Shuttles, by Margaret Friskey (New True Books)	Gr. 1-5
Spanish-American War, by Mary Collins (Cornerstones)*	Gr. 2-7
Spanish-American War, by Edward Dolan*	Gr. 5-8
Spanish-American War, by Kathlyn & Marvin Gay*	Gr. 5-9
Spies with Wings, by Arch Whitehouse	Gr. 4-12
Stagecoach Days and Stagecoach Kings, by Virginia Voight (How They Lived)	Gr. 3-8
Stagecoach Sam, by Sanford Tousey	Gr. 1-5
Star of Danger, by Jane Levin	Gr. 4-12
Steamboat! by Judith Gilliland*	Gr. 1-5
Steamboats to the West, by Edith McCall (Frontiers of America)	Gr. 2-6
Steinmetz: Wizard of Light, by Anne Guy	Gr. 3-8
Stephen Foster, by Catherine Peare	Gr. 4-9
Stephen Foster and His Little Dog Tray, by Opal Wheeler	Gr. 2-6
Stephen Foster: Boy Minstrel, by Helen Higgins (Childhood)	Gr. 1-6
Stone Knife Boy, by Alida Malkus	Gr. 5-12

Story of a Main Street, by John Goodall*   Gr. PreK-8
Story of Admiral Peary at the North Pole, by Zachary Kent (Cornerstones)*   Gr. 2-8
Story of Amelia Earhart, by Adele de Leeuw (Signature)   Gr. 3-8
Story of Annie Oakley, by Edmund Collier (Signature)   Gr. 3-8
Story of Annie Sullivan, by Bernice Selden (Dell)*   Gr. 3-7
Story of Apollo 11: First Man on the Moon, by R. Conrad Stein (Cornerstone)* Gr. 3-8
Story of Atomic Energy, by Laura Fermi (Landmark)   Gr. 4-12
Story of Babe Ruth, by Lisa Eisenberg   Gr. 3-10
Story of Booker T. Washington, by P. & F. McKissack (Cornerstones)*   Gr. 3-8
Story of Buffalo Bill, by Edmund Collier (Signature)   Gr. 3-8
Story of Crazy Horse, by Enid Meadowcroft (Signature)   Gr. 3-8
Story of D-Day, by Bruce Bliven, Jr. (Landmark)   Gr. 4-10
Story of D-Day, by R. Conrad Stein (Cornerstones)   Gr. 2-8
Story of Dwight D. Eisenhower, by Arthur Beckhard (Signature)   Gr. 3-8
Story of Edith Cavell, by Iris Vinton (Signature)   Gr. 3-8
Story of Ellis Island, by R. Conrad Stein (Cornerstones)*   Gr. 2-7
Story of Flight, by Mary Settle (Step-Up Books)   Gr. 1-5
Story of General Custer, by Margaret Leighton (Signature)   Gr. 3-8
Story of George Washington Carver, by Arna Bontemps (Signature)   Gr. 3-8
Story of George Washington Carver, by Eva Moore (Scholastic)*   Gr. 1-6
Story of Geronimo, by Jim Kjelgaard (Signature)*   Gr. 3-9
Story of Geronimo, by Zachary Kent (Cornerstones)*   Gr. 3-8
Story of Helen Keller, by Lorena Hickok (Signature)*   Gr. 3-8
Story of Henry Ford and the Automobile, by Zachary Kent (Cornerstones)   Gr. 2-7
Story of Jacqueline Kennedy, by Alida Malkus (Signature)   Gr. 5-12
Story of Jonas Salk and the Discovery of the Polio Vaccine, by Z. Kent (Cornerstone) Gr. 3-7
Story of Louis Pasteur, by Alida Malkus (Signature)   Gr. 3-8
Story of Louisa May Alcott, by Joan Howard (Signature)   Gr. 3-8
Story of Madame Curie, by Alice Thorne (Signature)   Gr. 3-8
Story of Mark Twain, by Joan Howard (Signature)   Gr. 3-8
Story of Mary McLeod Bethune, by P. & F. McKissack (Cornerstones)*   Gr. 3-8
Story of Mount Rushmore, by Marilyn Prolman (Cornerstone)   Gr. 2-6
Story of Oklahoma, by Lon Tinkle (Landmark)   Gr. 3-10
Story of Painting for Young People, by the H.W. & Dora Janson   Various
Story of President Kennedy, by Iris Vinton (Signature)   Gr. 5-12
Story of Ruby Bridges, by Robert Coles*   Gr. 1-4
Story of Seward's Folly, by Susan Clinton (Cornerstones)   Gr. 2-6
Story of Stephen Foster, by Esther Douty (Signature)   Gr. 3-8
Story of Television, by Zachary Kent (Cornerstones)   Gr. 3-7
Story of the Assassination of John F. Kennedy, by R. Conrad Stein (Corner...) Gr. 3-7
Story of the Battle for Iwo Jima, by R. Conrad Stein (Cornerstones)   Gr. 2-8
Story of the Battle of the Bulge, by R. Conrad Stein (Cornerstones)   Gr. 3-8
Story of the Brooklyn Bridge, by Zachary Kent (Cornerstones)   Gr. 2-7
Story of the Challenger Disaster, by Zachary Kent (Cornerstones)   Gr. 4-9

Story of the Chicago Fire, by R. Conrad Stein (Cornerstones)	Gr. 2-7
Story of the Chisholm Trail, by R. Conrad Stein (Cornerstones)	Gr. 2-7
Story of the Cold War, by Leila Foster (Cornerstones)	Gr. 2-7
Story of the Conestoga Wagon, by Kenneth Richards (Cornerstones)*	Gr. 2-7
Story of the Cuban Missile Crisis, by Susan Clinton (Cornerstones)*	Gr. 3-9
Story of the Empire State Building, by Patrick Clinton (Cornerstones)*	Gr. 3-10
Story of the Flight at Kitty Hawk, by R. Conrad Stein (Cornerstones)*	Gr. 2-7
Story of the Golden Spike, by R. Conrad Stein (Cornerstone)*	Gr. 2-7
Story of the Great Depression, by R. Conrad Stein (Cornerstones)*	Gr. 2-8
Story of the Great Republic, by H.A. Guerber*	Gr. 3-7
Story of the Great Society, by Leila Foster (Cornerstones)	Gr. 3-7
Story of the Homestead Act, by R. Conrad Stein (Cornerstones)	Gr. 2-7
Story of the Johnstown Flood, by R. Conrad Stein (Cornerstones)	Gr. 2-7
Story of the Lafayette Escadrille, by R. Conrad Stein (Cornerstones)	Gr. 2-6
Story of the Little Bighorn, by R. Conrad Stein (Cornerstones)*	Gr. 2-7
Story of the Mississippi Steamboats, by R. Conrad Stein (Cornerstones)*	Gr. 2-7
Story of the Montgomery Bus Boycott, by R. Conrad Stein (Cornerstones)*	Gr. 3-8
Story of the Panama Canal, by R.Conrad Stein (Cornerstones)*	Gr. 2-7
Story of the Paratroops, by George Weller (Landmark)	Gr. 4-12
Story of the Persian Gulf War, by Leila Foster (Cornerstones)	Gr. 2-7
Story of the Rough Riders, by Zachary Kent (Cornerstones)	Gr. 2-7
Story of the Saigon Airlift, by Zachary Kent (Cornerstones)	Gr. 2-8
Story of the San Francisco Earthquake, by R. Conrad Stein (Cornerstone)	Gr. 2-6
Story of the Sinking of the Battleship Maine, by Zachary Kent (Cornerstones)	Gr. 2-7
Story of the Spirit of St. Louis, by R. Conrad Stein (Cornerstones)	Gr. 2-6
Story of the Statue of Liberty, by Betsy Maestro*	Gr. K-3
Story of the Statue of Liberty, by Natalie Miller (Cornerstone)*	Gr. 1-6
Story of the Totem Pole, by Ruth Brindze	Gr. 3-9
Story of the Trapp Family Singers, by Maria Trapp*	Gr. 5-12
Story of the U.S.S. Arizona, by R. Conrad Stein (Cornerstones)	Gr. 2-7
Story of Theodore Roosevelt, by Winthrop Neilson (Signature)	Gr. 3-8
Story of Thomas Alva Edison, by Margaret Cousins (Landmark)*	Gr. 4-12
Story of Thomas Alva Edison, by Enid Meadowcroft (Signature)	Gr. 3-8
Story of Watergate, by Jim Hargrove (Cornerstones)	Gr. 3-7
Story of Winston Churchill, by Alida Malkus (Signature)	Gr. 3-8
Story of World War I, by Robert Leckie (Landmark Giant)	Gr. 4-12
Story of World War II, by Stewart Graff	Gr. 5-12
Story of World War II, by Robert Leckie (Landmark Giant)	Gr. 5-12
Story of Wounded Knee, by R. Conrad Stein (Cornerstones)	Gr. 3-8
Strawberry Girl, by Lois Lenski*	Gr. 3-12
Strawberry Roan, by Glen Rounds	Gr. K-2
Streets of Gold, adapted by Rosemary Wells, from Mary Antin*	Gr. 2-6
Stubby: Brave Soldier Dog, by Richard & Sally Glendinning	Gr. 1-6
Submarine Pioneer, by Frank Morriss	Gr. 5-12

Submarines in the Pacific, by G.C. Skipper (World at War)	Gr. 3-7
Survival in the Storm, by Katelan Janke (Dear America)*	Gr. 3-8
Survivor, by Robb White	Gr. 5-12
Suzannah series, by Elaine Schulte*	Gr. 4-10
Suzette and the Puppy: A Story of Mary Cassatt, by Joan Sweeney*	Gr. 1-4
Swift Rivers, by Cornelia Meigs*	Gr. 4-10
Sword is Drawn, by André Norton	Gr. 5-12
Take Me Out to the Airfield! by Robert Quackenbush	Gr. 2-6
Taking Flight, by Stephen Krensky (Ready-to-Read)*	Gr. 1-3
Talking Wire, by O.J. Stevenson	Gr. 5-12
Tall Boy and the Coyote, by Edna Walker Chandler	Gr. K-2
Teammates, by Peter Golenbock*	Gr. 1-4
Teddy Roosevelt, by Edd Parks (Childhood)*	Gr. 1-6
Teddy Roosevelt and the Rough Riders, by Henry Castor (Landmark)	Gr. 3-9
Teddy Roosevelt: Rough Rider, by Louis Sabin (Troll Easy Biography)*	Gr. 1-3
Ten Mile Day, by Mary Ann Fraser*	Gr. 3-8
Ten Tall Texans, by Lee McGiffin	Gr. 3-12
Ten Texas Tales, by R. Gilstrap	Gr. 4-12
Teresa of Calcutta, by D. Jeanne Watson (Sower Series)*	Gr. 5-12
Teton Sioux, by Nancy Bonvillain (Junior Library of American Indians)*	Gr. 4-12
Texans Ride North: Story of the Cattle Trails, by John Jakes (Winston Adventure)	Gr. 3-9
Texas Rangers, by Will Henry (Landmark)	Gr. 4-12
Texas Roundup, by Catherine Chambers (Adventures in Frontier America)*	Gr. 2-4
Texas Star, by Enid Meadowcroft	Gr. 1-6
That Denmark Might Live, by Irving Werstein	Gr. 5-12
Theodore Roosevelt, by Sibyl Hancock (See and Read)	Gr. 1-3
Theodore Roosevelt, by Clara Ingram Judson	Gr. 5-12
Theodore Roosevelt, by Zachary Kent (Encyclopedia of Presidents)*	Gr. 5-12
Theodore Roosevelt: An Initial Biography, by Genevieve Foster	Gr. 3-8
Theodore Roosevelt: Man of Action, by James Beach (Garrard Discovery)	Gr. 1-5
Theodore Roosevelt's Boys, by Stewart Graff	Gr. 1-5
There'll Be a Hot Time in the Old Town, by Robert Quackenbush	Gr. 1-6
They Sought a New World, by William Kurelek	Gr. 4-12
Thirty Seconds Over Tokyo, by Ted Lawson (Landmark)	Gr. 4-12
This Country of Ours, by H.E. Marshall*	Gr. 3-8
This is Cape Canaveral, by Miroslav Sasek	Gr. 1-4
This is New York, by Miroslav Sasek	Gr. 1-5
Thomas Alva Edison, Inventor, by R. Weir (Makers of America)	Gr. 2-7
Thomas Alva Edison: Young Inventor, by Louis Sabin (Troll Easy Bio)*	Gr. 1-3
Thomas Edison, by Nicholas Nirgiotis (Cornerstones "Second" series)*	Gr. 3-7
Thomas Edison and Electricity, by Steve Parker (Science Discoveries)*	Gr. 3-9
Thomas Edison: Miracle Maker, by Mervyn Kaufman (Garrard Discovery)	Gr. 1-5
Three Little Indians, by George Stuart (National Geographic)*	Gr. K-4
Three Names, by Patricia MacLachlan*	Gr. 1-5

Three Together, by Lois Mills	Gr. 3-9
Thunder Rolling in the Mountains, by Scott O'Dell*	Gr. 5-12
Thunderhoof, by Syd Hoff (I Can Read)	Gr. K-1
Ticket to the Twenties, by Mary Blocksma*	Gr. 3-9
Tidewater Valley, by Lundy (Land of the Free)	Gr. 4-12
Timber, by Walter Buehr	Gr. 3-10
Timber! by Aileen Fisher (Aladdin's American Heritage)	Gr. 4-10
Time of the Wolves, by Verne Davis	Gr. 2-6
Time of Trial, Time of Hope, by Milton Meltzer	Gr. 5-12
Time to Keep, by Tasha Tudor*	Various
Tin Lizzie, by Peter Spier	Gr. 3-6
Titanic: Lost...and Found, by Judy Donnelly (Step Into Read 3)*	Gr. K-4
T-Model Tommy, by Stephen Meader	Gr. 5-12
To Be a Logger, by Lois Lenski	Gr. 3-9
To Be a Pioneer, by Paul Burns	Gr. 3-8
To Fly, by Wendie Old*	Gr. 2-5
Toby Tyler, by James Otis	Gr. 4-10
Tom Edison, by Sue Guthridge (Childhood)*	Gr. 1-6
Tom Logan series, by Edna Walker Chandler	Gr. 1-5
Trail Blazer of the Seas, by Jean Lee Latham	Gr. 4-12
Trail Boss in Pigtails, by Marjorie Stover	Gr. 3-12
Train Song, by Diane Siebert*	Gr. K-4
Train to Somewhere, by Eve Bunting*	Gr. 1-5
Treeless Plains, by Glen Rounds	Gr. 3-10
Trouble River, by Betsy Byars*	Gr. 3-9
True Book of Indians, by Teri Martini (True Books)	Gr. K-3
True Book of Pioneers, by Mabel Harmer (True Books)	Gr. K-3
Trumpeter's Tale: Louis Armstrong, by Jeanette Eaton	Gr. 5-12
Turkey Red, by Esther Vogt	Gr. 4-9
Turn Homeward, Hannalee, by Patricia Beatty*	Gr. 3-10
Turn of the Century, by Robert Hoare	Gr. 5-12
Twenty and Ten, by Claire Bishop*	Gr. 2-9
U.S. Frogmen of World War II, by Wyatt Blassingame (Landmark)	Gr. 4-12
Uncle Fonzo's Ford, by Miska Miles	Gr. 3-8
Underground, by David Macaulay*	Gr. 3-12
Understood Betsy, by Dorothy Canfield Fisher*	Gr. 4-10
United States Holocaust Memorial Museum, by P. Brooks (Cornerstones)*	Gr. 3-7
Unsung Heroes, by Nathan Aaseng*	Gr. 5-12
Up in the Air: The Story of Bessie Coleman, by Philip Hart (Carolrhoda)*	Gr. 3-6
Up Periscope, by Robb White	Gr. 5-12
Up the Hill, by Marguerite de Angeli	Gr. 3-9
Up the Trail from Texas, by J. Frank Dobie (Landmark)	Gr. 3-9
V is for Victory, by Sylvia Whitman	Gr. 5-12

Value of Believing in Yourself: Louis Pasteur, by Spencer Johnson (ValueTale)	Gr. 1-6
Value of Creativity: Thomas Edison, by Ann Johnson (ValueTale)	Gr. 1-6
Value of Humor: Will Rogers, by Spencer Johnson (ValueTales)	Gr. 1-4
Value of Learning: Marie Curie, by Ann Johnson (ValueTales)	Gr. 1-5
Value of Patience: The Wright Brothers, by Spencer Johnson (ValueTale)	Gr. 2-6
Value of Self-Discipline: Alexander Graham Bell, by Ann Johnson (ValueTale)	Gr. 2-6
Value of Sharing: Mayo Brothers, by Spencer Johnson (ValueTales)	Gr. 1-4
Value of Truth and Trust: Cochise, by Ann Johnson (ValueTales)	Gr. 1-5
Vanished! by Monica Killing (Step into Reading 4)*	Gr. 2-4
Vietnam Veterans Memorial, by David Wright (Cornerstones)	Gr. 2-8
Vietnam War, by John Devaney*	Gr. 5-12
Vietnam Women's Memorial, by Deborah Kent (Cornerstones)	Gr. 2-8
Virgil I. Grissom, by Carl Chappell (Childhood)	Gr. 1-6
Voice of Liberty: Emma Lazarus, by Eve Merriam	Gr. 5-12
Voyage on the Great Titanic, by Ellen White (Dear America)*	Gr. 3-9
Wagon Wheels, by Barbara Brenner (I Can Read)*	Gr. K-2
Wall of Names, by Judy Donnelly (Step Into Reading 4)*	Gr. 1-5
Wall, by Eve Bunting*	Gr. 3-7
Walter Chrysler: Boy Machinist, by Ethel Weddle (Childhood)	Gr. 1-6
Walter Reed, by Lynn Groh (Americans All)	Gr. 2-7
Walter Reed, by Helen Higgins (Childhood)	Gr. 1-6
Walter Reed, by L. Wood (Messner)	Gr. 5-12
War Boy, by Michael Foreman*	Gr. 3-8
War in Korea, by Robert Leckie (Landmark)	Gr. 4-12
Warren Harding, by Linda Wade (Encyclopedia of Presidents)*	Gr. 5-12
Warsaw Ghetto, by R. Conrad Stein (World at War)	Gr. 3-7
Watch the Stars Come Out, by Riki Levinson*	Gr. 1-3
Water Buffalo Days, by Huynh Quang Nhuong*	Gr. 3-7
Waterless Mountain, by Laura Armer*	Gr. 3-12
Way We Lived, by Martin Sandler*	Gr. 5-12
We Have Conquered Pain, by Dennis Fradin*	Gr. 5-12
We Live in the City, by Lois Lenski	Gr. 1-6
We Were There at Pearl Harbor, by Felix Sutton (We Were There)	Gr. 3-8
We Were There at the Battle for Bataan, by Benjamin Appel (We Were There)	Gr. 3-8
We Were There at the Battle of Britain, by Clayton Knight (We Were There)	Gr. 3-8
We Were There at the Battle of the Bulge, by David Shepherd (We Were There)	Gr. 3-8
We Were There at the Driving of the Golden Spike, by David Shepherd (We...)	Gr. 3-9
We Were There at the First Airplane Flight, by Felix Sutton (We Were There)	Gr. 3-8
We Were There at the Normandy Invasion, by Clayton Knight (We Were There)	Gr. 3-8
We Were There at the Oklahoma Land Run, by Jim Kjelgaard (We Were There)	Gr. 3-8
We Were There at the Opening of the Atomic Era, by James Munves (We Were...)	Gr. 3-8
We Were There in the Klondike Gold Rush, by Benjamin Appel (We Were There)	Gr. 3-8
We Were There on the Chisholm Trail, by Ross Taylor (We Were There)	Gr. 3-8

We Were There on the Nautilus, by Robert Webb (We Were There)   Gr. 3-8
We Were There with Byrd at the South Pole, by Charles Strong (We Were There)   Gr. 3-8
We Were There with the California Rancheros, by Stephen Holt (We Were...)   Gr. 3-8
We Were There with the Lafayette Escadrille, by Clayton Knight (We Were There)   Gr. 3-8
We'll Race You, Henry, by Barbara Mitchell (Creative Minds)*   Gr. 2-6
Weed is Not a Flower, by Aliki   Gr. 3-6
Weekend with Winslow Homer, by Ann Beneduce   Gr. 4-9
Wells Fargo, by Ralph Moody (North Star)   Gr. 5-12
Wes Powell: Conqueror of the Grand Canyon, by Leonard Wibberley   Gr. 4-12
Westward Ho! by Laurie Carlson*   Various
What is a Space Shuttle? by Chris Arvetis *et al* (Just Ask)   Gr. K-2
What Makes a Cassatt a Cassatt? by Richard Muhlberger   Gr. 5-12
What You Know First, by Patricia MacLachlan*   Gr. 1-6
Wheels of Time, by Catherine Gourley*   Gr. 3-8
When a Ton of Gold Reached Seattle, by E. Montgomery (How They Lived)   Gr. 3-8
When Chicago Was Young, by James McCague (How They Lived)   Gr. 3-10
When Christmas Comes Again, by Beth Levine (Dear America)*   Gr. 3-8
When Cowboys Rode the Chisholm Trail, by James McCague (How They Lived)   Gr. 3-8
When Grandpa Wore Knickers, by Fern Brown   Gr. 1-6
When Hitler Stole the Pink Rabbit, by Judith Kerr*   Gr. 4-10
When I Was Nine, by James Stevenson   Gr. 1-4
When Jo Louis Won the Title, by Belinda Rochelle*   Gr. K-3
When John & Caroline Lived in the White House, by Laurie Coulter*   Gr. 4-8
When Men First Flew, by James McCague (How They Lived)   Gr. 3-8
When Men Panned Gold in the Klondike, by Edward Janes (How They Lived)   Gr. 3-8
When the Rails Ran West, by James McCague (How They Lived)   Gr. 3-8
When the Saboteurs Came, by William Wise   Gr. 5-12
When the Sirens Wailed, by Noel Streatfeild   Gr. 5-12
When the Typhoon Blows, by Elizabeth Lewis   Gr. 5-12
When Willard Met Babe Ruth, by Donald Hall*   Gr. 2-6
Where the Buffalo Roam, by Jacqueline Geis   Gr. K-5
Where the Red Fern Grows, by Wilson Rawls*   Gr. 5-12
Whitey Ropes and Rides series, by Glen Rounds   Gr. 1-5
Whitney Young, Jr.: Crusader for Equality, by Peggy Mann (Garr. Am. All)   Gr. 3-8
Who Shot the President? by Judy Donnelly (Step into Reading 4)*   Gr. 2-5
Who was Albert Einstein? by Jess Braillier*   Gr. 3-5
Who's That Girl with a Gun? A Story of Annie Oakley, by Robert Quackenbush   Gr. 1-5
Why Cowboys Sing, In Texas, by LeGrand   Gr. 1-5
Wilbur & Orville Wright, by Louis Sabin (Troll Easy Biographies)*   Gr. 1-4
Wilbur and Orville Wright, by Augusta Stevenson (Childhood)*   Gr. 1-6
Wild Bill Hickok, by A.M. Anderson (American Adventure, older series)   Gr. 3-8
Wild Bill Hickok, by Carl Green   Gr. 4-12
Wild Bill Hickok, by Sanford Tousey   Gr. 2-7

Wild Bill Hickok Tames the West, by Stewart Holbrook (Landmark)	Gr. 3-9
Wild West Days, by David King*	Various
Wild, Wild West, by James Daugherty	Gr. 5-12
Will and Charlie: Boy Doctors, by Marie Hammontree (Childhood)	Gr. 1-6
Will and Orv, by Walter Schulz (Carolrhoda's On My Own)*	Gr. 1-3
Will Rogers, by Guernsey Van Riper, Jr. (Childhood)	Gr. 1-5
Will Rogers: Cowboy Philosopher, by Eliz. Montgomery (Americans All)	Gr. 2-7
Will Rogers: Immortal Cowboy, by Shannon Garst (Messner)	Gr. 4-12
William C. Handy: Father of the Blues, by Elizabeth Montgomery (Gar. Am. All)	Gr. 2-8
William Crawford Gorgas, by Beryl Williams & Sam Epstein	Gr. 5-12
William Fargo, by Katharine Wilkie (Childhood)	Gr. 1-6
Willie Jasper's Golden Eagle, by F.N. Monjo	Gr. 2-10
Willow Whistle, by Cornelia Meigs	Gr. 2-6
Wilma Unlimited, by Kathleen Krull*	Gr. 1-6
Winged Watchman, by Hilda van Stockum*	Gr. 5-12
Winning of the West, by Harold McCracken	Gr. 3-8
Winslow Homer, by Jean Gould	Gr. 10-12
Winston Churchill, by Quentin Reynolds (Landmark)	Gr. 5-12
With Daring Faith, by R. Davis*	Gr. 5-10
Wizard of Sound, by Barbara Mitchell (Creative Minds)*	Gr. 1-5
World of Knowing, by Andy Bowen (Creative Minds)*	Gr. 3-10
World of Little House, by Carolyn Collins*	Gr. 3-10
World of Young Herbert Hoover, by Suzanne Hilton	Gr. 5-12
World War I, by Tom McGowen*	Gr. 4-11
World War I Tommy, by Martin Windrow (Soldier Through the Ages)	Gr. 3-12
World War II, by Tom McGowen*	Gr. 4-12
World War II Days, by David King*	Various
World War II Submarine, by Richard Humble (Inside Story)*	Gr. 4-12
World's Greatest Showman: P.T. Barnum, by Joe Bryan (Landmark)	Gr. 3-8
Wound of Peter Wayne, by Leonard Wibberley	Gr. 5-12
Wright Brothers, by Quentin Reynolds (Landmark)	Gr. 3-9
Wright Brothers and Aviation, by Steve Parker (Science Discoveries)*	Gr. 3-9
Wright Brothers at Kitty Hawk, by Donald Sobol	Gr. 4-9
Wright Brothers: First to Fly, by Madge Haines (Makers of America)	Gr. 1-6
Wright Brothers: Kings of the Air, by Mervyn Kaufman (Garrard Discovery)	Gr. 1-5
Wyatt Earp, by Carl Green	Gr. 4-12
Wyatt Earp: U.S. Marshal, by Stewart Holbrook (Landmark)	Gr. 3-9
Yellow Star, by Carmen Deedy*	Gr. 1-4
Yippe-Yay! A Book about Cowboys and Cowgirls, by Gail Gibbons*	Gr. 1-4
Young Albert Einstein, by Laurence Santrey (Troll)	Gr. 1-4
Young Amelia Earhart, by Susan Alcott (Troll First-Start)*	Gr. K-3
Young Bat Masterson, by Richard O'Connor	Gr. 5-12
Young Eleanor Roosevelt, by Francene Sabin (Troll Easy Biographies)*	Gr. 1-4

Young Hawk, by Edna Walker Chandler	Gr. 2-7
Young Helen Keller, by Anne Benjamin (Troll First-Start)*	Gr. K-2
Young Man in a Hurry, by Jean Lee Latham	Gr. 4-12
Young Man of the House, by Mabel Leigh Hunt	Gr. 2-6
Young Mark Twain, by Louis Sabin (Troll Easy Biographies)*	Gr. 1-4
Young Mark Twain and the Mississippi, by Harnett Kane (Landmark)	Gr. 3-8
Young Martin Luther King, Jr.: I Have a Dream, by J. Mattern (Troll First-Start)*	Gr. 1-3
Young Orville and Wilbur Wright, by Andrew Woods (Troll First-Start)*	Gr. K-2
Young People's Story of Architecture: Gothic-Modern, by V.M. Hillyer & E.G. Huey	Gr. 2-8
Young People's Story of Fine Art: Last Two Hundred Years, by Hillyer & Huey	Gr. 2-8
Young People's Story of Sculpture, by V.M. Hillyer & E.G. Huey	Gr. 2-8
Young Pioneers, by Rose Wilder Lane (formerly titled, *Let the Hurricane Roar*)*	Gr. 5-12
Young Reader's Christian Library series:	Gr. 1-5
Billy Graham, Luis Palau, D.L. Moody, Samuel Morris, etc.*	
Young Rosa Parks: Civil Rights Heroine, by Anne Benjamin (Troll First-Start)	Gr. 1-3
Young Sand Hills Cowboy, by Frances Kroll (Young Heroes Library)	Gr. 2-8
Young Sioux Warrior, by Frances Kroll (Young Hero Library)	Gr. 2-7
Young Teddy Roosevelt, by Cheryl Harness*	Gr. 3-8
Yukon Gold, by Charlotte Jones*	Unknown
Zia, by Scott O'Dell*	Gr. 4-12

This booklist is only for those persons who have already purchased the companion *TruthQuest History* guide.

Films/Videos: *All should be pre-approved by parents!*

◆ Remember, there are also film versions of many of the famous books/novels mentioned in the guide; they're too numerous to mention.

Adventures of Mark Twain, starring Frederic March
Albert Einstein: Light to the Power of 2 (Inventors' Specials)* (Very questionable worldview.)
Bataan, starring Robert Taylor*
Balto
Big Buildings, by David Macaulay*

Bridge on the River Kwai, starring Alec Guinness and William Holden*
*Christy**
Command Decision, starring Clark Gable*
Diary of Anne Frank, starring Millie Perkins*
Edison, the Man, starring Spencer Tracy*
Edison: The Wizard of Light (Inventors' Specials)*
Glory & Honor (I know nothing about this film; just saw it cited.)*
Gunfight at OK Corral, starring Gary Cooper*
How Should We Then Live? by Francis Schaeffer* (For parents only.)
Inn of the Sixth Happiness, starring Ingrid Bergman*
It's a Wonderful Life, starring Jimmy Stewart*
*Jesse Owens Story**
Journey for Margaret, starring Robert Young*
Judgment at Nuremberg, starring Spencer Tracy*
Longest Day, starring Henry Fonda, John Wayne, Richard Burton*
Louis Pasteur (Animated Hero Classics)*
Madame Curie, starring Greer Garson and Walter Pidgeon*
Marie Curie: More than Meets the Eye (Inventors' Specials)*
Mark Twain, a film by Ken Burns*
Mary Cassatt: American Impressionist (Artists' Specials)*
Miracle at Moreaux, starring Loretta Swit
Miracle of the White Stallions, starring Robert Taylor
Miracle Worker, starring Ann Bancroft and Patty Duke*
Miss Rose White, starring Kyra Sedgwick and Maximilian Schell*
Mortal Storm, starring Jimmy Stewart*
*Night to Remember**
Origins of the Indians, by Richard "Little Bear" Wheeler*
*Orphan Train** (I have NOT seen this.)
*Pollyanna**
*Rascal**
Rebecca of Sunnybrook Farm, starring Shirley Temple*
Sands of Iwo Jima, starring John Wayne*
Scarlet and the Black, starring Gregory Peck*
Sergeant York, starring Gary Cooper*
Showdown at O.K. Corral, by Richard "Little Bear" Wheeler*
Sink the Bismarck, starring Kenneth More*
Sound of Music, starring Julie Andrews*
Story of Alexander Graham Bell, starring Don Ameche & Henry Fonda*
Story of Louis Pasteur, starring Paul Muni*
Thirty Seconds Over Tokyo, starring Spencer Tracy & Van Johnson*
*Titanic's Last Hero**
Tora! Tora! Tora! starring Martin Balsam, Joseph Cotten, E.G. Marshall*
Twelve O'Clock High, starring Gregory Peck*
Why We Fight, directed by Frank Capra*
Winslow Homer: An American Original (Artists' Specials)*
Young Tom Edison, starring Mickey Rooney*

Audio:

Bonhoeffer: Cost of Freedom (Focus on the Family)*	Parental decision
History Alive Through Music: Westward Ho! by Diana Waring*	Various
New Coat for Anna, by Harriet Ziefert*	Gr. K-4
*Your Story Hour–Volume 6 & 7**	Various

BIBLIOGRAPHY

Bloom, Jan. *Who Should We Then Read?* Cokato, MN: Booksbloom, 2001.

Breese, Dave. *Seven Men Who Rule the World from the Grave.* Chicago: Moody Press, 1990.

Carson, Clarence. *The Sections and the Civil War: A Basic History of the United States–Vol. 3.* Wadley, AL: American Textbook Company, 1985.

_____. *The Growth of America: A Basic History of the United States–Vol. 4.* Wadley, AL: American Textbook Company, 1985.

_____. *The Welfare State: A Basic History of the United States–Vol. 5.* Wadley, AL: American Textbook Company, 1986.

Craven, Thomas. *The Rainbow Book of Art.* Cleveland: World Publishing Company, 1956.

Folsom, Burton, Jr. *The Spirit of Freedom: Essays in American History.* Irvington-on-Hudson, NY: Foundation for Economic Education, Ind., 1994.

Galbraith, John Kenneth. *The Age of Uncertainty.* Boston: Houghton Mifflin, 1977.

Grun, Bernard. *The Timetables of History.* New York: Touchstone Books, published by Simon & Schuster, 1991.

Hotchkiss, Jeanette. *American Historical Fiction and Biography for Children and Young People.* Metuchen, NJ:Scarecrow Press, 1973.

_____. *European Historical Fiction for Children and Young People.* Metuchen, NJL Scarecrow Press, 1967.

Jackson, Jeremy. *No Other Foundation: The Church Through Twenty Centuries.* Westchester, IL: Cornerstone, 1980.

Janson, H.W. and Dora Janson. *The Story of Painting.* New York: Harry N. Abrams, Inc., 1966.

Keller, Kathy. *Turning Back the Pages of Time.* New Berlin, WI: Pilgrim Enterprises, 1993.

LaFarge, Oliver. *The American Indian.* New York: Golden Press, 1960.

Lutzer, Erwin. *Hitler's Cross.* Chicago: Moody Press, 1995.

McManus, Patrick. *Never Sniff a Gift Fish.* New York: Holt, Rinehart and Winston, 1979-1983.

Maybury, Richard. *World War I.* Placerville, CA: Bluestocking Press, 2002.

_____. *World War II.* Placerville, CA: Bluestocking Press, 2002.

Merriam-Webster's Encyclopedia of Literature. Springfield, MA: Merriam-Webster, 1995.

Metzner, Seymour. *American History in Juvenile Books.* New York: H.N. Wilson, 1966.

_____. *World History in Juvenile Books.* New York: H.N. Wilson, 1973.

Miller, Douglas. *Then was the Future.* New York: Alfred A. Knopf, 1973.

Morris, Richard. *Encyclopedia of American History.* New York: Harper & Brothers, 1953.

Potter, William. *The Boy's Guide to the Historical Adventures of G.A. Henty.* Bulverde, TX: Vision Forum, 2000.

Quigley, Lillian, ad. *The Blind Men and the Elephant.* New York: Scribner's, 1959.

Rowley, Gill (editor). *The Book of Music.* Englewood Cliffs, NJ: Prentice-Hall, 1978.

Schaeffer, Francis. *How Should We Then Live?* Old Tappan, NJ: Revell, 1976.

Stein, R. Conrad. *The Siege of Leningrad (World at War).* Chicago: Childrens Press, 1983.

Strickland, Carol and John Boswell. *The Annotated Mona Lisa.* Kansas City: Andrews and McMeel, 1992.

Webster's Biographical Dictionary. Springfield, MA: G. & C. Merriam, 1943.

Webster's New Collegiate Dictionary. Springfield, MA: G. & C. Merriam, 1977.